MARVEL

CIVIL WAR

CAPTAIN AMERICA

PRELUDE

MAY 18 2016

MARVEL'S *IRON MAN 3* SCREENPLAY BY **DREW PEARCE & SHANE BLACK**
MARVEL'S *CAPTAIN AMERICA: THE WINTER SOLDIER* SCREENPLAY BY
CHRISTOPHER MARKUS & STEPHEN MCFEELY

WRITER: **WILL CORONA PILGRIM**
ARTISTS: **SZYMON KUDRANSKI** (#1-2) &
LEE FERGUSON (#3-4)
COLORISTS: **GURU-eFX** (#1-2) &
DONO SANCHEZ ALMAR
LETTERER: **VC'S TRAVIS LA**
EDITOR: **EMILY SHAW**

D1445044

INFINITE COMIC
WRITER: **WILL CORONA PILGRIM**   ART (BUCKY): **LEE FERGUSON**
ART (RUMLOW): **GORAN SUDŽUKA**   ART (CAPTAIN AMERICA): **GUILLERMO MOGORRON**
COLORIST: **RACHELLE ROSENBERG** LETTERER: **VC'S TRAVIS LANHAM**
PRODUCTION: **ANNIE CHEUNG**   PRODUCTION MANAGER: **TIM SMITH 3**   EDITOR: **EMILY SHAW**

CAPTAIN AMERICA CREATED BY **JOE SIMON & JACK KIRBY**

MARVEL STUDIOS
DIRECTOR OF PRODUCTION & DEVELOPMENT: **TRINH TRAN**
SVP PRODUCTION & DEVELOPMENT: **STEPHEN BROUSSARD**
SVP PRODUCTION & DEVELOPMENT: **NATE MOORE**
PRESIDENT: **KEVIN FEIGE**

COLLECTION EDITOR: **JENNIFER GRÜNWALD** ASSOCIATE EDITOR: **SARAH BRUNSTAD**
ASSOCIATE MANAGING EDITOR: **ALEX STARBUCK**   EDITOR, SPECIAL PROJECTS: **MARK D. BEAZLEY**
VP, PRODUCTION & SPECIAL PROJECTS: **JEFF YOUNGQUIST** SVP PRINT, SALES & MARKETING: **DAVID GABRIEL**

EDITOR IN CHIEF: **AXEL ALONSO**   CHIEF CREATIVE OFFICER: **JOE QUESADA**
PUBLISHER: **DAN BUCKLEY**   EXECUTIVE PRODUCER: **ALAN FINE**

VEL'S CAPTAIN AMERICA: CIVIL WAR PRELUDE. Contains material originally published in magazine form as MARVEL'S CAPTAIN AMERICA: CIVIL WAR PRELUDE #1-4 and INFINITE COMIC #1, and CIVIL WAR #1.
printing 2016. ISBN# 978-0-7851-9440-8. Published by MARVEL WORLDWIDE, INC., a subsidiary of MARVEL ENTERTAINMENT, LLC. OFFICE OF PUBLICATION: 135 West 50th Street, New York, NY 10020. Copyright
16 MARVEL No similarity between any of the names, characters, persons, and/or institutions in this magazine with those of any living or dead person or institution is intended, and any such similarity which may
is purely coincidental. **Printed in the U.S.A.** ALAN FINE, President, Marvel Entertainment; DAN BU
blishing; DAVID BOGART, SVP of Business Affairs & Operations, Publishing & Partnership; C.B. CEB
GQUIST, VP of Production & Special Projects; DAN CARR, Executive Director of Publishing Techno

MARVEL'S CAPTAIN AMERICA: CIVIL WAR PRELUDE #1

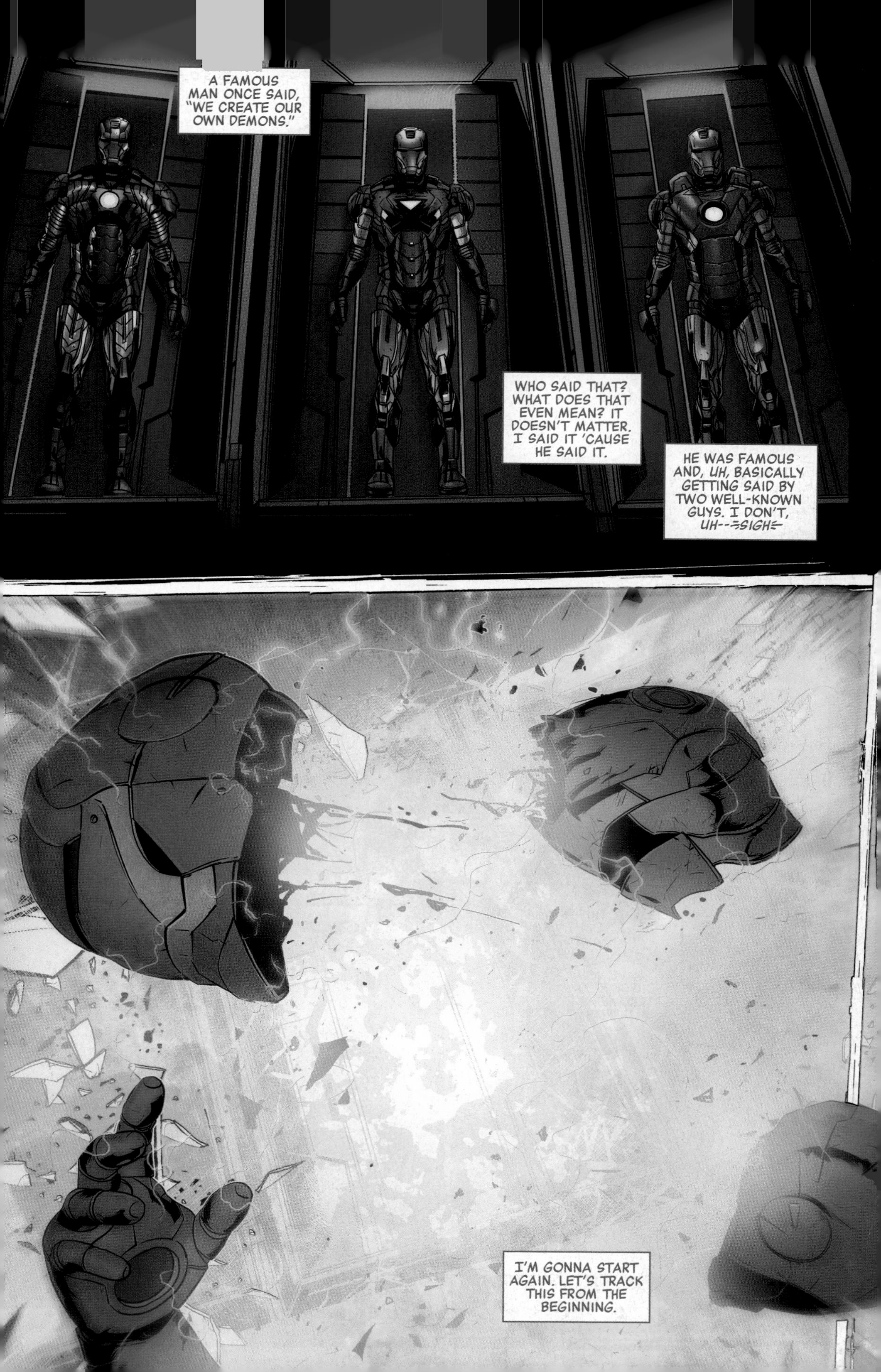
A FAMOUS MAN ONCE SAID, "WE CREATE OUR OWN DEMONS."
WHO SAID THAT? WHAT DOES THAT EVEN MEAN? IT DOESN'T MATTER. I SAID IT 'CAUSE HE SAID IT.
HE WAS FAMOUS AND, UH, BASICALLY GETTING SAID BY TWO WELL-KNOWN GUYS. I DON'T, UH-- =SIGH=
I'M GONNA START AGAIN. LET'S TRACK THIS FROM THE BEGINNING.

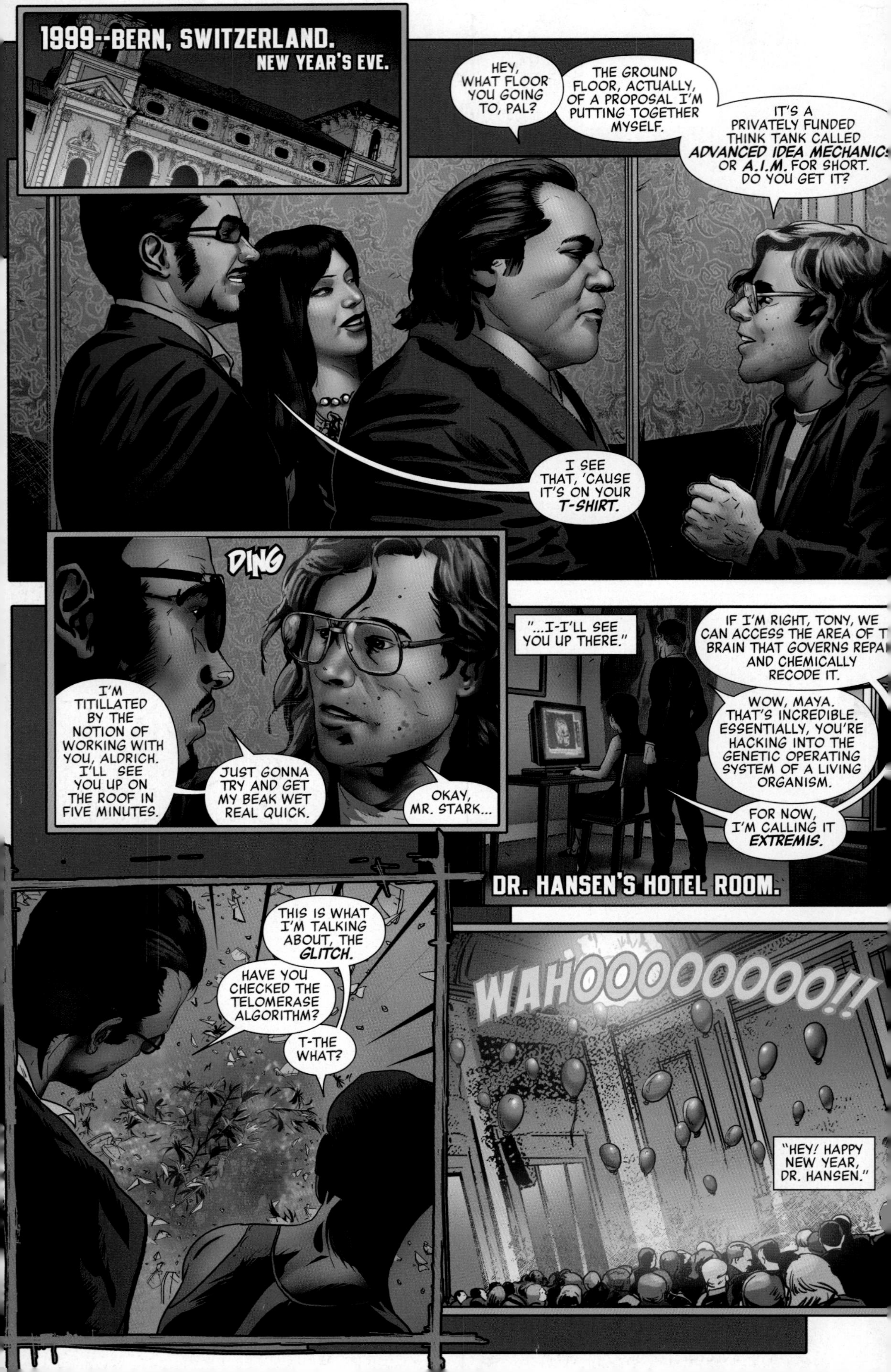

1999--BERN, SWITZERLAND.
NEW YEAR'S EVE.
HEY, WHAT FLOOR YOU GOING TO, PAL?
THE GROUND FLOOR, ACTUALLY, OF A PROPOSAL I'M PUTTING TOGETHER MYSELF.
IT'S A PRIVATELY FUNDED THINK TANK CALLED ADVANCED IDEA MECHANICS OR A.I.M. FOR SHORT. DO YOU GET IT?
I SEE THAT, 'CAUSE IT'S ON YOUR T-SHIRT.
DING
I'M TITILLATED BY THE NOTION OF WORKING WITH YOU, ALDRICH. I'LL SEE YOU UP ON THE ROOF IN FIVE MINUTES.
JUST GONNA TRY AND GET MY BEAK WET REAL QUICK.
OKAY, MR. STARK...
"...I-I'LL SEE YOU UP THERE."
IF I'M RIGHT, TONY, WE CAN ACCESS THE AREA OF T BRAIN THAT GOVERNS REPA AND CHEMICALLY RECODE IT.
WOW, MAYA. THAT'S INCREDIBLE. ESSENTIALLY, YOU'RE HACKING INTO THE GENETIC OPERATING SYSTEM OF A LIVING ORGANISM.
FOR NOW, I'M CALLING IT EXTREMIS.
DR. HANSEN'S HOTEL ROOM.
THIS IS WHAT I'M TALKING ABOUT, THE GLITCH.
HAVE YOU CHECKED THE TELOMERASE ALGORITHM?
T-THE WHAT?
WAHOOOOOOOOO!!
"HEY! HAPPY NEW YEAR, DR. HANSEN."

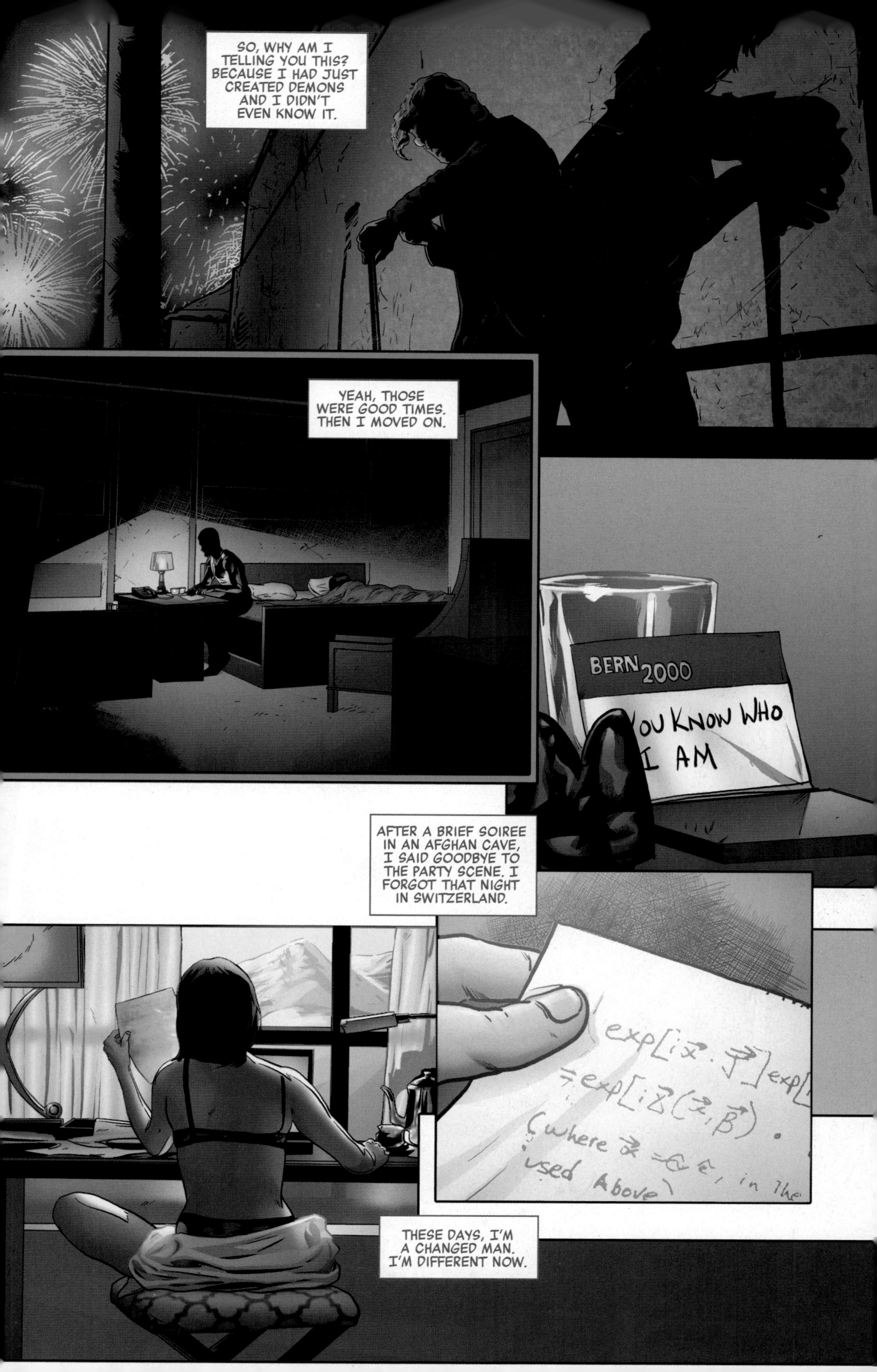
SO, WHY AM I TELLING YOU THIS? BECAUSE I HAD JUST CREATED DEMONS AND I DIDN'T EVEN KNOW IT.
YEAH, THOSE WERE GOOD TIMES. THEN I MOVED ON.
BERN 2000
YOU KNOW WHO I AM
AFTER A BRIEF SOIREE IN AN AFGHAN CAVE, I SAID GOODBYE TO THE PARTY SCENE. I FORGOT THAT NIGHT IN SWITZERLAND.
THESE DAYS, I'M A CHANGED MAN. I'M DIFFERENT NOW.

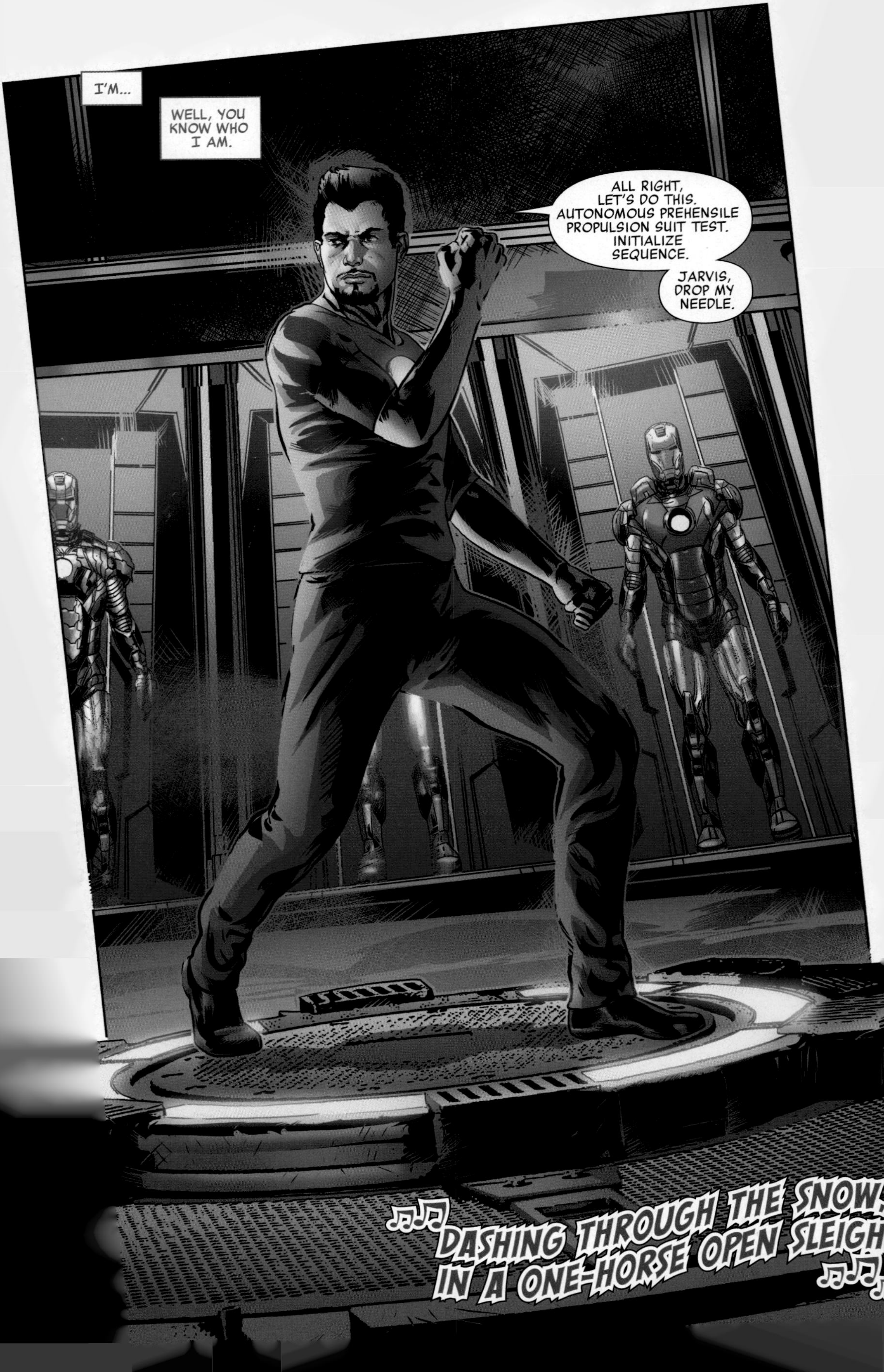

I'M...
WELL, YOU KNOW WHO I AM.
ALL RIGHT, LET'S DO THIS. AUTONOMOUS PREHENSILE PROPULSION SUIT TEST. INITIALIZE SEQUENCE.
JARVIS, DROP MY NEEDLE.
♫DASHING THROUGH THE SNOW, IN A ONE-HORSE OPEN SLEIGH♫

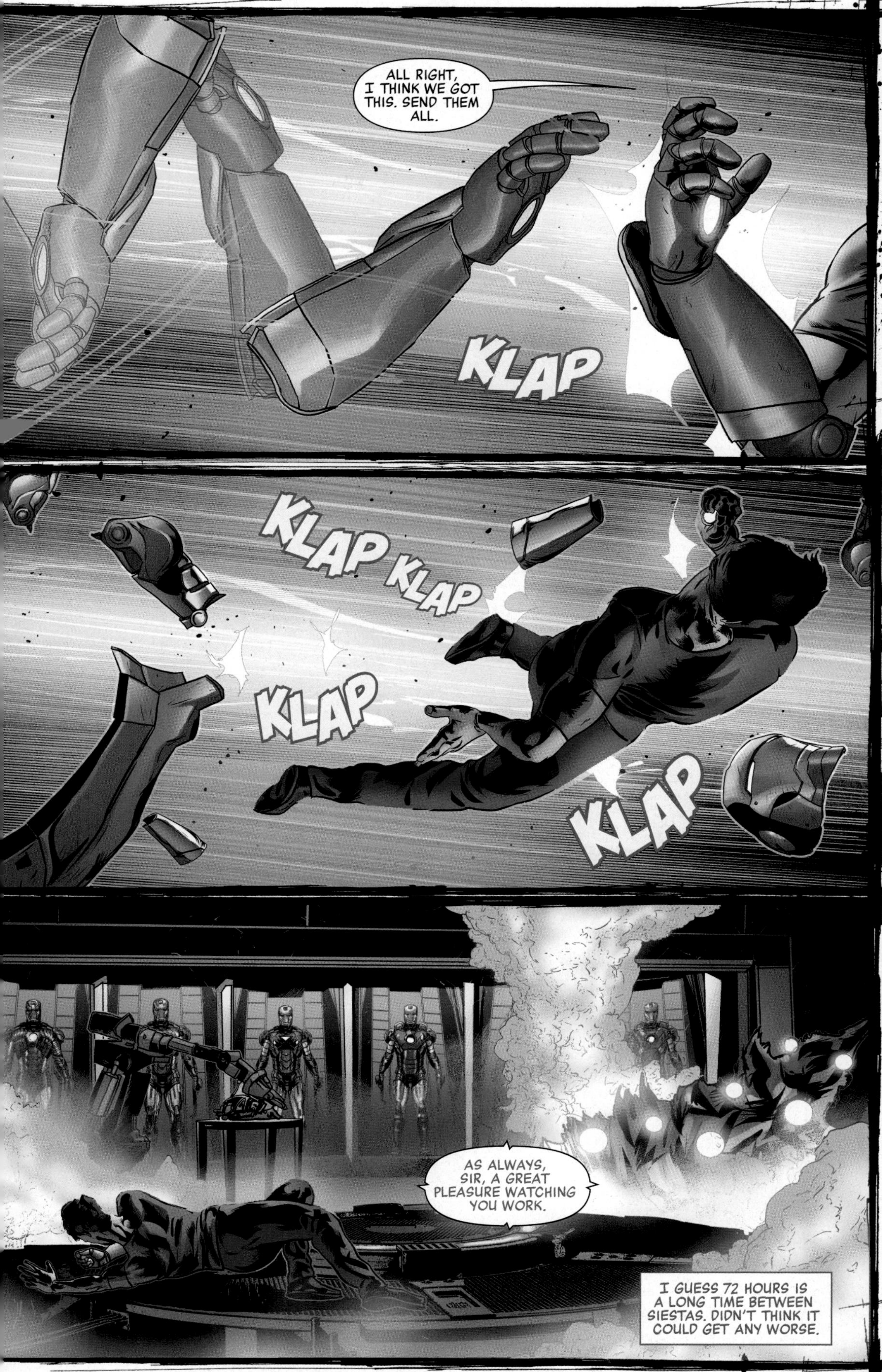

ALL RIGHT, I THINK WE GOT THIS. SEND THEM ALL.
KLAP
KLAP KLAP
KLAP
KLAP
AS ALWAYS, SIR, A GREAT PLEASURE WATCHING YOU WORK.
I GUESS 72 HOURS IS A LONG TIME BETWEEN SIESTAS. DIDN'T THINK IT COULD GET ANY WORSE.

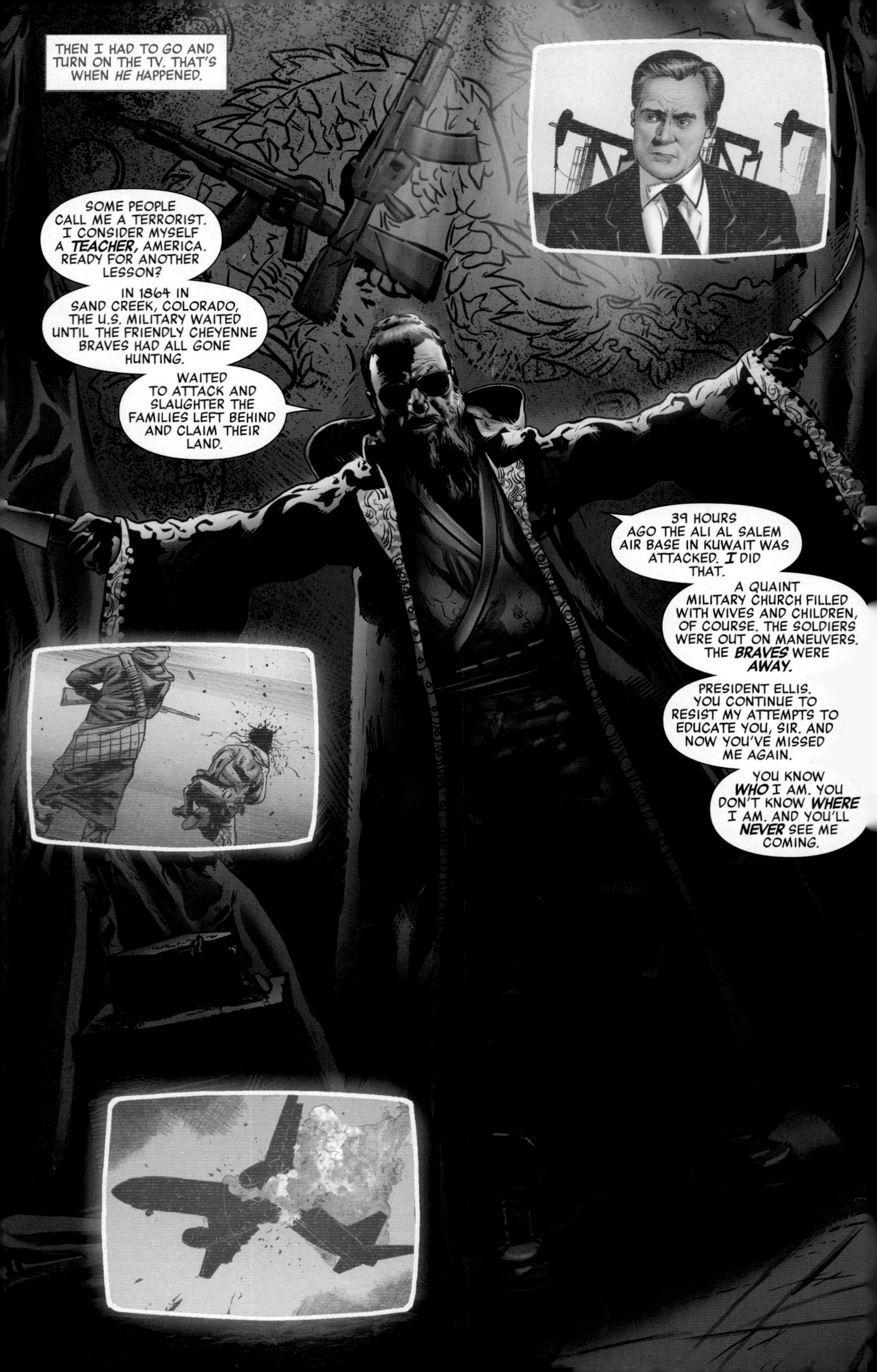

THEN I HAD TO GO AND TURN ON THE TV. THAT'S WHEN HE HAPPENED.
SOME PEOPLE CALL ME A TERRORIST. I CONSIDER MYSELF A TEACHER, AMERICA. READY FOR ANOTHER LESSON?
IN 1864 IN SAND CREEK, COLORADO, THE U.S. MILITARY WAITED UNTIL THE FRIENDLY CHEYENNE BRAVES HAD ALL GONE HUNTING.
WAITED TO ATTACK AND SLAUGHTER THE FAMILIES LEFT BEHIND AND CLAIM THEIR LAND.
39 HOURS AGO THE ALI AL SALEM AIR BASE IN KUWAIT WAS ATTACKED. I DID THAT.
A QUAINT MILITARY CHURCH FILLED WITH WIVES AND CHILDREN, OF COURSE. THE SOLDIERS WERE OUT ON MANEUVERS. THE BRAVES WERE AWAY.
PRESIDENT ELLIS. YOU CONTINUE TO RESIST MY ATTEMPTS TO EDUCATE YOU, SIR. AND NOW YOU'VE MISSED ME AGAIN.
YOU KNOW WHO I AM. YOU DON'T KNOW WHERE I AM. AND YOU'LL NEVER SEE ME COMING.

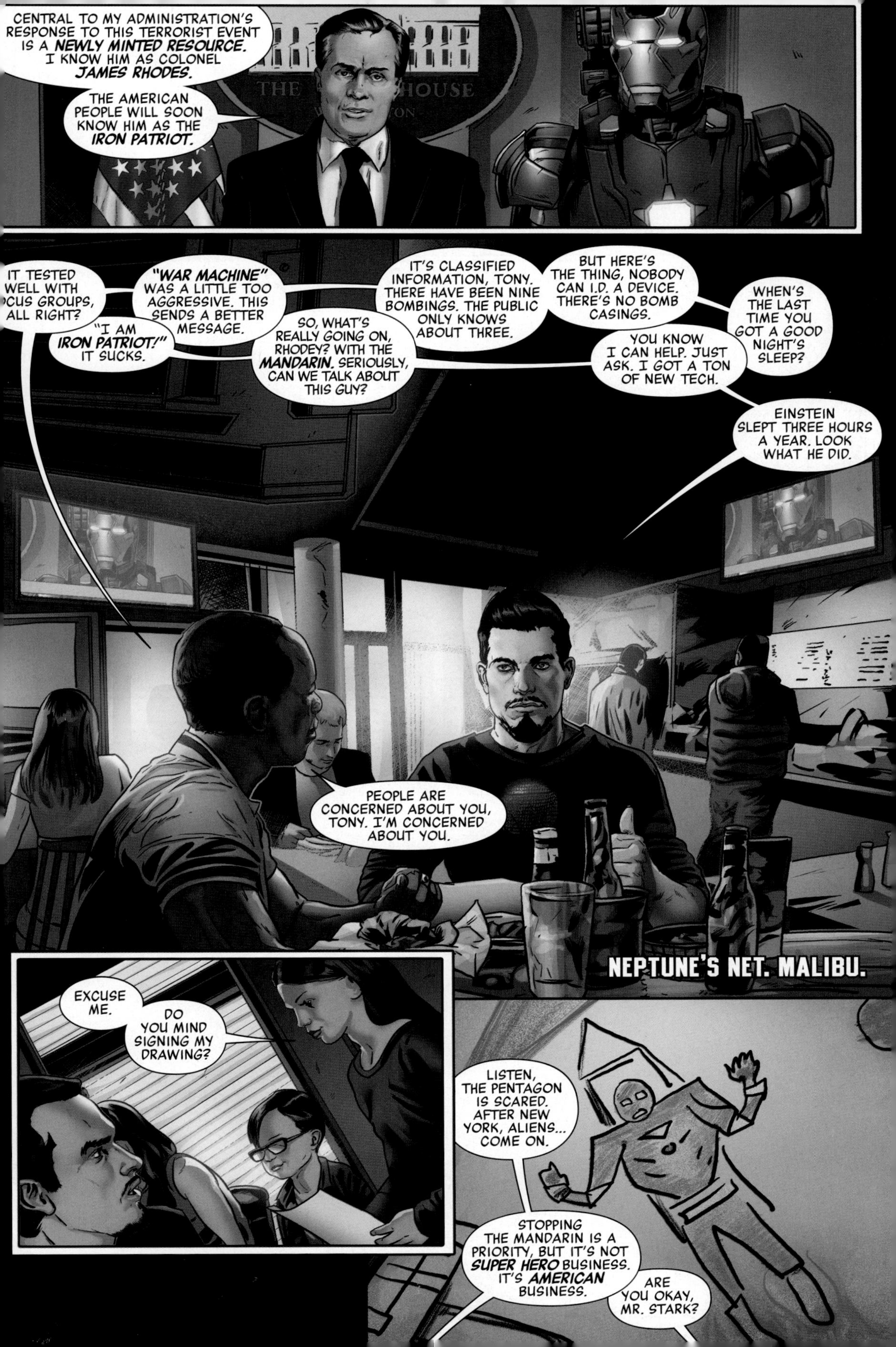
CENTRAL TO MY ADMINISTRATION'S RESPONSE TO THIS TERRORIST EVENT IS A NEWLY MINTED RESOURCE. I KNOW HIM AS COLONEL JAMES RHODES.
THE AMERICAN PEOPLE WILL SOON KNOW HIM AS THE IRON PATRIOT.
IT TESTED WELL WITH FOCUS GROUPS, ALL RIGHT?
"WAR MACHINE" WAS A LITTLE TOO AGGRESSIVE. THIS SENDS A BETTER MESSAGE.
"I AM IRON PATRIOT!" IT SUCKS.
SO, WHAT'S REALLY GOING ON, RHODEY? WITH THE MANDARIN. SERIOUSLY, CAN WE TALK ABOUT THIS GUY?
IT'S CLASSIFIED INFORMATION, TONY. THERE HAVE BEEN NINE BOMBINGS. THE PUBLIC ONLY KNOWS ABOUT THREE.
BUT HERE'S THE THING, NOBODY CAN I.D. A DEVICE. THERE'S NO BOMB CASINGS.
YOU KNOW I CAN HELP. JUST ASK. I GOT A TON OF NEW TECH.
WHEN'S THE LAST TIME YOU GOT A GOOD NIGHT'S SLEEP?
EINSTEIN SLEPT THREE HOURS A YEAR. LOOK WHAT HE DID.
PEOPLE ARE CONCERNED ABOUT YOU, TONY. I'M CONCERNED ABOUT YOU.
NEPTUNE'S NET. MALIBU.
EXCUSE ME.
DO YOU MIND SIGNING MY DRAWING?
LISTEN, THE PENTAGON IS SCARED. AFTER NEW YORK, ALIENS... COME ON.
STOPPING THE MANDARIN IS A PRIORITY, BUT IT'S NOT SUPER HERO BUSINESS. IT'S AMERICAN BUSINESS.
ARE YOU OKAY, MR. STARK?

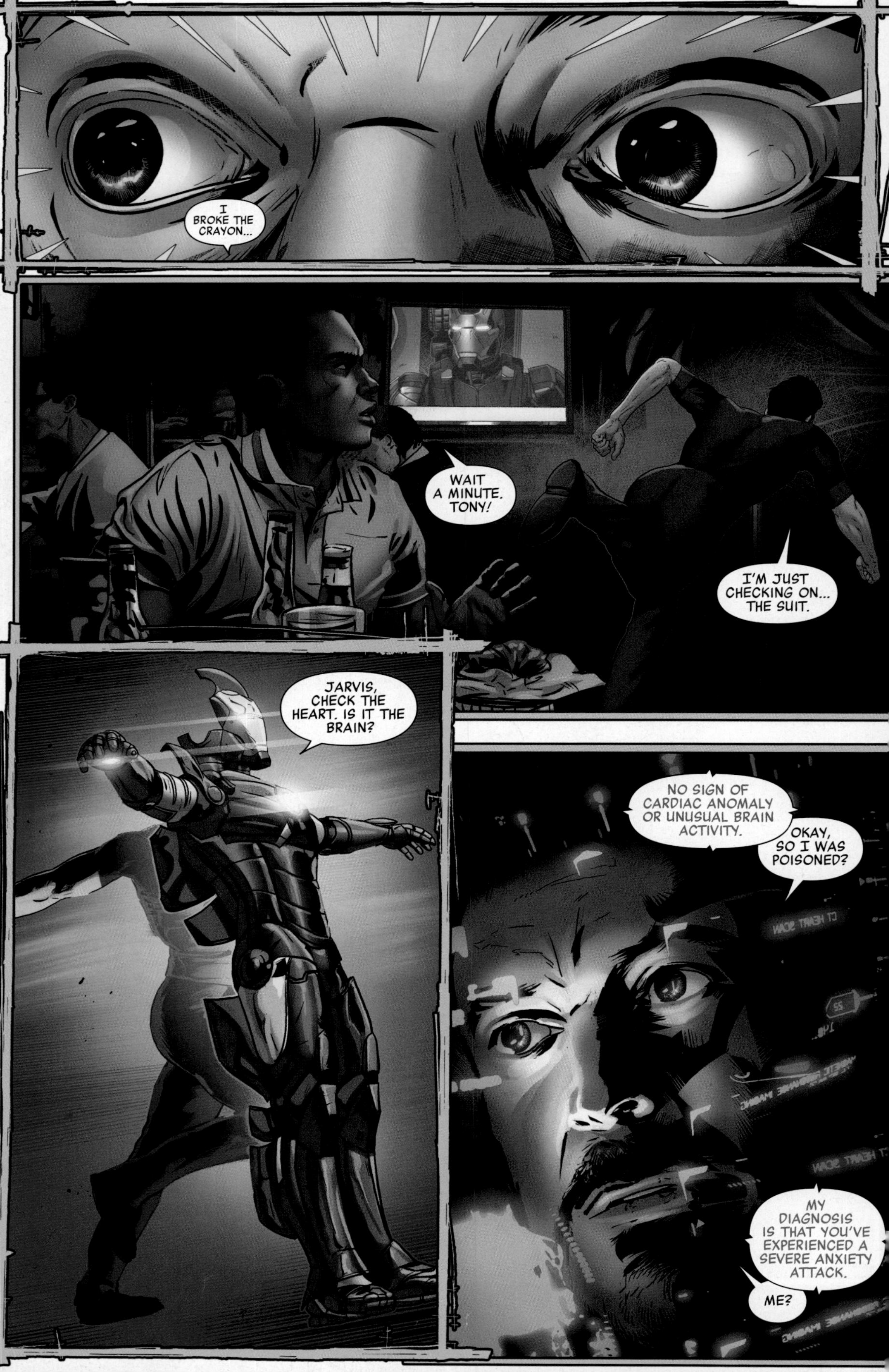
I BROKE THE CRAYON...
WAIT A MINUTE. TONY!
I'M JUST CHECKING ON... THE SUIT.
JARVIS, CHECK THE HEART. IS IT THE BRAIN?
NO SIGN OF CARDIAC ANOMALY OR UNUSUAL BRAIN ACTIVITY.
OKAY, SO I WAS POISONED?
MY DIAGNOSIS IS THAT YOU'VE EXPERIENCED A SEVERE ANXIETY ATTACK.
ME?

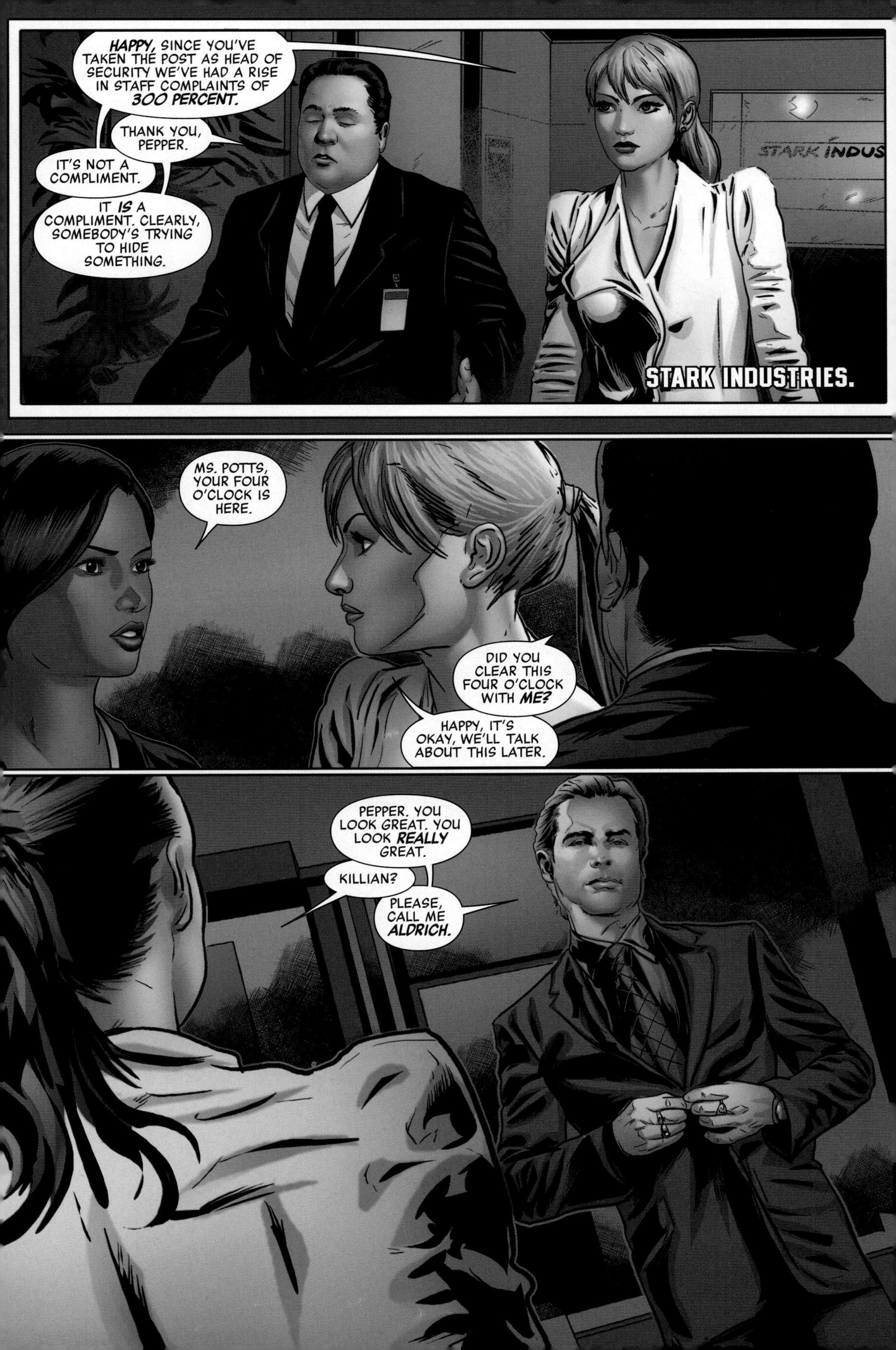
HAPPY, SINCE YOU'VE TAKEN THE POST AS HEAD OF SECURITY WE'VE HAD A RISE IN STAFF COMPLAINTS OF 300 PERCENT.
THANK YOU, PEPPER.
IT'S NOT A COMPLIMENT.
IT IS A COMPLIMENT. CLEARLY, SOMEBODY'S TRYING TO HIDE SOMETHING.
STARK INDUS
STARK INDUSTRIES.
MS. POTTS, YOUR FOUR O'CLOCK IS HERE.
DID YOU CLEAR THIS FOUR O'CLOCK WITH ME?
HAPPY, IT'S OKAY, WE'LL TALK ABOUT THIS LATER.
PEPPER. YOU LOOK GREAT. YOU LOOK REALLY GREAT.
KILLIAN?
PLEASE, CALL ME ALDRICH.

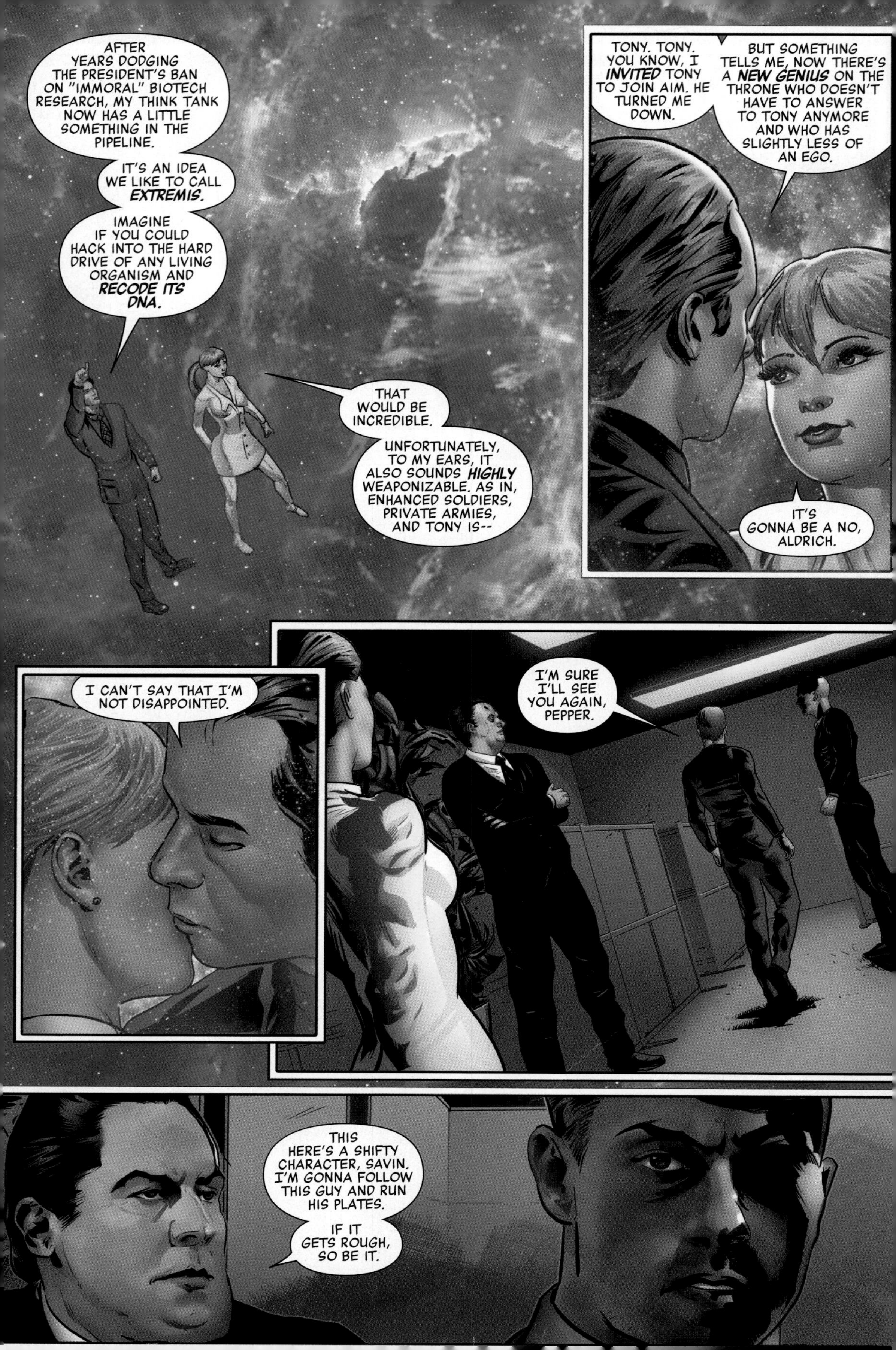
AFTER YEARS DODGING THE PRESIDENT'S BAN ON "IMMORAL" BIOTECH RESEARCH, MY THINK TANK NOW HAS A LITTLE SOMETHING IN THE PIPELINE.
IT'S AN IDEA WE LIKE TO CALL ***EXTREMIS.***
IMAGINE IF YOU COULD HACK INTO THE HARD DRIVE OF ANY LIVING ORGANISM AND ***RECODE ITS DNA.***
THAT WOULD BE INCREDIBLE.
UNFORTUNATELY, TO MY EARS, IT ALSO SOUNDS ***HIGHLY*** WEAPONIZABLE. AS IN, ENHANCED SOLDIERS, PRIVATE ARMIES, AND TONY IS--
TONY. TONY. YOU KNOW, I ***INVITED*** TONY TO JOIN AIM. HE TURNED ME DOWN.
BUT SOMETHING TELLS ME, NOW THERE'S A ***NEW GENIUS*** ON THE THRONE WHO DOESN'T HAVE TO ANSWER TO TONY ANYMORE AND WHO HAS SLIGHTLY LESS OF AN EGO.
IT'S GONNA BE A NO, ALDRICH.
I CAN'T SAY THAT I'M NOT DISAPPOINTED.
I'M SURE I'LL SEE YOU AGAIN, PEPPER.
THIS HERE'S A SHIFTY CHARACTER, SAVIN. I'M GONNA FOLLOW THIS GUY AND RUN HIS PLATES.
IF IT GETS ROUGH, SO BE IT.

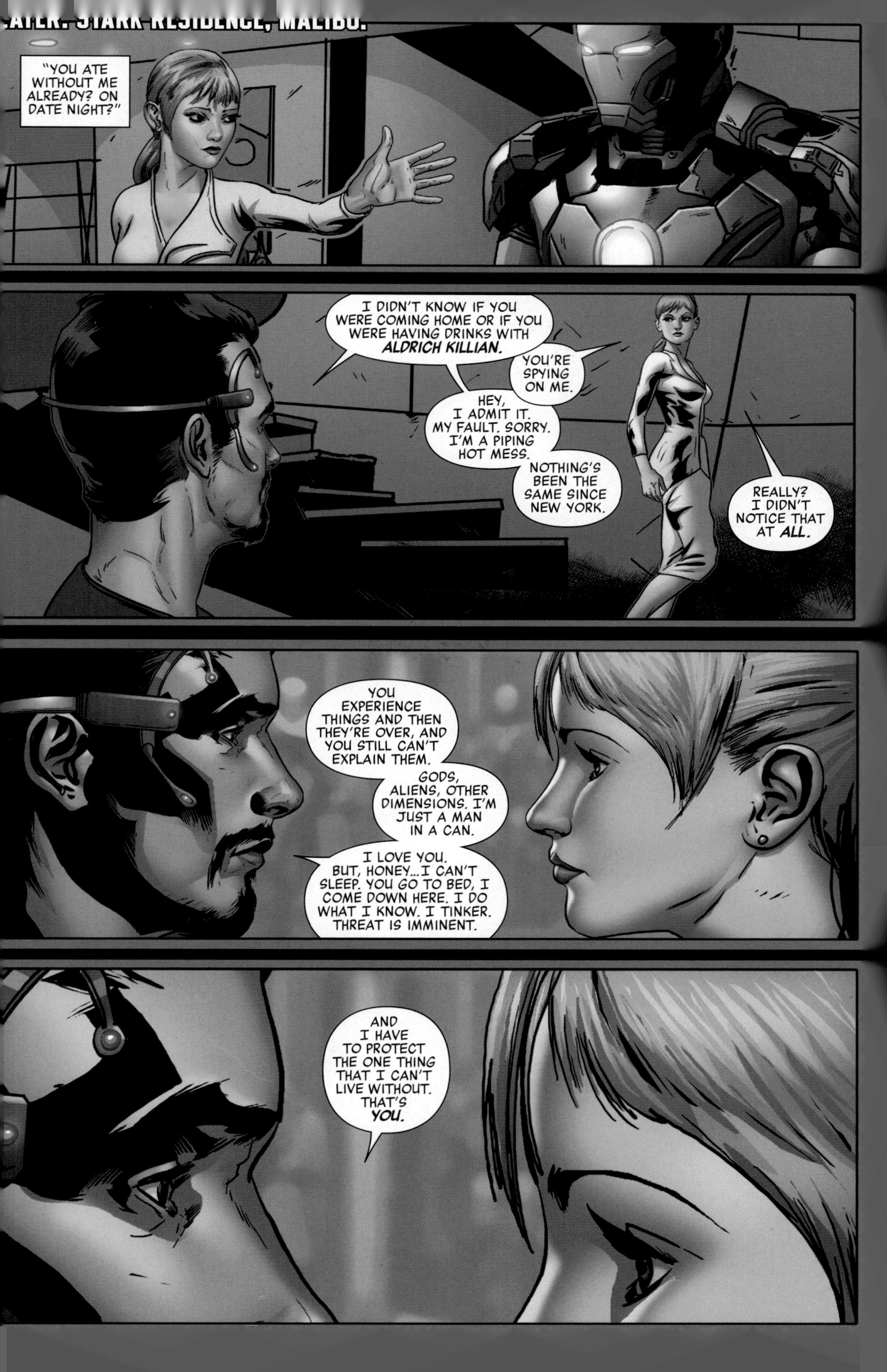
STARK RESIDENCE, MALIBU.
"YOU ATE WITHOUT ME ALREADY? ON DATE NIGHT?"
I DIDN'T KNOW IF YOU WERE COMING HOME OR IF YOU WERE HAVING DRINKS WITH **ALDRICH KILLIAN.**
YOU'RE SPYING ON ME.
HEY, I ADMIT IT. MY FAULT. SORRY. I'M A PIPING HOT MESS.
NOTHING'S BEEN THE SAME SINCE NEW YORK.
REALLY? I DIDN'T NOTICE THAT AT **ALL.**
YOU EXPERIENCE THINGS AND THEN THEY'RE OVER, AND YOU STILL CAN'T EXPLAIN THEM.
GODS, ALIENS, OTHER DIMENSIONS. I'M JUST A MAN IN A CAN.
I LOVE YOU. BUT, HONEY... I CAN'T SLEEP. YOU GO TO BED, I COME DOWN HERE. I DO WHAT I KNOW. I TINKER. THREAT IS IMMINENT.
AND I HAVE TO PROTECT THE ONE THING THAT I CAN'T LIVE WITHOUT. THAT'S **YOU.**

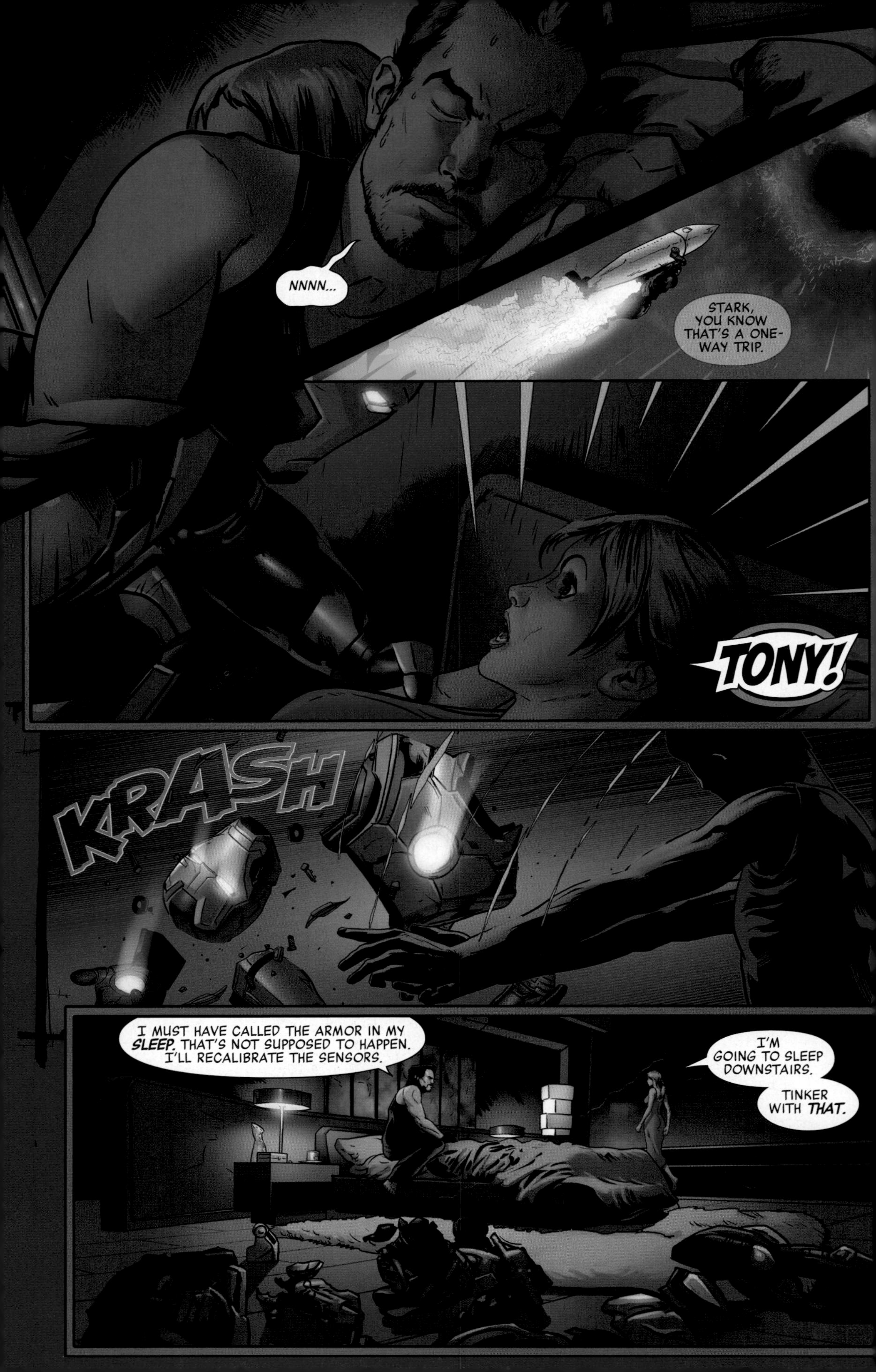
NNNN...
STARK, YOU KNOW THAT'S A ONE-WAY TRIP.
TONY!
KRASH
I MUST HAVE CALLED THE ARMOR IN MY SLEEP. THAT'S NOT SUPPOSED TO HAPPEN. I'LL RECALIBRATE THE SENSORS.
I'M GOING TO SLEEP DOWNSTAIRS.
TINKER WITH THAT.

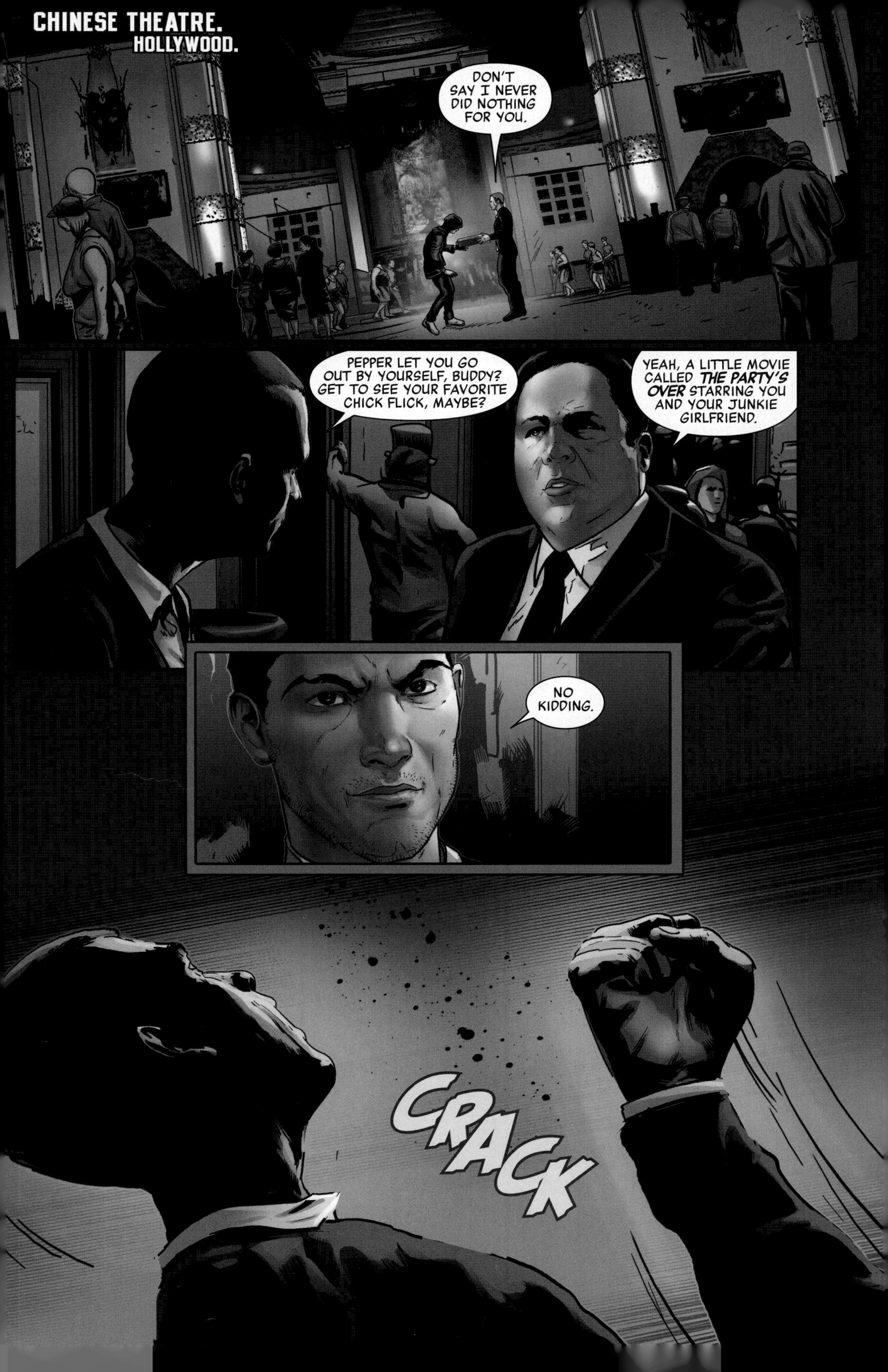
CHINESE THEATRE.
HOLLYWOOD.
DON'T SAY I NEVER DID NOTHING FOR YOU.
PEPPER LET YOU GO OUT BY YOURSELF, BUDDY? GET TO SEE YOUR FAVORITE CHICK FLICK, MAYBE?
YEAH, A LITTLE MOVIE CALLED THE PARTY'S OVER STARRING YOU AND YOUR JUNKIE GIRLFRIEND.
NO KIDDING.
CRACK

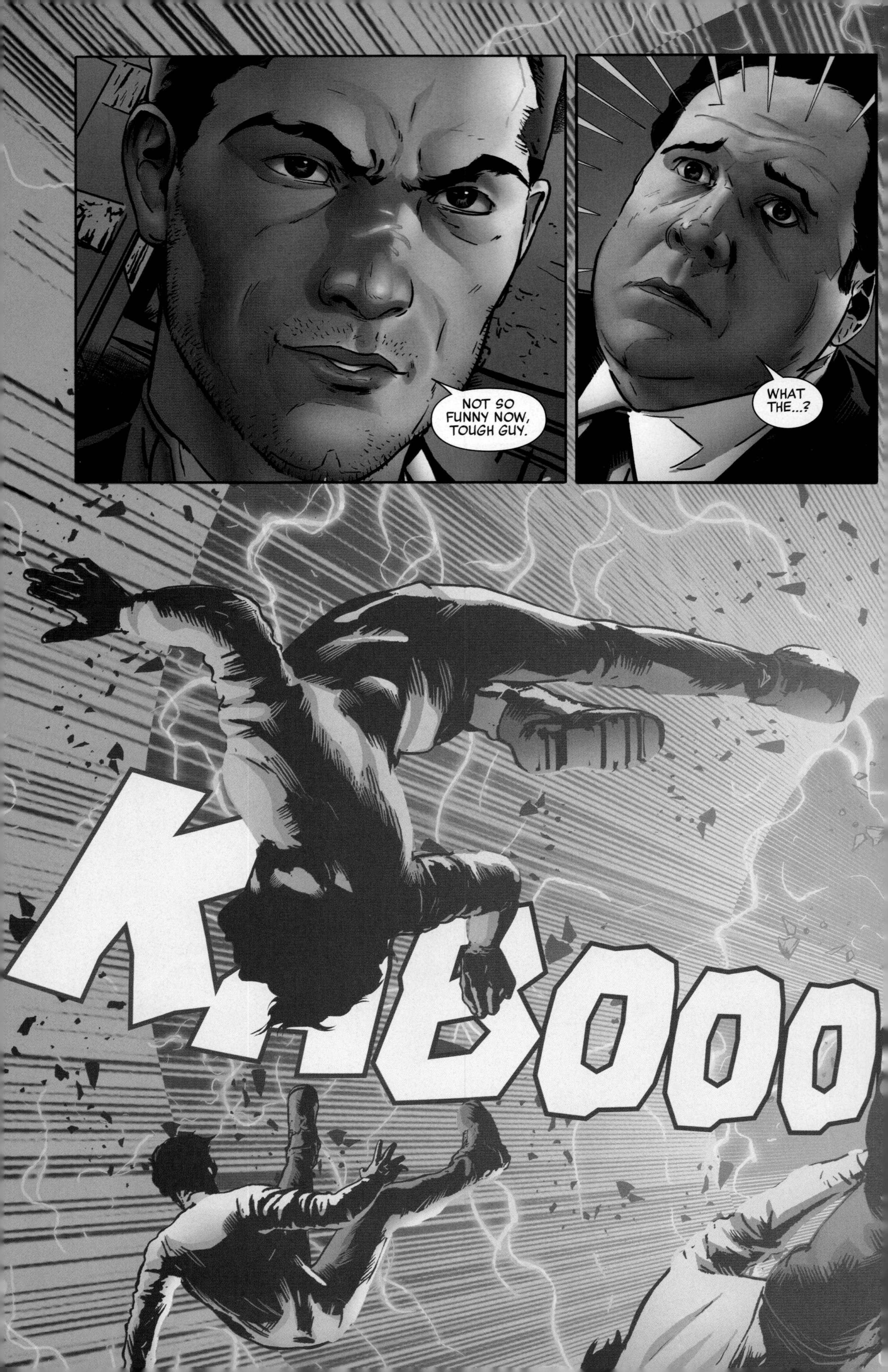
NOT SO FUNNY NOW, TOUGH GUY.
WHAT THE...?

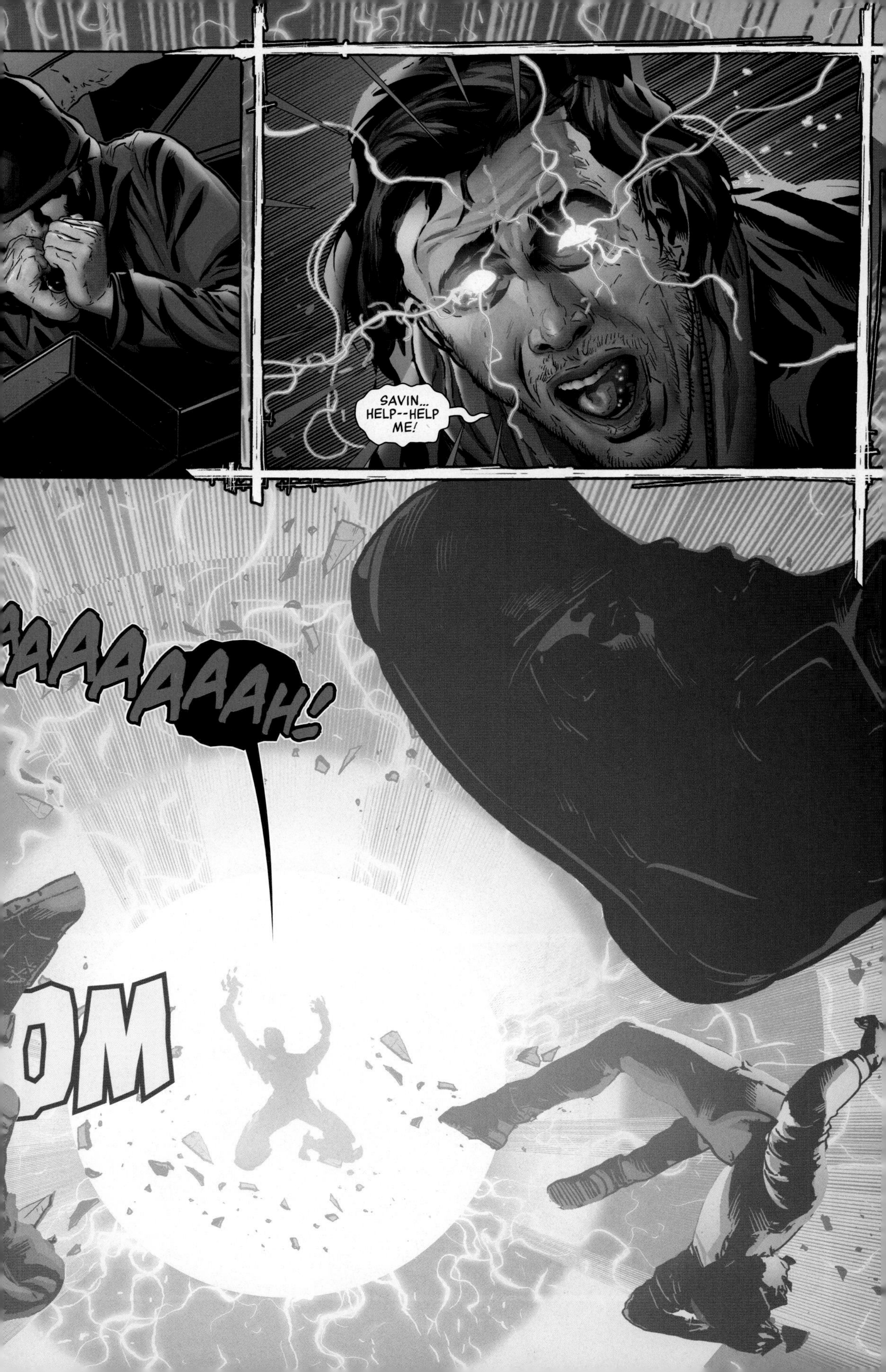
SAVIN... HELP--HELP ME!
AAAAAAAAH!
OM

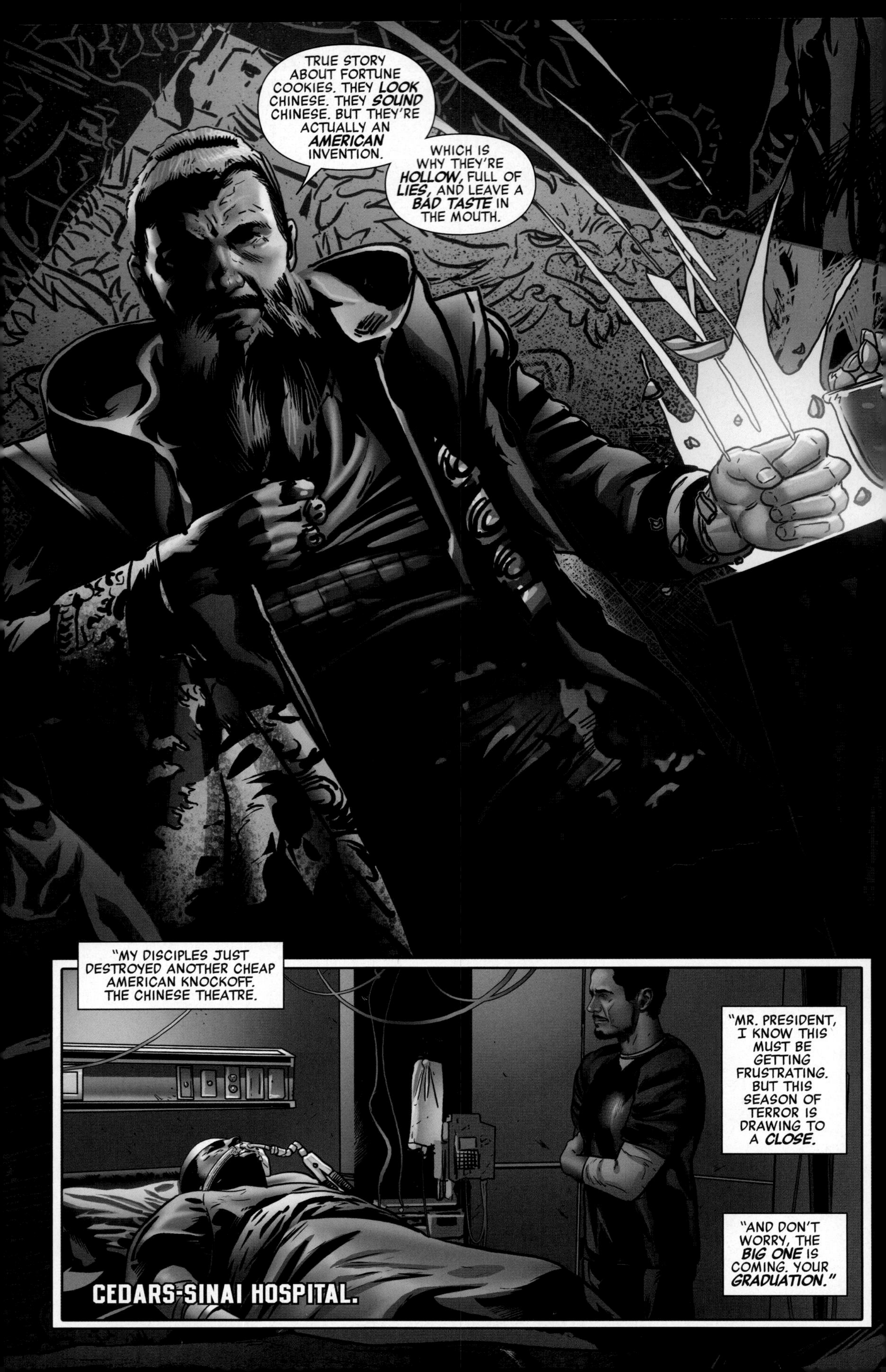
TRUE STORY ABOUT FORTUNE COOKIES. THEY LOOK CHINESE. THEY SOUND CHINESE. BUT THEY'RE ACTUALLY AN AMERICAN INVENTION.
WHICH IS WHY THEY'RE HOLLOW, FULL OF LIES, AND LEAVE A BAD TASTE IN THE MOUTH.
"MY DISCIPLES JUST DESTROYED ANOTHER CHEAP AMERICAN KNOCKOFF. THE CHINESE THEATRE.
"MR. PRESIDENT, I KNOW THIS MUST BE GETTING FRUSTRATING. BUT THIS SEASON OF TERROR IS DRAWING TO A CLOSE.
"AND DON'T WORRY, THE BIG ONE IS COMING. YOUR GRADUATION."
CEDARS-SINAI HOSPITAL.

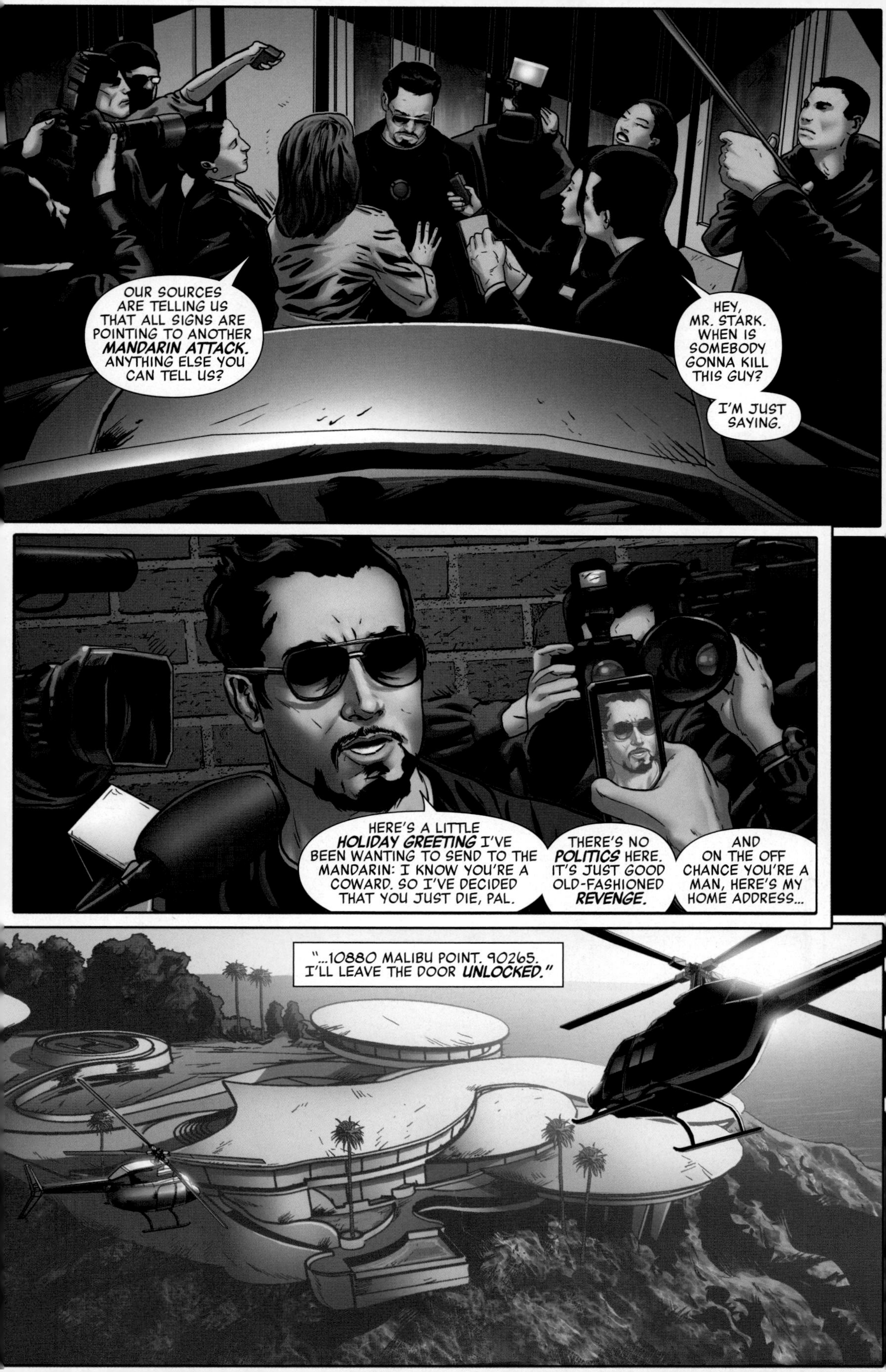
OUR SOURCES ARE TELLING US THAT ALL SIGNS ARE POINTING TO ANOTHER MANDARIN ATTACK. ANYTHING ELSE YOU CAN TELL US?
HEY, MR. STARK. WHEN IS SOMEBODY GONNA KILL THIS GUY?
I'M JUST SAYING.
HERE'S A LITTLE HOLIDAY GREETING I'VE BEEN WANTING TO SEND TO THE MANDARIN: I KNOW YOU'RE A COWARD. SO I'VE DECIDED THAT YOU JUST DIE, PAL.
THERE'S NO POLITICS HERE. IT'S JUST GOOD OLD-FASHIONED REVENGE.
AND ON THE OFF CHANCE YOU'RE A MAN, HERE'S MY HOME ADDRESS...
"...10880 MALIBU POINT. 90265. I'LL LEAVE THE DOOR UNLOCKED."

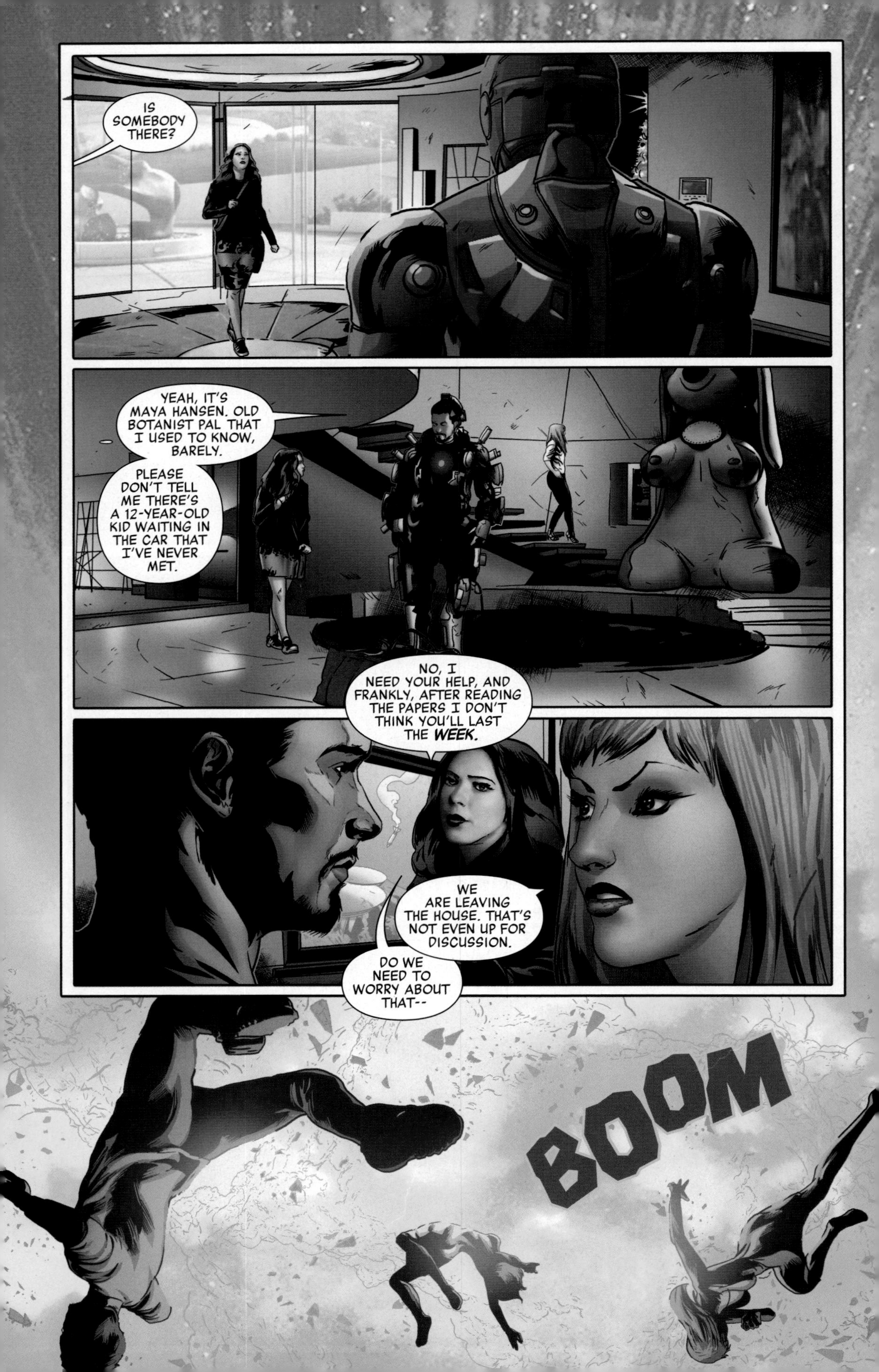
IS SOMEBODY THERE?
YEAH, IT'S MAYA HANSEN. OLD BOTANIST PAL THAT I USED TO KNOW, BARELY.
PLEASE DON'T TELL ME THERE'S A 12-YEAR-OLD KID WAITING IN THE CAR THAT I'VE NEVER MET.
NO, I NEED YOUR HELP, AND FRANKLY, AFTER READING THE PAPERS I DON'T THINK YOU'LL LAST THE WEEK.
WE ARE LEAVING THE HOUSE. THAT'S NOT EVEN UP FOR DISCUSSION.
DO WE NEED TO WORRY ABOUT THAT--
BOOM

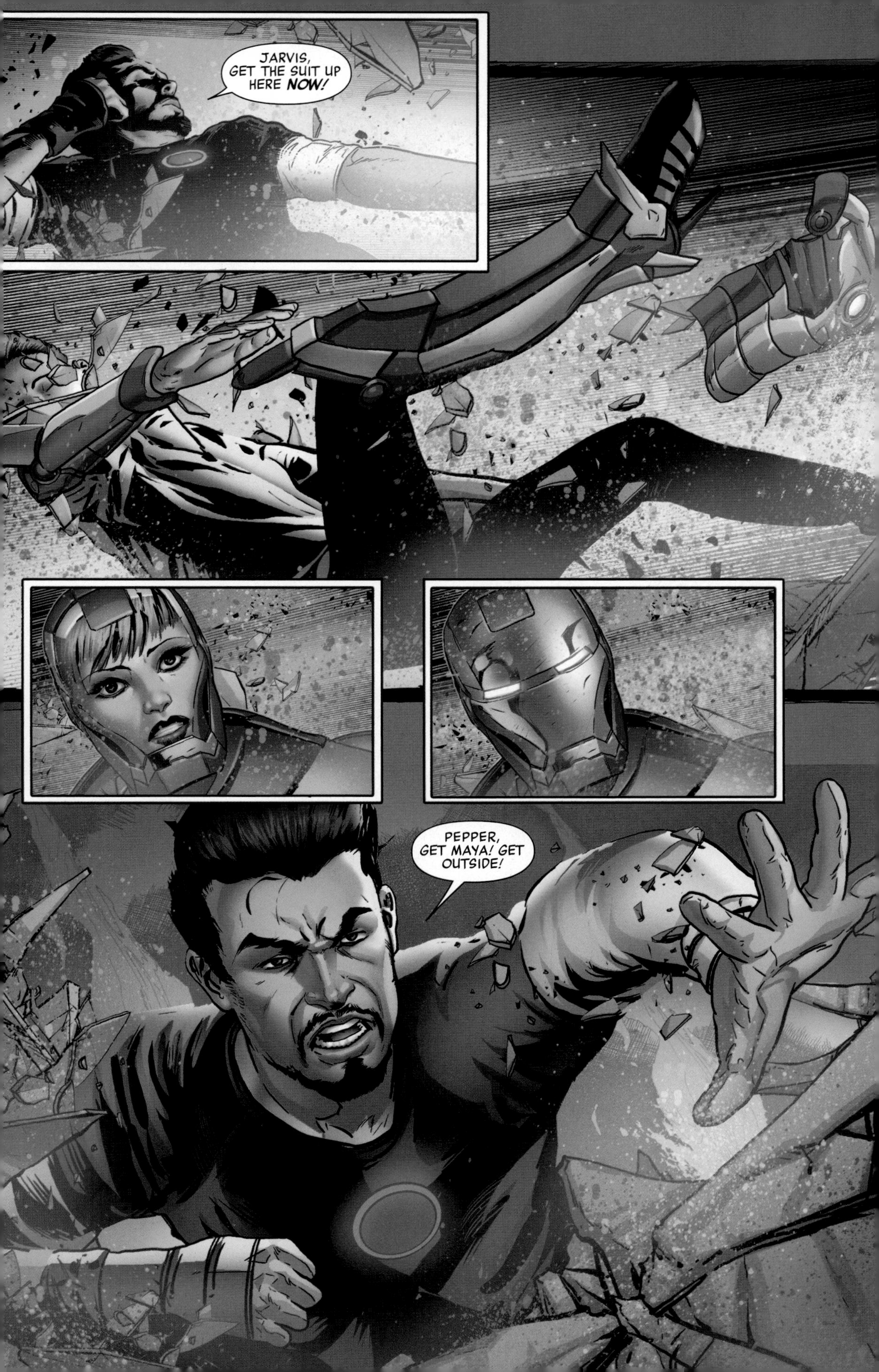
JARVIS, GET THE SUIT UP HERE **NOW!**
PEPPER, GET MAYA! GET OUTSIDE!

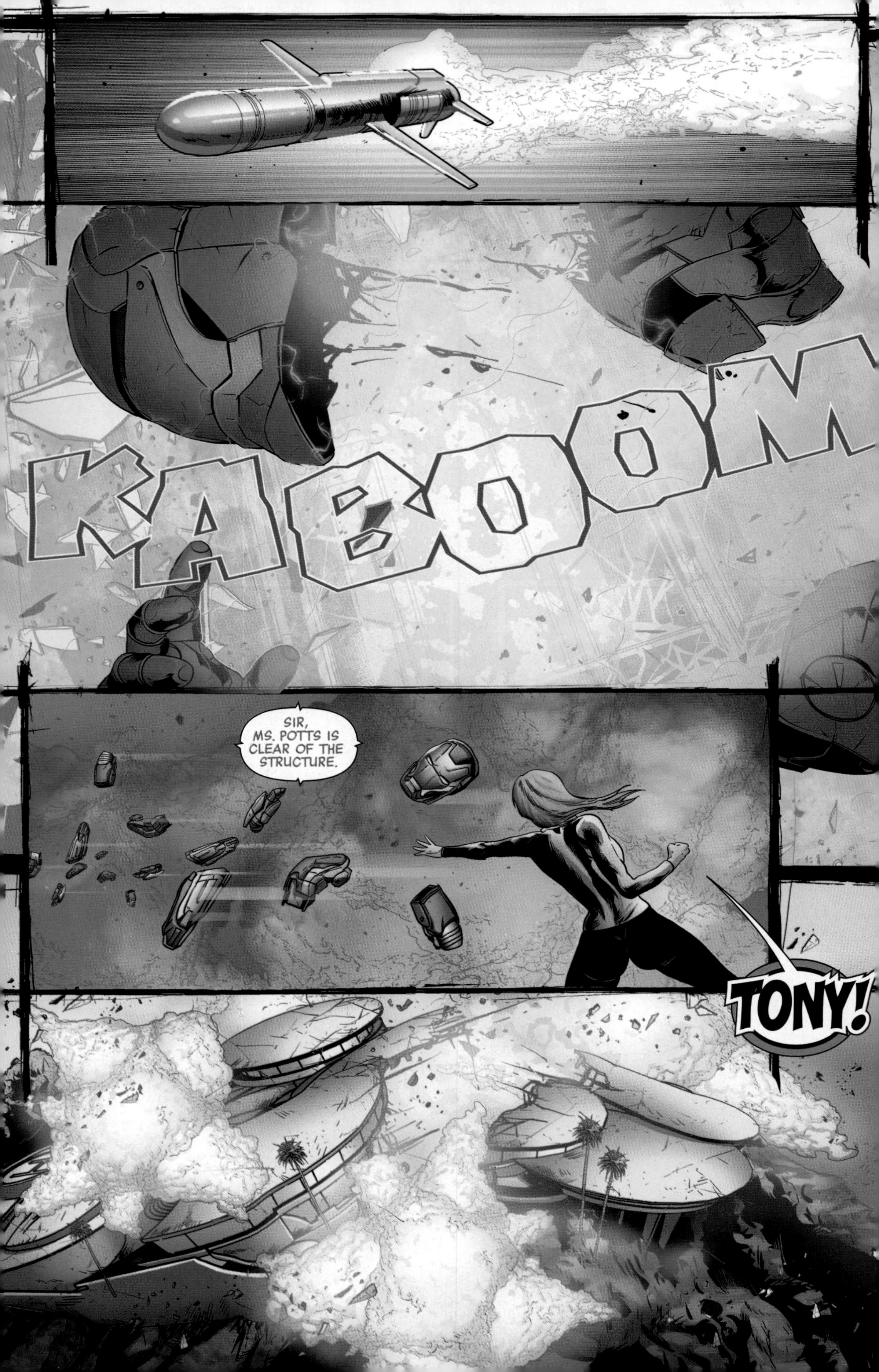
KABOOM
SIR, MS. POTTS IS CLEAR OF THE STRUCTURE.
TONY!

MARVEL'S CAPTAIN AMERICA: CIVIL WAR PRELUDE #2

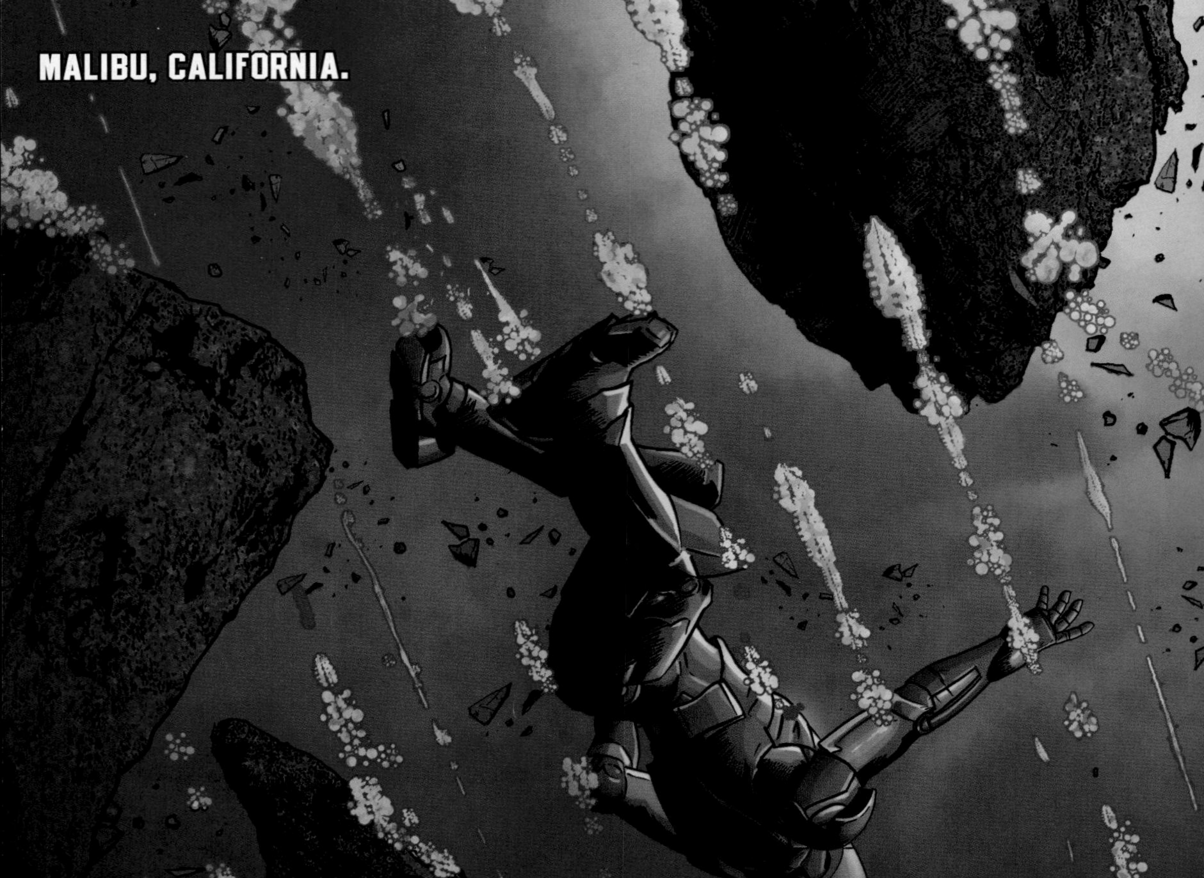
MALIBU, CALIFORNIA.

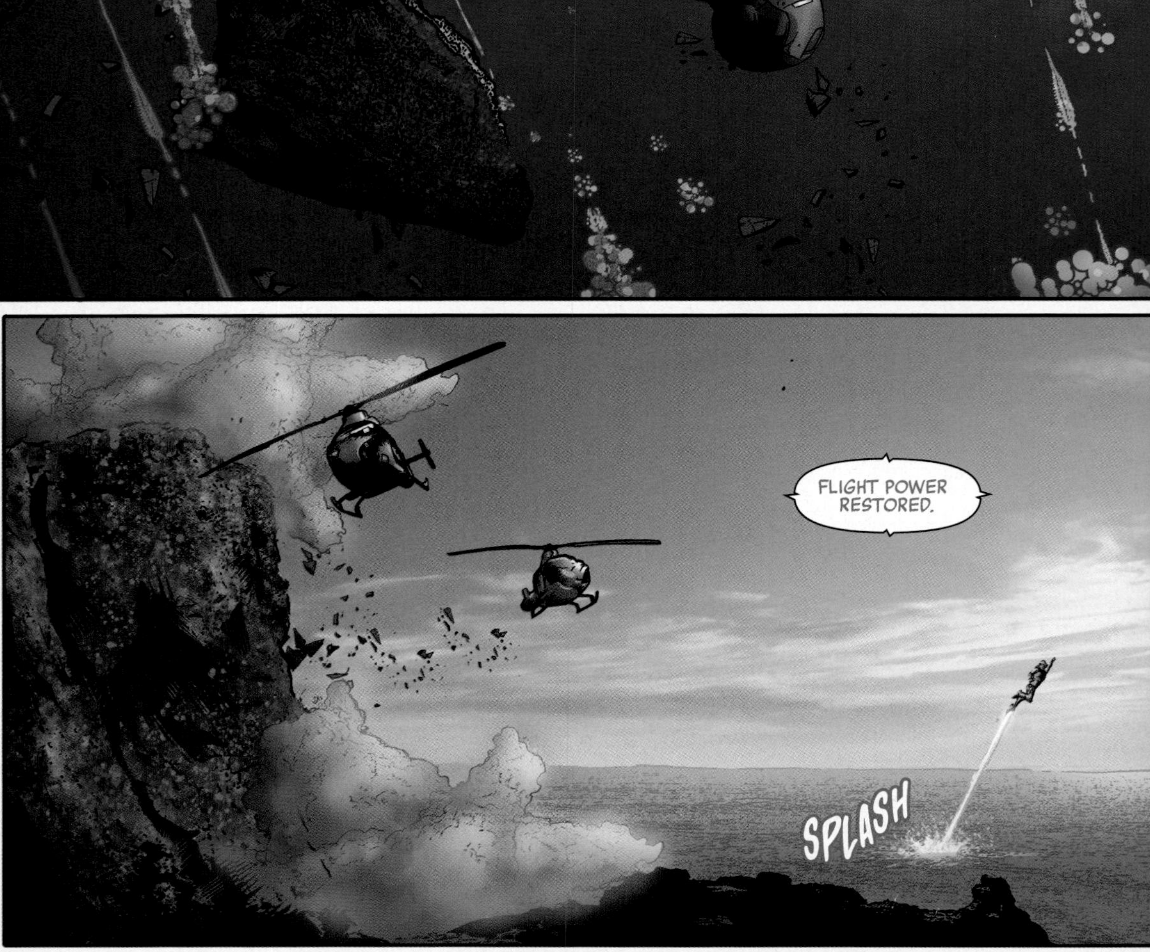
FLIGHT POWER RESTORED.
SPLASH

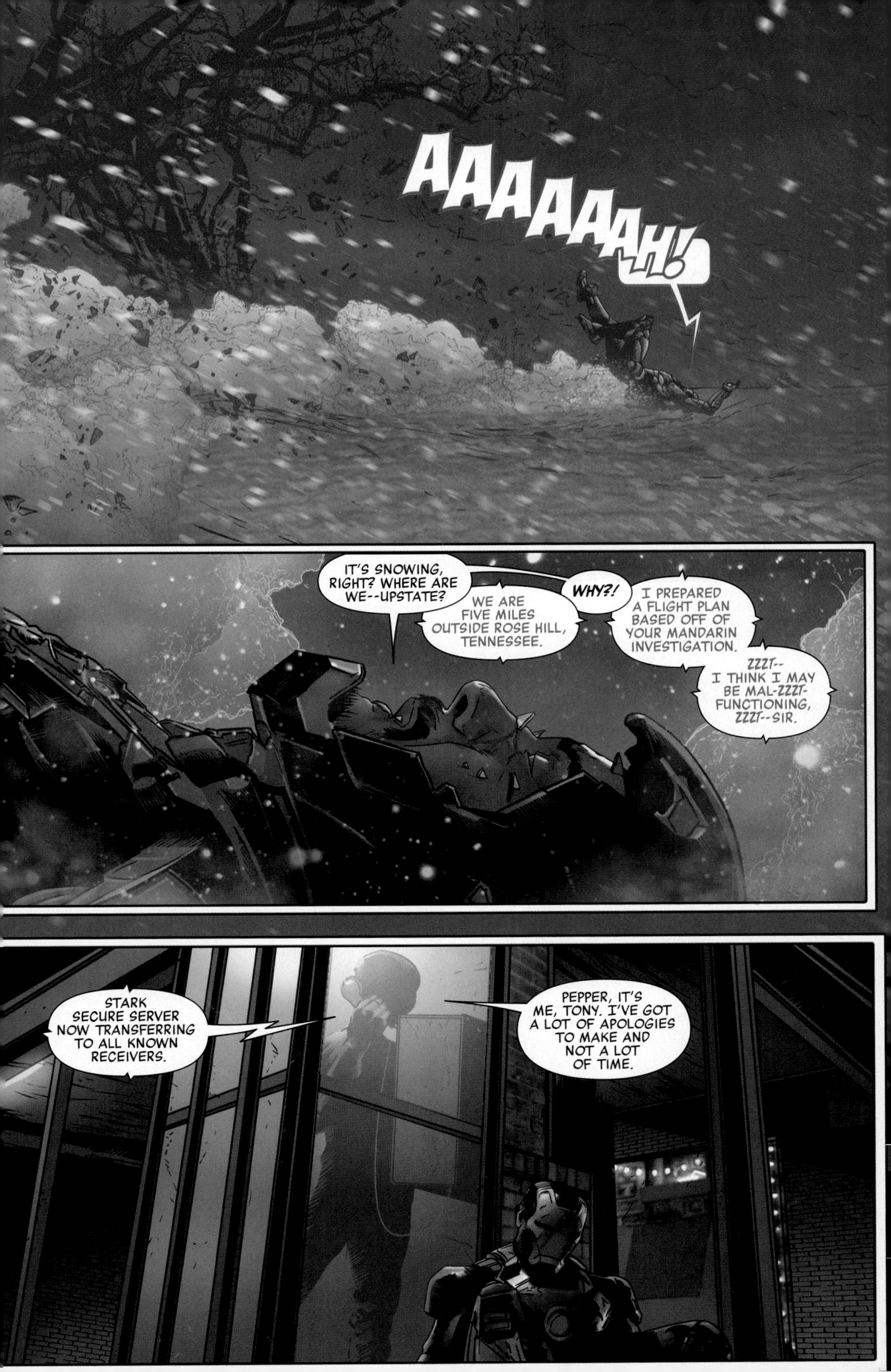
AAAAAAAH!
IT'S SNOWING, RIGHT? WHERE ARE WE--UPSTATE? WHY?!
WE ARE FIVE MILES OUTSIDE ROSE HILL, TENNESSEE.
I PREPARED A FLIGHT PLAN BASED OFF OF YOUR MANDARIN INVESTIGATION.
ZZZT-- I THINK I MAY BE MAL-ZZZT-FUNCTIONING, ZZZT--SIR.
STARK SECURE SERVER NOW TRANSFERRING TO ALL KNOWN RECEIVERS.
PEPPER, IT'S ME, TONY. I'VE GOT A LOT OF APOLOGIES TO MAKE AND NOT A LOT OF TIME.

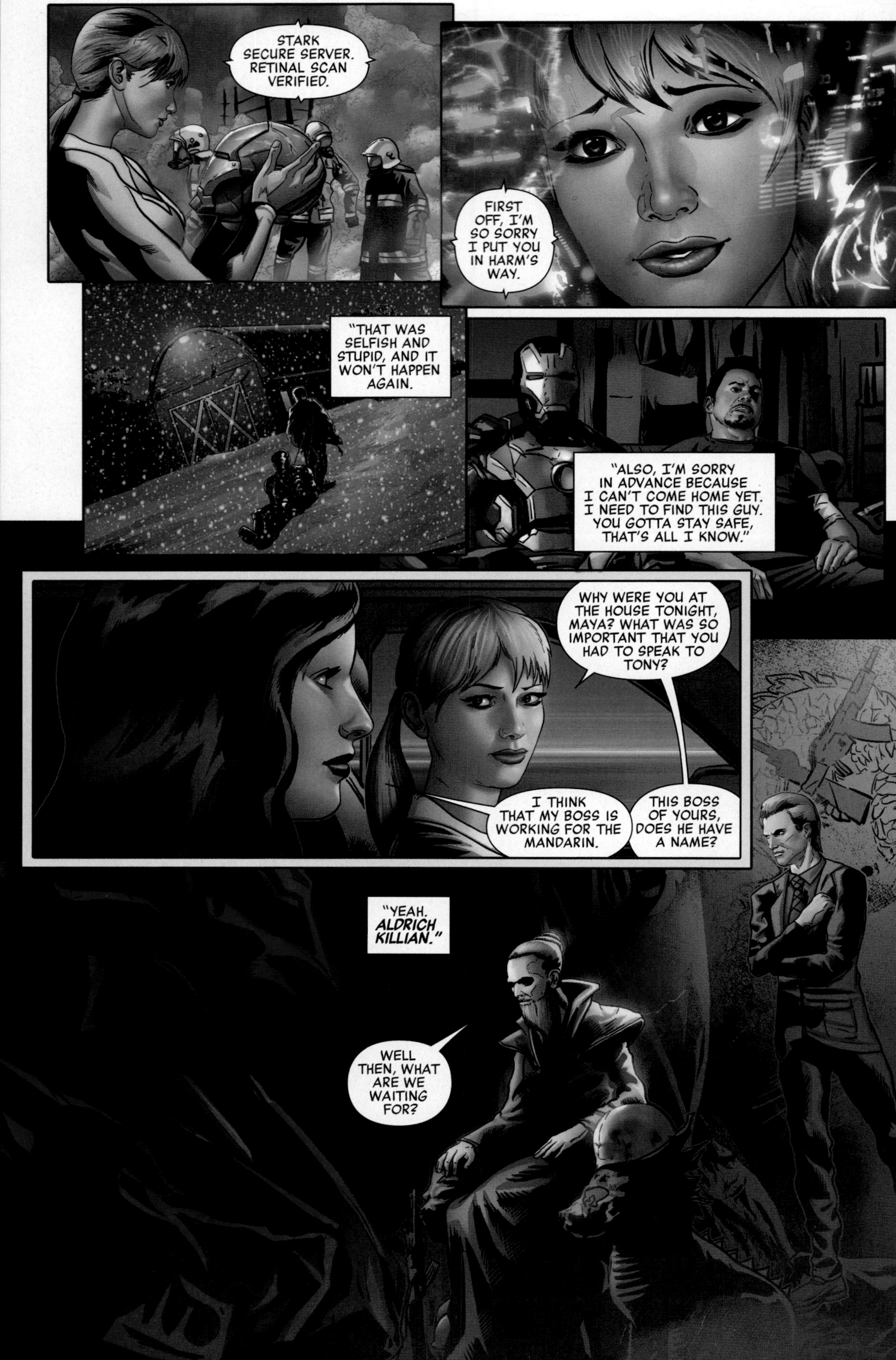
STARK SECURE SERVER. RETINAL SCAN VERIFIED.
FIRST OFF, I'M SO SORRY I PUT YOU IN HARM'S WAY.
"THAT WAS SELFISH AND STUPID, AND IT WON'T HAPPEN AGAIN.
"ALSO, I'M SORRY IN ADVANCE BECAUSE I CAN'T COME HOME YET. I NEED TO FIND THIS GUY. YOU GOTTA STAY SAFE, THAT'S ALL I KNOW."
WHY WERE YOU AT THE HOUSE TONIGHT, MAYA? WHAT WAS SO IMPORTANT THAT YOU HAD TO SPEAK TO TONY?
I THINK THAT MY BOSS IS WORKING FOR THE MANDARIN.
THIS BOSS OF YOURS, DOES HE HAVE A NAME?
"YEAH. *ALDRICH KILLIAN.*"
WELL THEN, WHAT ARE WE WAITING FOR?

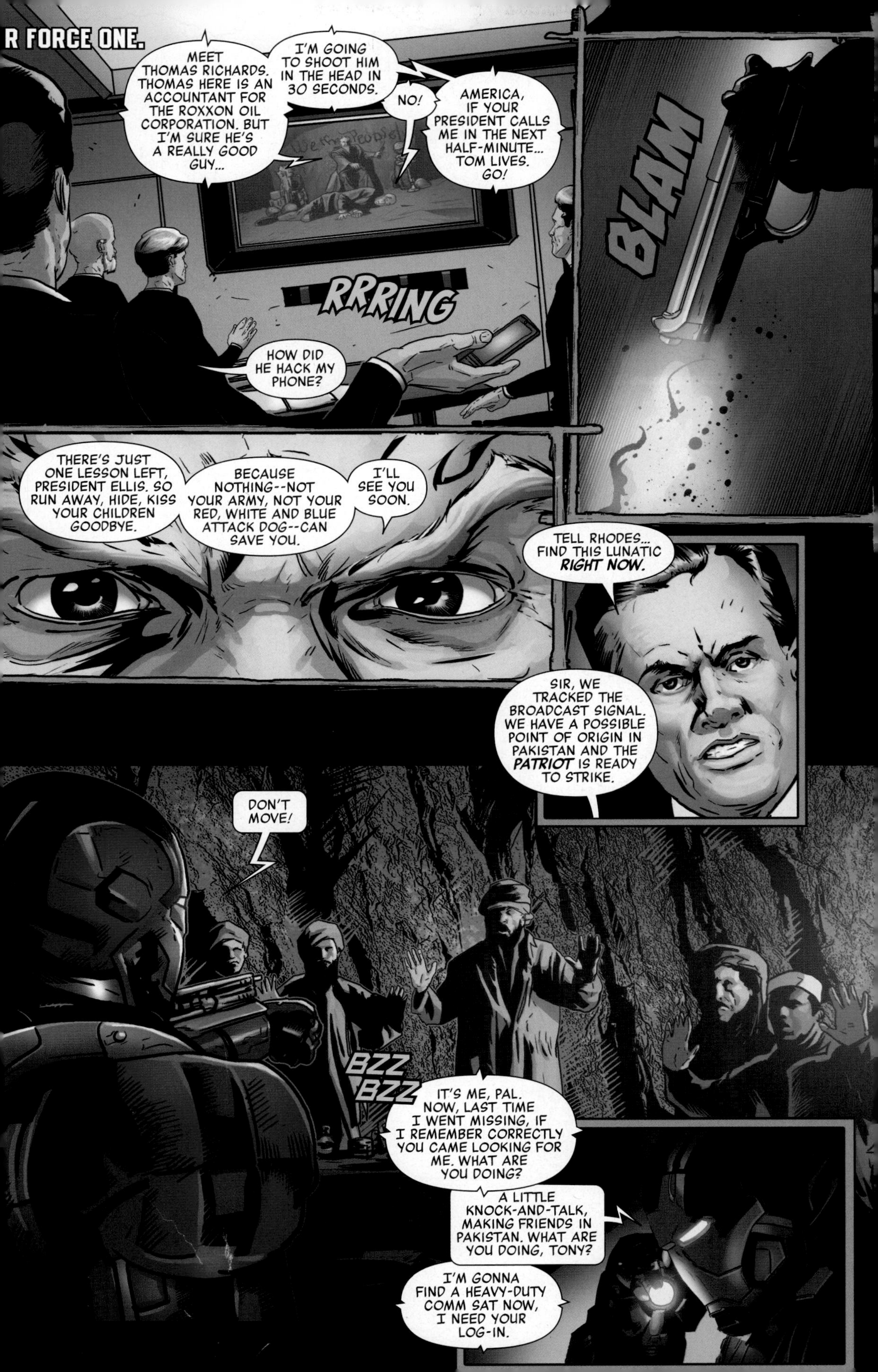
R FORCE ONE.
MEET THOMAS RICHARDS. THOMAS HERE IS AN ACCOUNTANT FOR THE ROXXON OIL CORPORATION. BUT I'M SURE HE'S A REALLY GOOD GUY...
I'M GOING TO SHOOT HIM IN THE HEAD IN 30 SECONDS.
NO!
AMERICA, IF YOUR PRESIDENT CALLS ME IN THE NEXT HALF-MINUTE... TOM LIVES. GO!
RRRING
HOW DID HE HACK MY PHONE?
BLAM
THERE'S JUST ONE LESSON LEFT, PRESIDENT ELLIS. SO RUN AWAY, HIDE, KISS YOUR CHILDREN GOODBYE.
BECAUSE NOTHING--NOT YOUR ARMY, NOT YOUR RED, WHITE AND BLUE ATTACK DOG--CAN SAVE YOU.
I'LL SEE YOU SOON.
TELL RHODES... FIND THIS LUNATIC RIGHT NOW.
SIR, WE TRACKED THE BROADCAST SIGNAL. WE HAVE A POSSIBLE POINT OF ORIGIN IN PAKISTAN AND THE PATRIOT IS READY TO STRIKE.
DON'T MOVE!
BZZ BZZ
IT'S ME, PAL. NOW, LAST TIME I WENT MISSING, IF I REMEMBER CORRECTLY YOU CAME LOOKING FOR ME. WHAT ARE YOU DOING?
A LITTLE KNOCK-AND-TALK, MAKING FRIENDS IN PAKISTAN. WHAT ARE YOU DOING, TONY?
I'M GONNA FIND A HEAVY-DUTY COMM SAT NOW, I NEED YOUR LOG-IN.

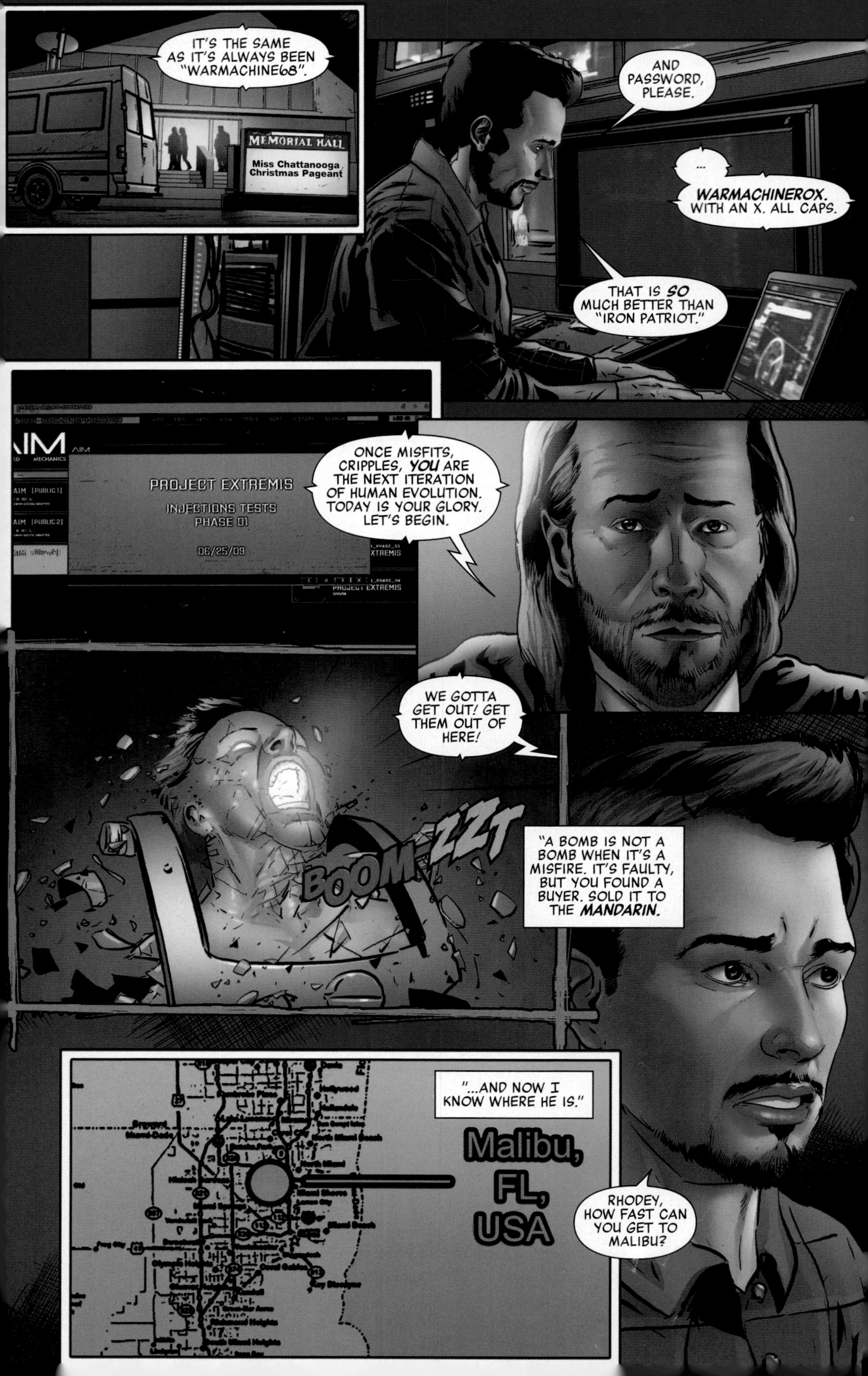
IT'S THE SAME AS IT'S ALWAYS BEEN "WARMACHINE68".
MEMORIAL HALL
Miss Chattanooga Christmas Pageant
AND PASSWORD, PLEASE.
...
WARMACHINEROX. WITH AN X. ALL CAPS.
THAT IS SO MUCH BETTER THAN "IRON PATRIOT."
AIM
PROJECT EXTREMIS
INJECTIONS TESTS
PHASE 01
06/25/09
ONCE MISFITS, CRIPPLES, YOU ARE THE NEXT ITERATION OF HUMAN EVOLUTION. TODAY IS YOUR GLORY. LET'S BEGIN.
WE GOTTA GET OUT! GET THEM OUT OF HERE!
BOOM-ZZZT
"A BOMB IS NOT A BOMB WHEN IT'S A MISFIRE. IT'S FAULTY, BUT YOU FOUND A BUYER. SOLD IT TO THE MANDARIN.
"...AND NOW I KNOW WHERE HE IS."
Malibu, FL, USA
RHODEY, HOW FAST CAN YOU GET TO MALIBU?

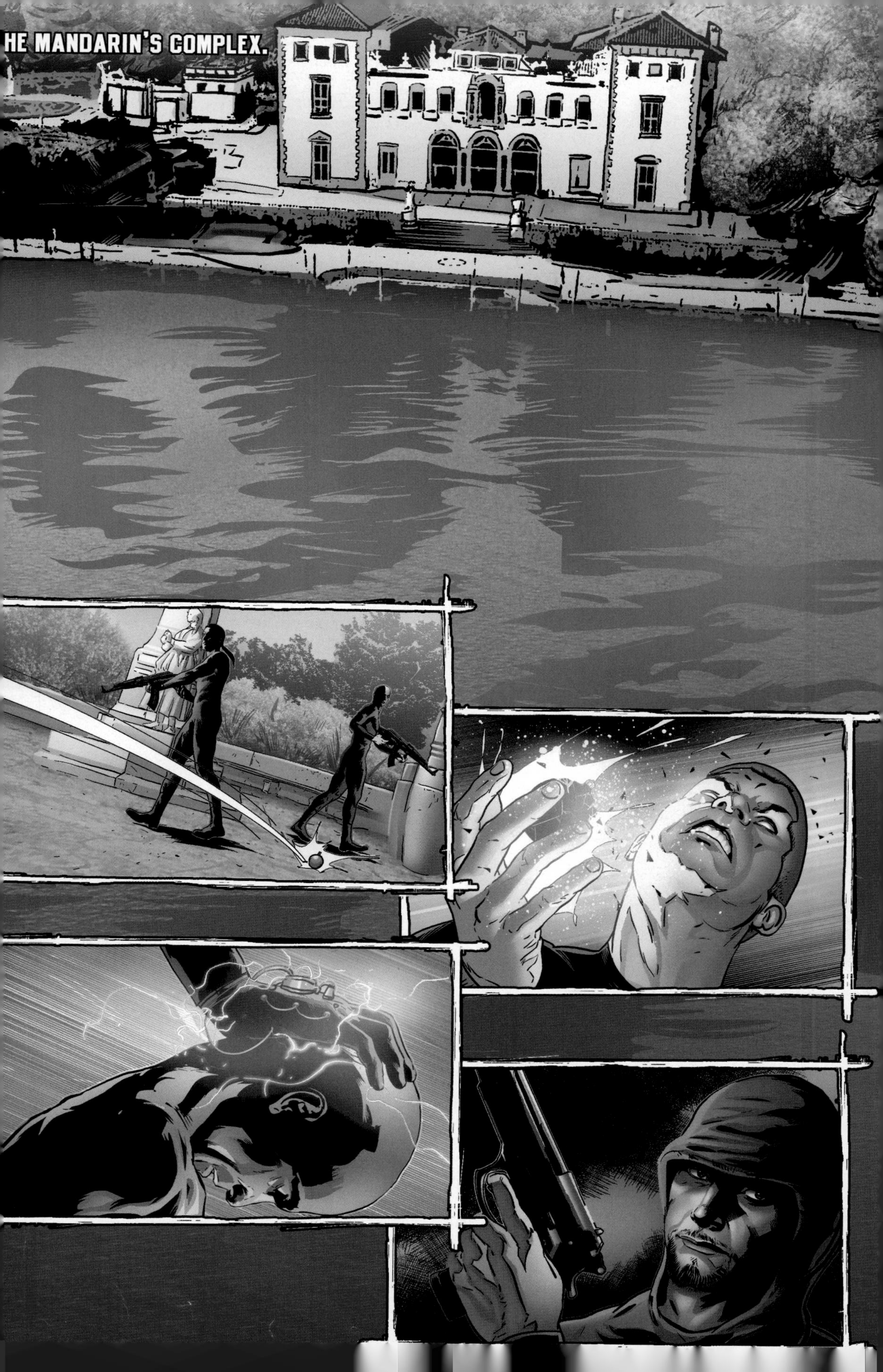
HE MANDARIN'S COMPLEX.

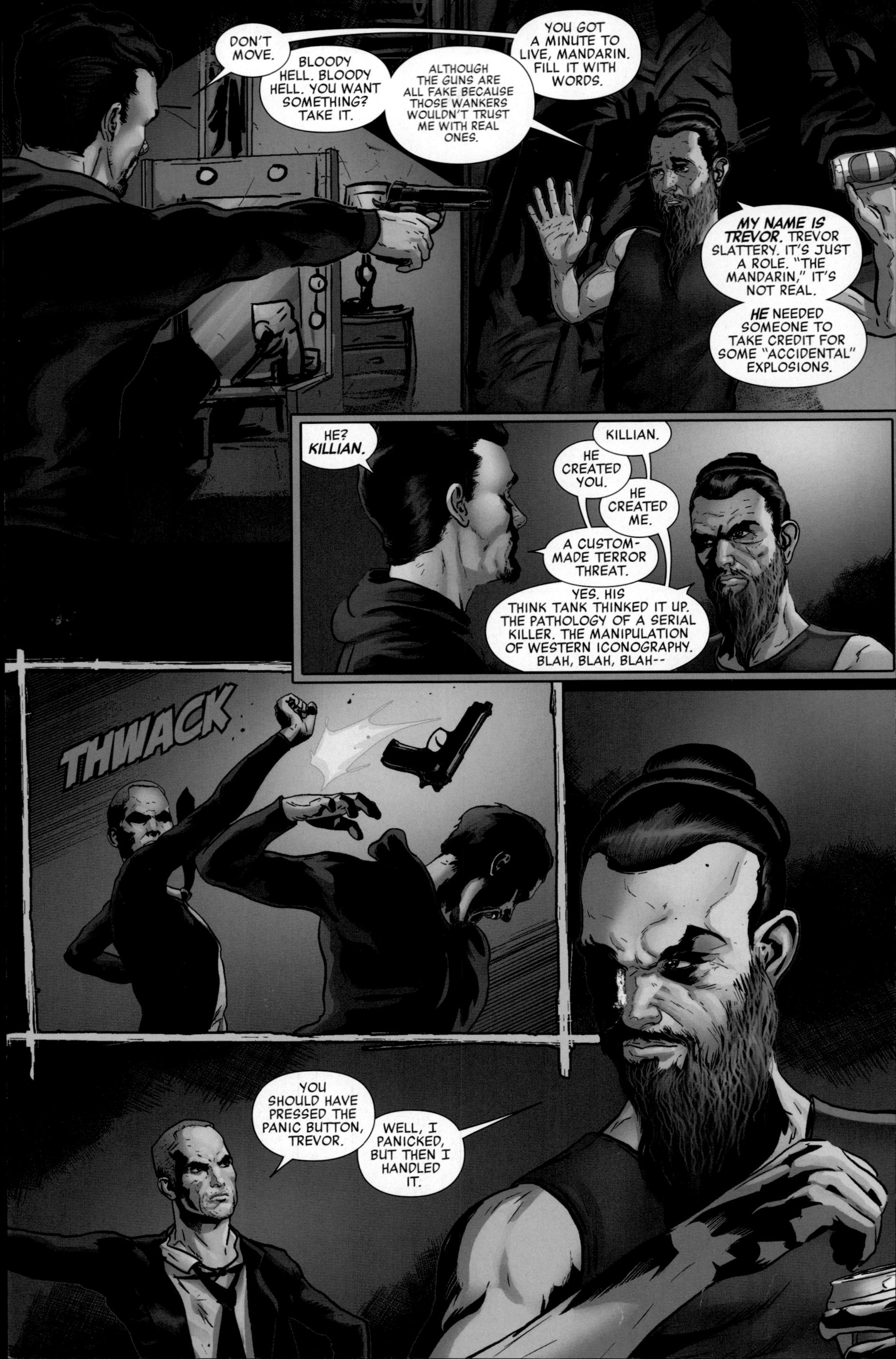
DON'T MOVE.
BLOODY HELL. BLOODY HELL. YOU WANT SOMETHING? TAKE IT.
ALTHOUGH THE GUNS ARE ALL FAKE BECAUSE THOSE WANKERS WOULDN'T TRUST ME WITH REAL ONES.
YOU GOT A MINUTE TO LIVE, MANDARIN. FILL IT WITH WORDS.
MY NAME IS TREVOR. TREVOR SLATTERY. IT'S JUST A ROLE. "THE MANDARIN," IT'S NOT REAL.
HE NEEDED SOMEONE TO TAKE CREDIT FOR SOME "ACCIDENTAL" EXPLOSIONS.
HE? KILLIAN.
KILLIAN.
HE CREATED YOU.
HE CREATED ME.
A CUSTOM-MADE TERROR THREAT.
YES. HIS THINK TANK THINKED IT UP. THE PATHOLOGY OF A SERIAL KILLER. THE MANIPULATION OF WESTERN ICONOGRAPHY. BLAH, BLAH, BLAH--
THWACK
YOU SHOULD HAVE PRESSED THE PANIC BUTTON, TREVOR.
WELL, I PANICKED, BUT THEN I HANDLED IT.

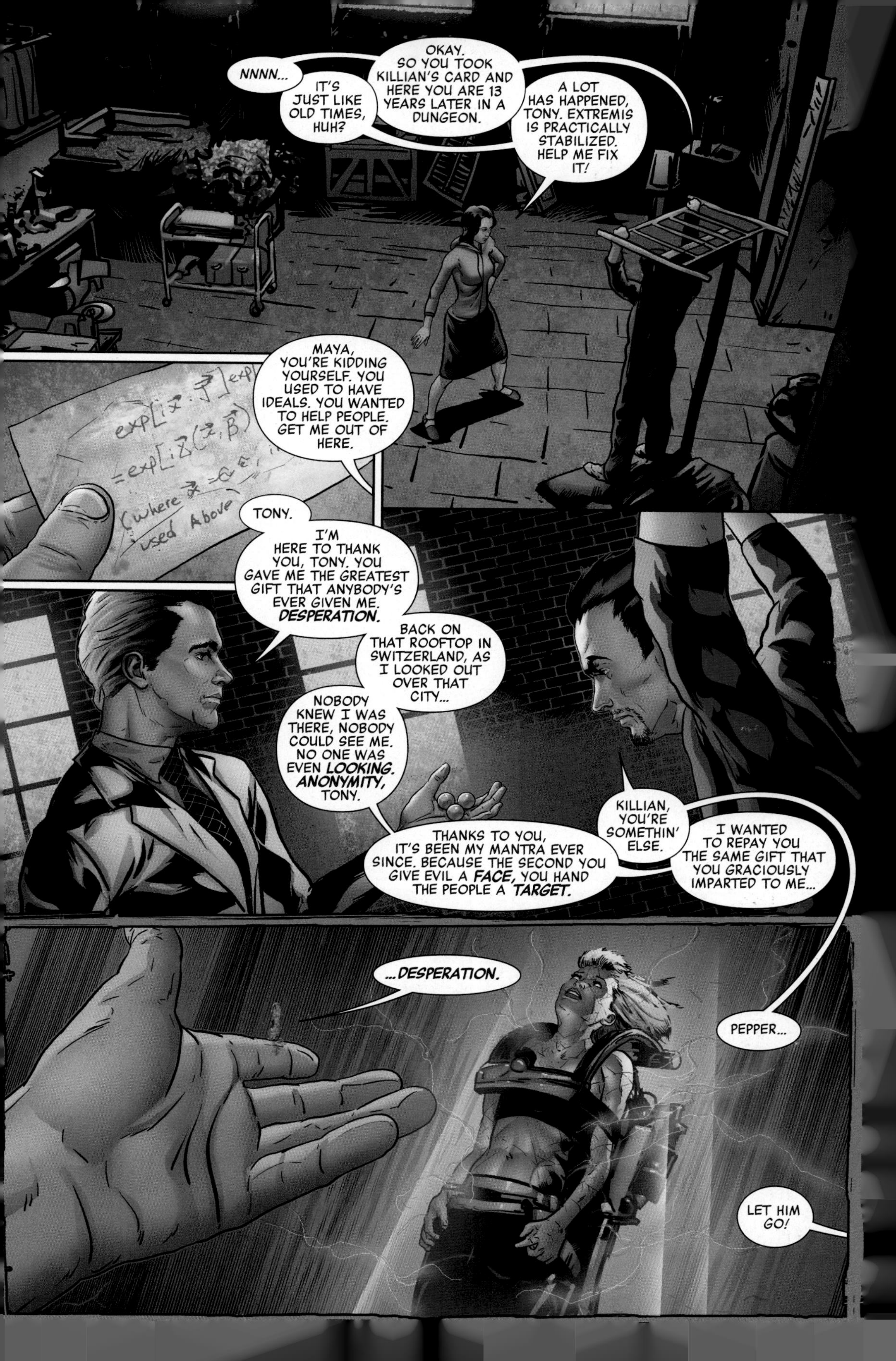
NNNN...
IT'S JUST LIKE OLD TIMES, HUH?
OKAY. SO YOU TOOK KILLIAN'S CARD AND HERE YOU ARE 13 YEARS LATER IN A DUNGEON.
A LOT HAS HAPPENED, TONY. EXTREMIS IS PRACTICALLY STABILIZED. HELP ME FIX IT!
MAYA, YOU'RE KIDDING YOURSELF. YOU USED TO HAVE IDEALS. YOU WANTED TO HELP PEOPLE. GET ME OUT OF HERE.
TONY.
I'M HERE TO THANK YOU, TONY. YOU GAVE ME THE GREATEST GIFT THAT ANYBODY'S EVER GIVEN ME. **DESPERATION.**
BACK ON THAT ROOFTOP IN SWITZERLAND, AS I LOOKED OUT OVER THAT CITY...
NOBODY KNEW I WAS THERE, NOBODY COULD SEE ME. NO ONE WAS EVEN **LOOKING. ANONYMITY,** TONY.
THANKS TO YOU, IT'S BEEN MY MANTRA EVER SINCE. BECAUSE THE SECOND YOU GIVE EVIL A **FACE,** YOU HAND THE PEOPLE A **TARGET.**
KILLIAN, YOU'RE SOMETHIN' ELSE.
I WANTED TO REPAY YOU THE SAME GIFT THAT YOU GRACIOUSLY IMPARTED TO ME...
...DESPERATION.
PEPPER...
LET HIM GO!

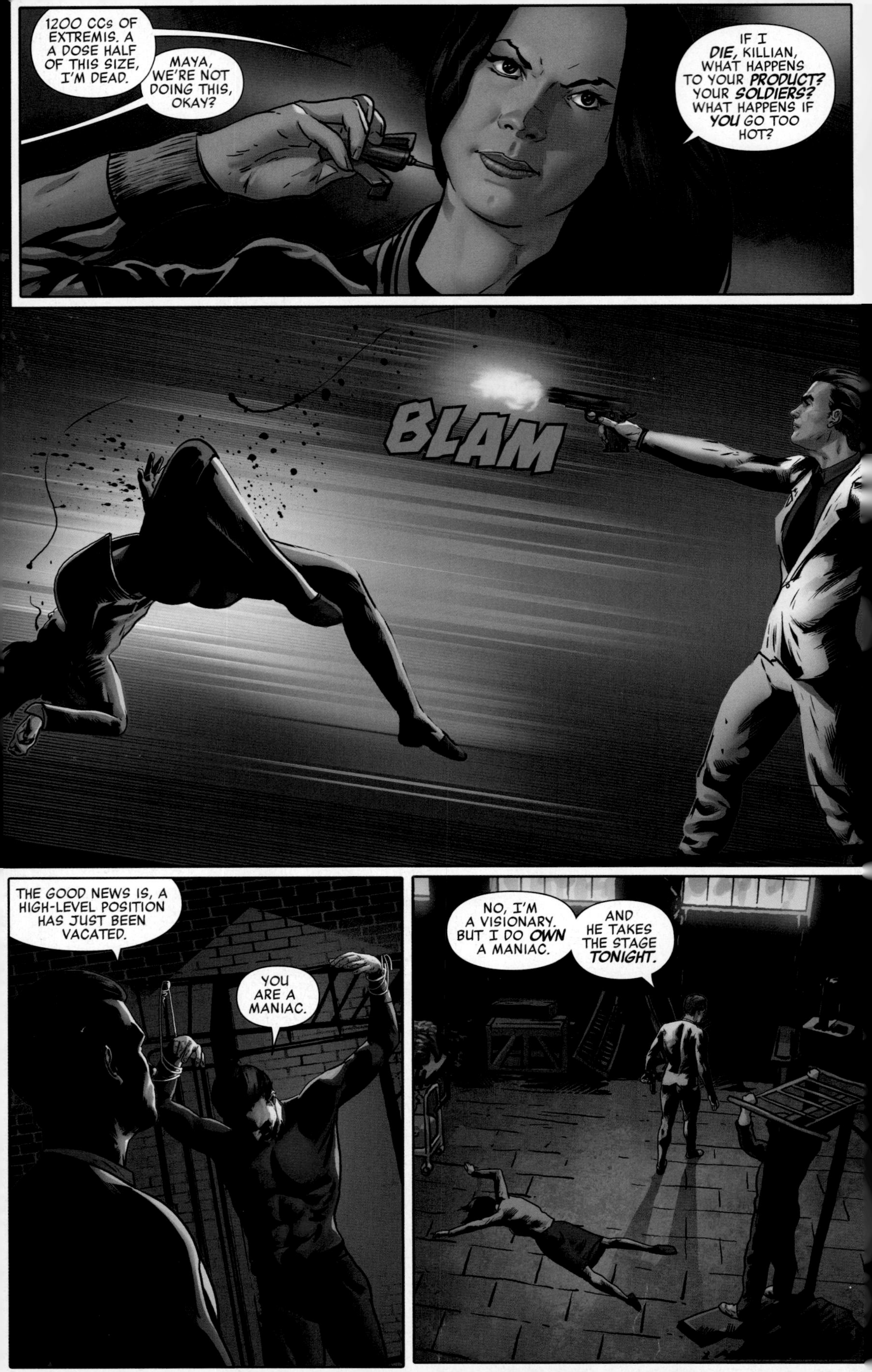
1200 CCs OF EXTREMIS. A A DOSE HALF OF THIS SIZE, I'M DEAD.
MAYA, WE'RE NOT DOING THIS, OKAY?
IF I DIE, KILLIAN, WHAT HAPPENS TO YOUR PRODUCT? YOUR SOLDIERS? WHAT HAPPENS IF YOU GO TOO HOT?
BLAM
THE GOOD NEWS IS, A HIGH-LEVEL POSITION HAS JUST BEEN VACATED.
YOU ARE A MANIAC.
NO, I'M A VISIONARY. BUT I DO OWN A MANIAC.
AND HE TAKES THE STAGE TONIGHT.

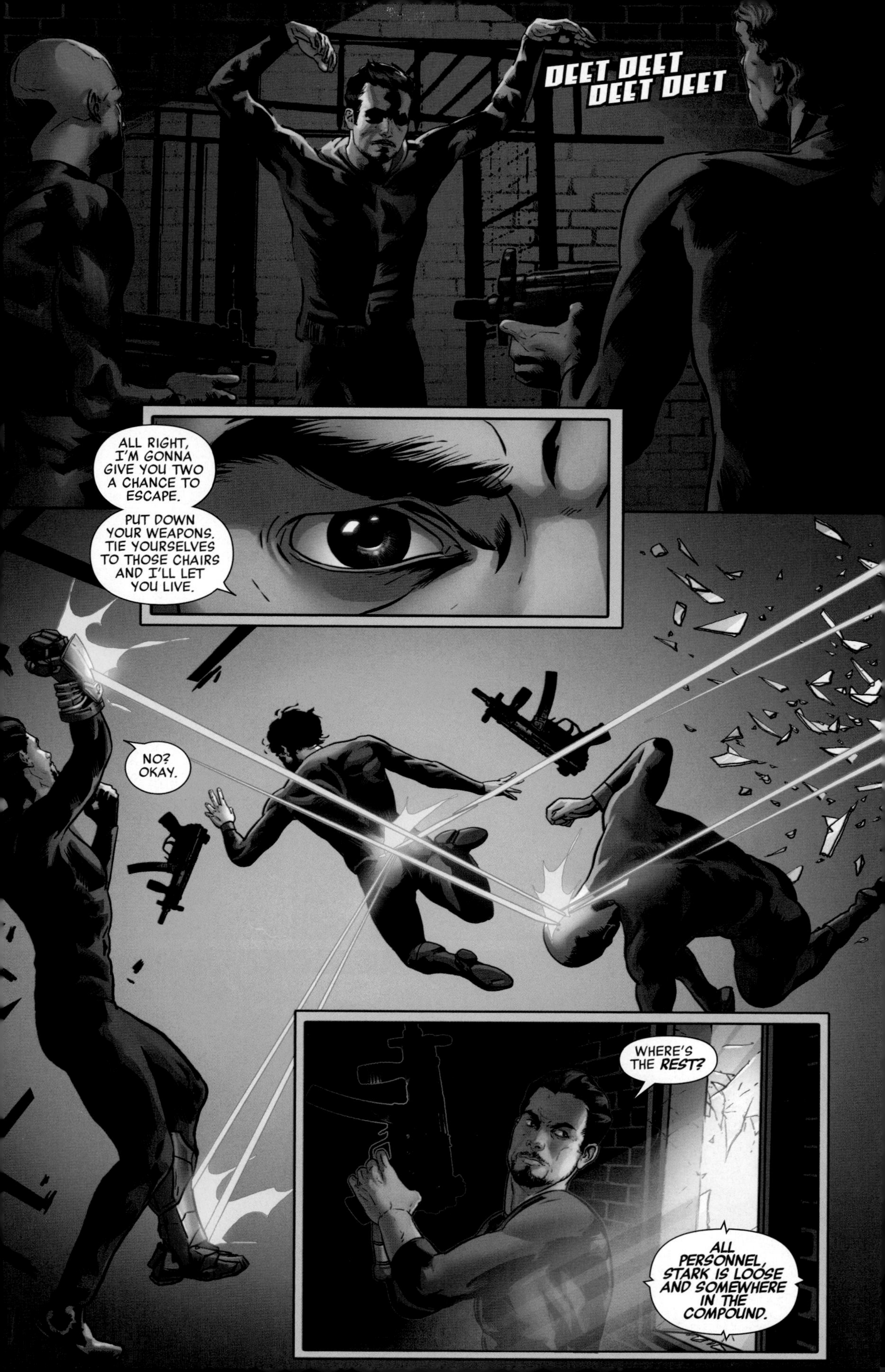
DEET DEET
DEET DEET
ALL RIGHT, I'M GONNA GIVE YOU TWO A CHANCE TO ESCAPE.
PUT DOWN YOUR WEAPONS. TIE YOURSELVES TO THOSE CHAIRS AND I'LL LET YOU LIVE.
NO? OKAY.
WHERE'S THE REST?
ALL PERSONNEL, STARK IS LOOSE AND SOMEWHERE IN THE COMPOUND.

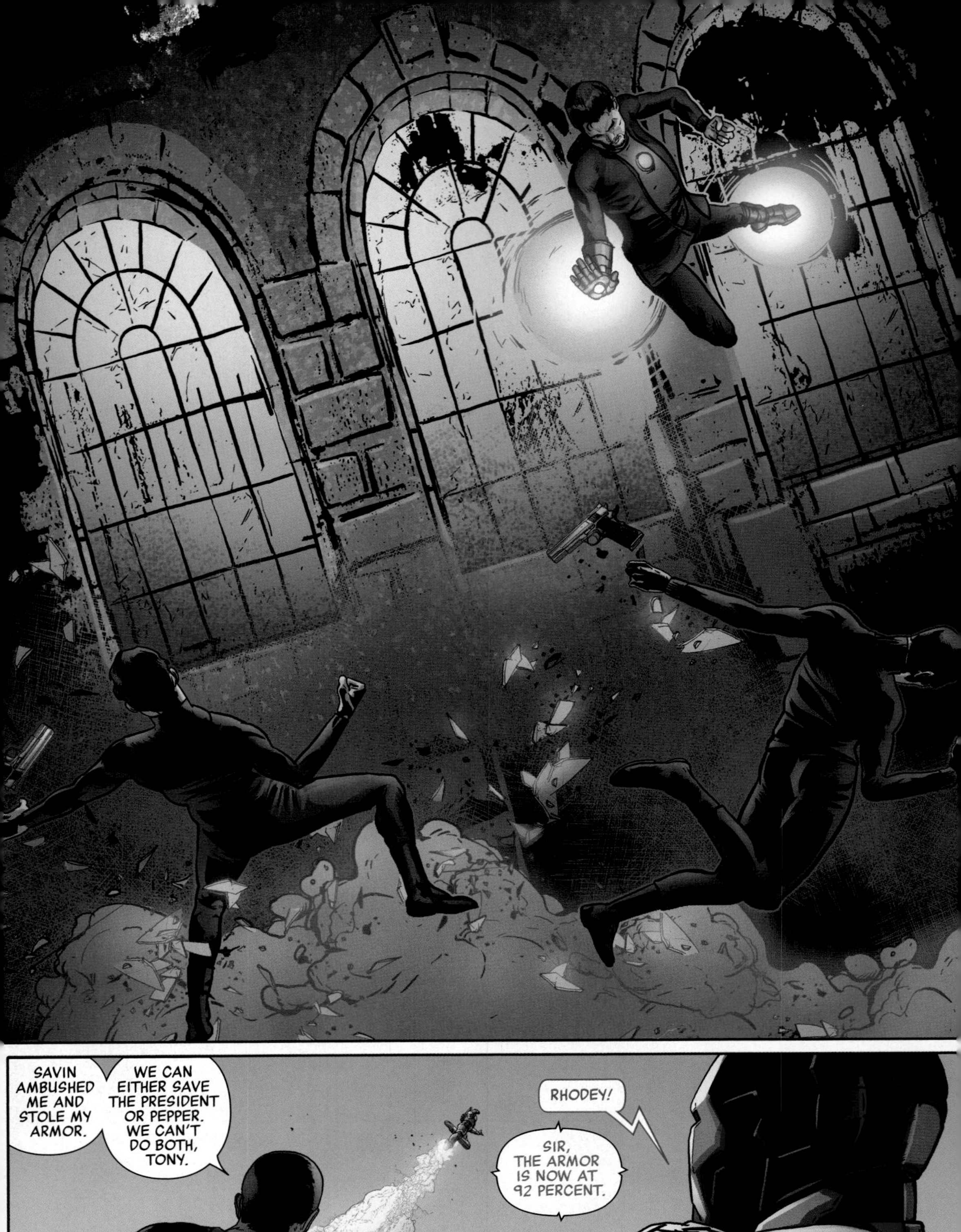

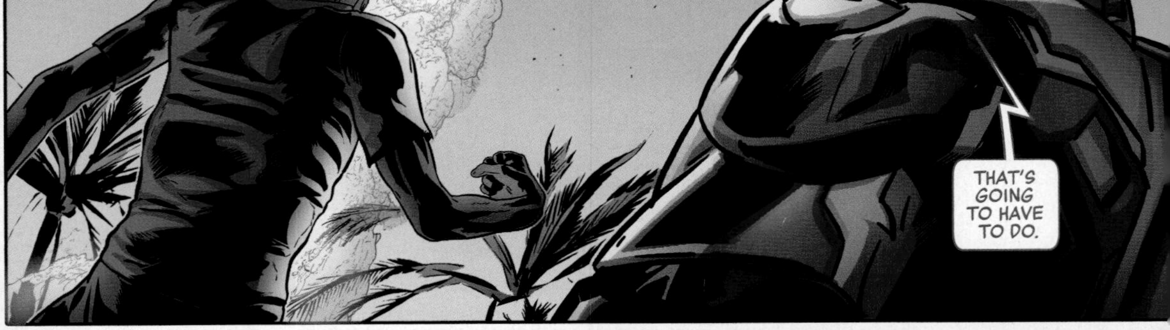
SAVIN AMBUSHED ME AND STOLE MY ARMOR.
WE CAN EITHER SAVE THE PRESIDENT OR PEPPER. WE CAN'T DO BOTH, TONY.
RHODEY!
SIR, THE ARMOR IS NOW AT 92 PERCENT.
THAT'S GOING TO HAVE TO DO.

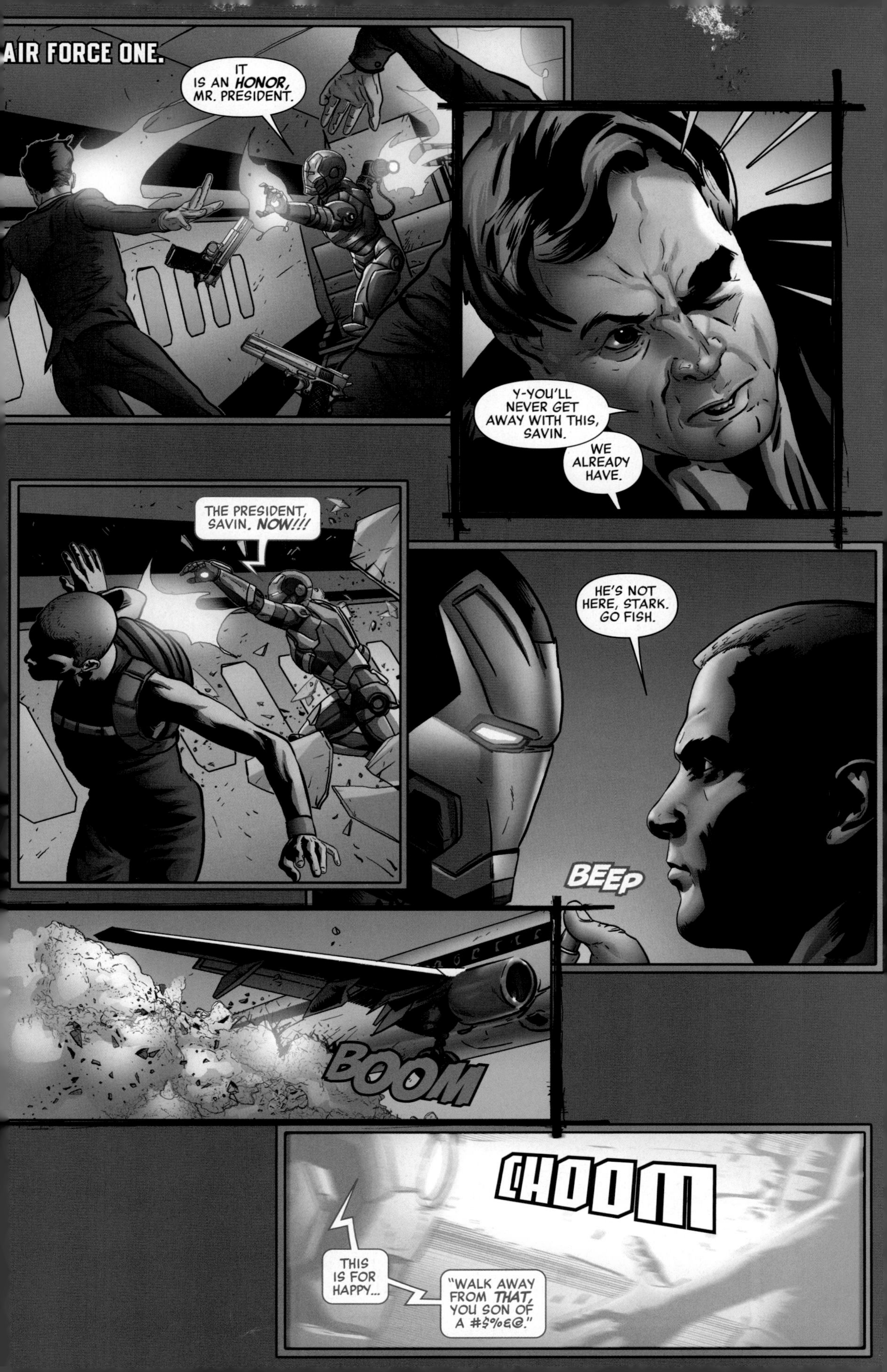
AIR FORCE ONE.
IT IS AN HONOR, MR. PRESIDENT.
Y-YOU'LL NEVER GET AWAY WITH THIS, SAVIN.
WE ALREADY HAVE.
THE PRESIDENT, SAVIN. NOW!!!
HE'S NOT HERE, STARK. GO FISH.
BEEP
BOOM
CHOOM
THIS IS FOR HAPPY...
"WALK AWAY FROM THAT, YOU SON OF A #$%&@."

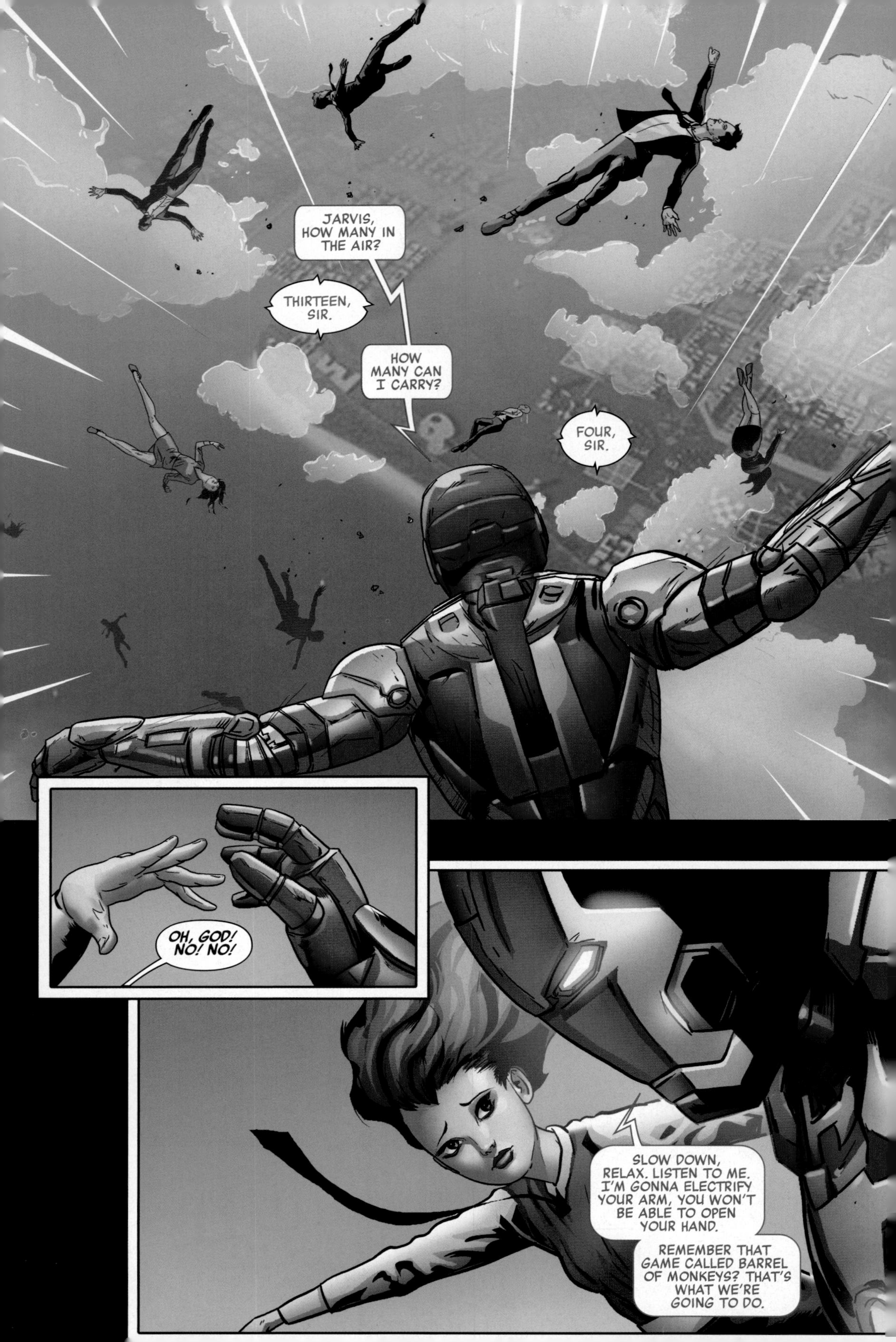
JARVIS, HOW MANY IN THE AIR?
THIRTEEN, SIR.
HOW MANY CAN I CARRY?
FOUR, SIR.
OH, GOD! NO! NO!
SLOW DOWN, RELAX. LISTEN TO ME. I'M GONNA ELECTRIFY YOUR ARM, YOU WON'T BE ABLE TO OPEN YOUR HAND.
REMEMBER THAT GAME CALLED BARREL OF MONKEYS? THAT'S WHAT WE'RE GOING TO DO.

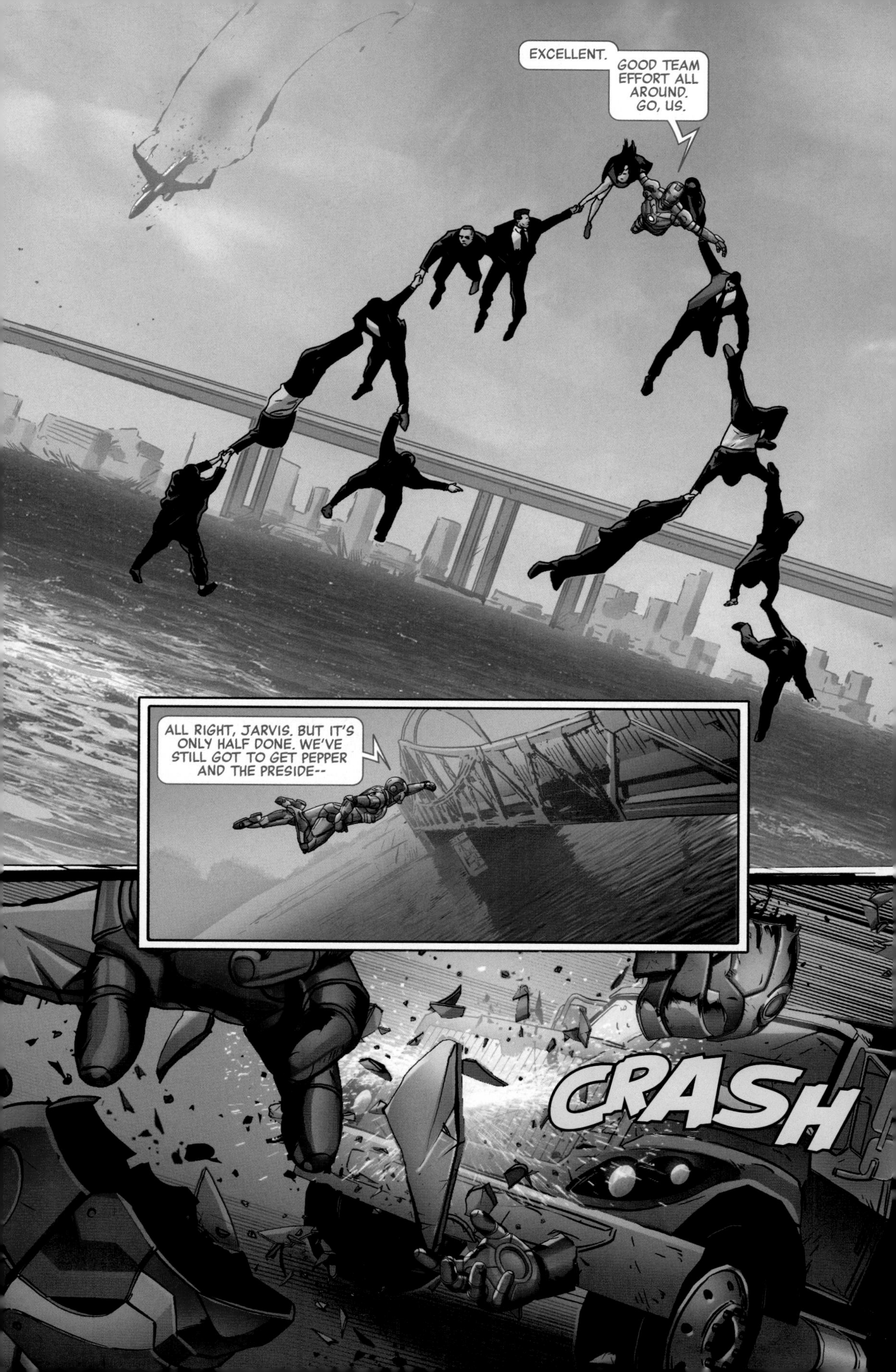
EXCELLENT.
GOOD TEAM EFFORT ALL AROUND. GO, US.
ALL RIGHT, JARVIS. BUT IT'S ONLY HALF DONE. WE'VE STILL GOT TO GET PEPPER AND THE PRESIDE--
CRASH

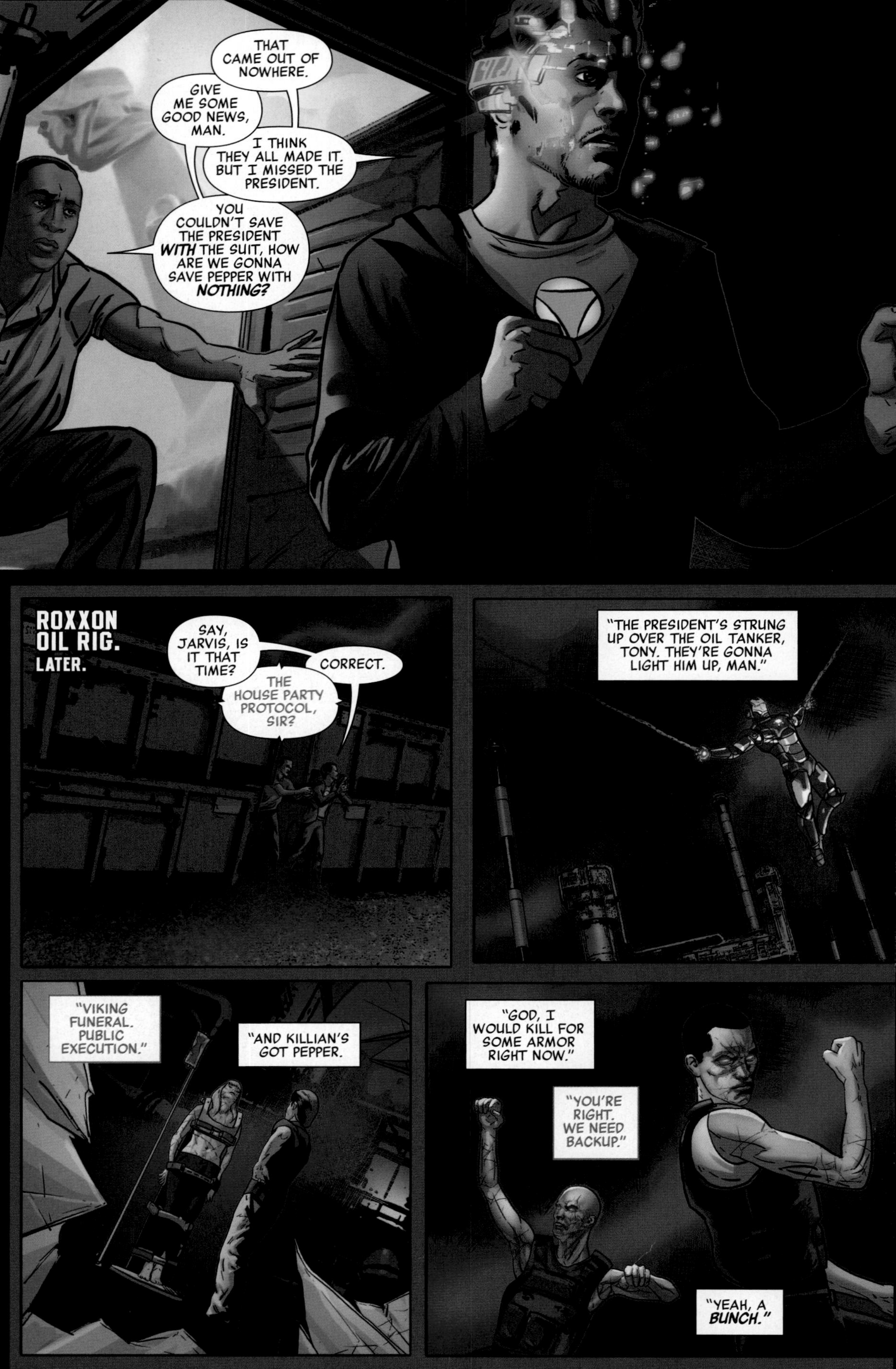
THAT CAME OUT OF NOWHERE.
GIVE ME SOME GOOD NEWS, MAN.
I THINK THEY ALL MADE IT. BUT I MISSED THE PRESIDENT.
YOU COULDN'T SAVE THE PRESIDENT WITH THE SUIT, HOW ARE WE GONNA SAVE PEPPER WITH NOTHING?
ROXXON OIL RIG. LATER.
SAY, JARVIS, IS IT THAT TIME?
THE HOUSE PARTY PROTOCOL, SIR?
CORRECT.
"THE PRESIDENT'S STRUNG UP OVER THE OIL TANKER, TONY. THEY'RE GONNA LIGHT HIM UP, MAN."
"VIKING FUNERAL. PUBLIC EXECUTION."
"AND KILLIAN'S GOT PEPPER.
"GOD, I WOULD KILL FOR SOME ARMOR RIGHT NOW."
"YOU'RE RIGHT. WE NEED BACKUP."
"YEAH, A BUNCH."

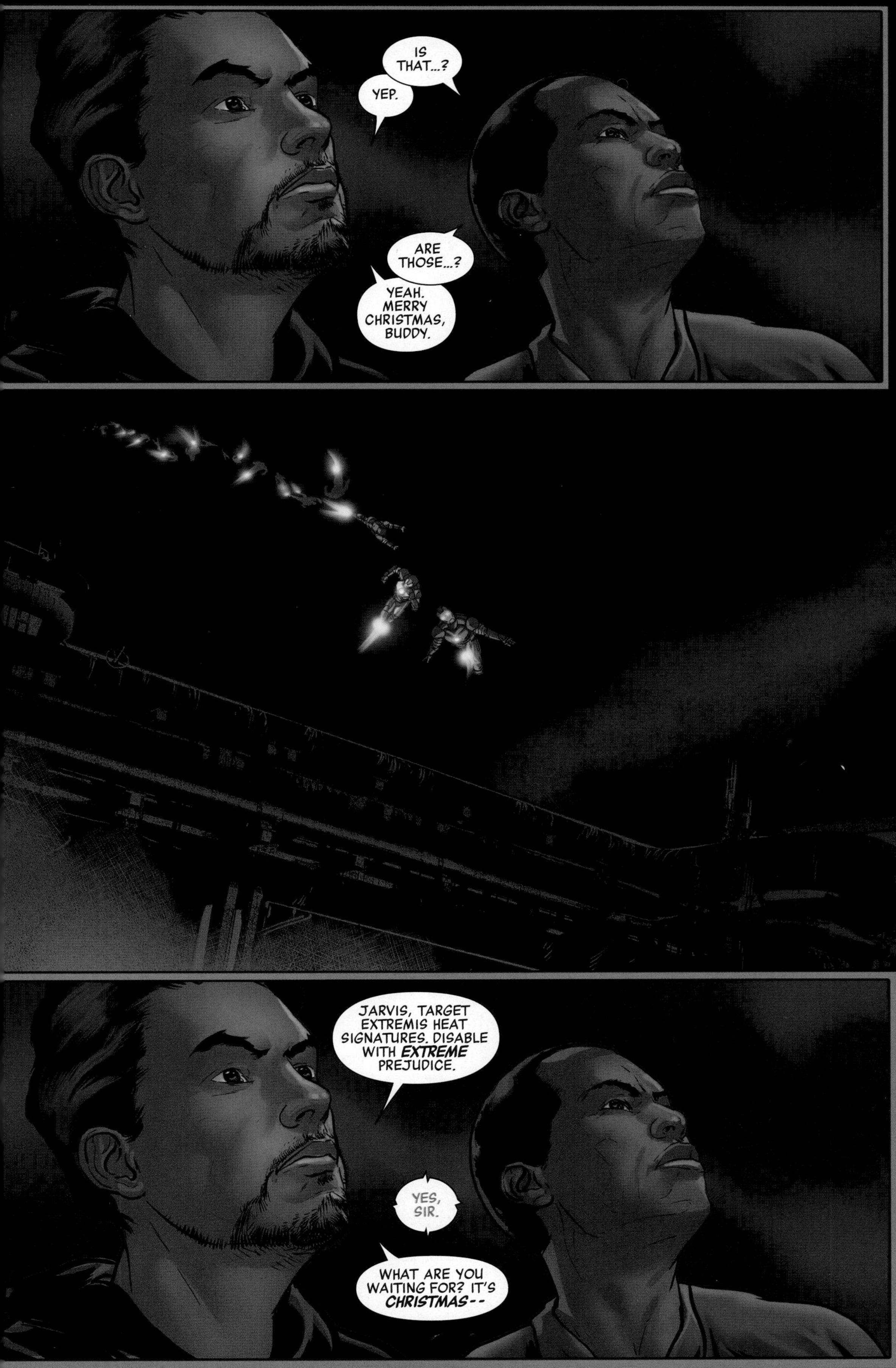
IS THAT...?
YEP.
ARE THOSE...?
YEAH. MERRY CHRISTMAS, BUDDY.
JARVIS, TARGET EXTREMIS HEAT SIGNATURES. DISABLE WITH EXTREME PREJUDICE.
YES, SIR.
WHAT ARE YOU WAITING FOR? IT'S CHRISTMAS--

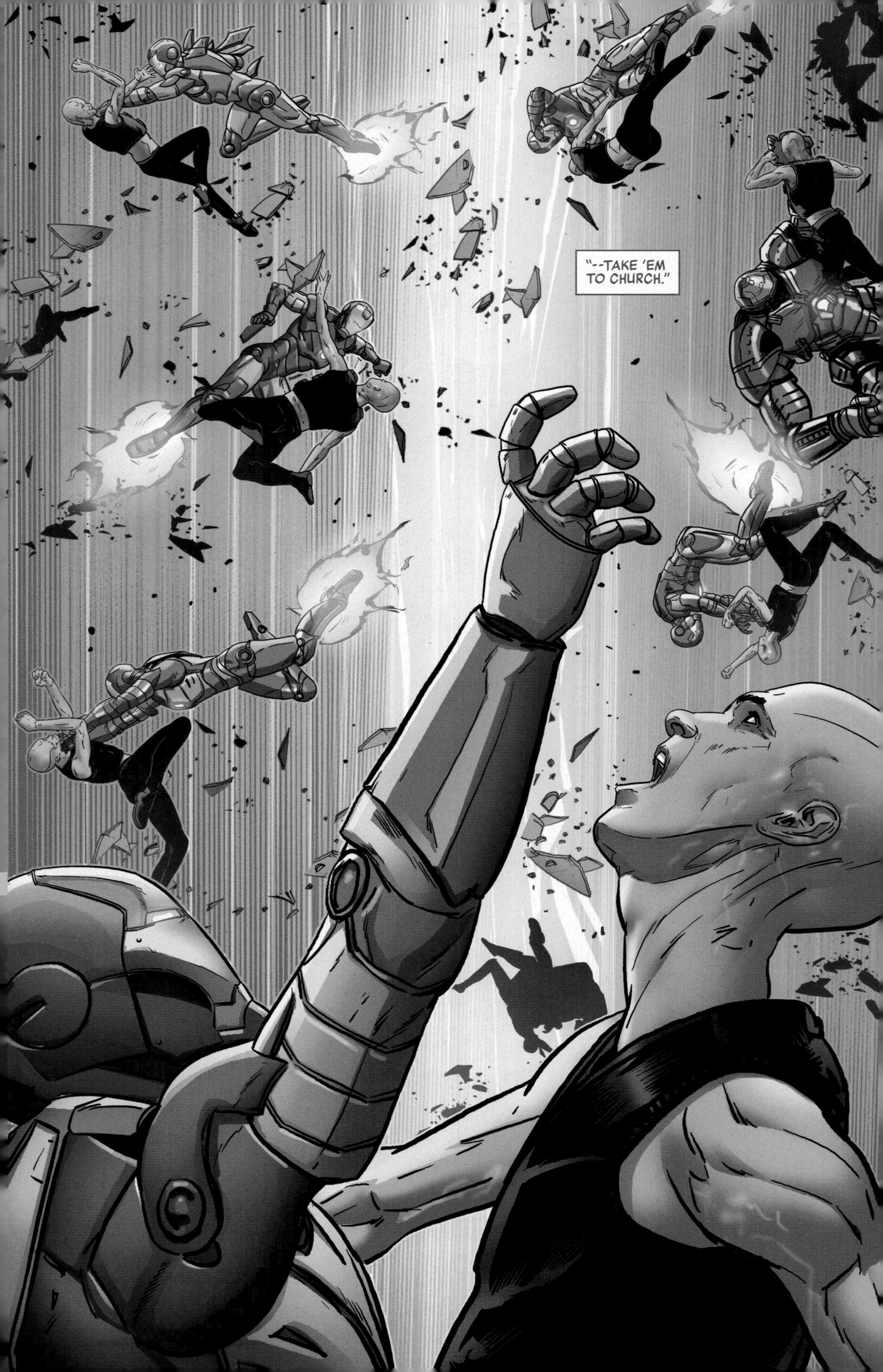
"--TAKE 'EM TO CHURCH."

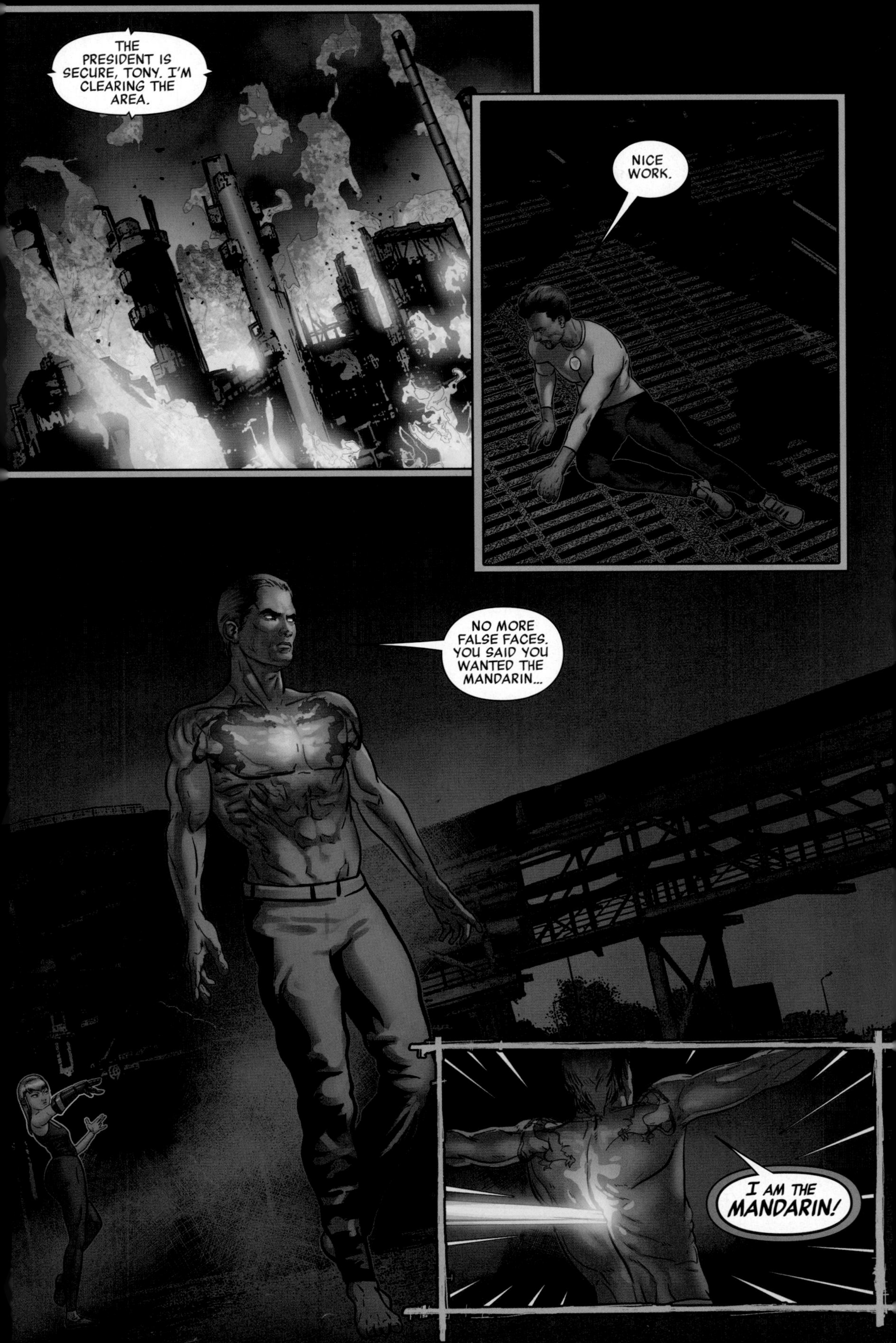
THE PRESIDENT IS SECURE, TONY. I'M CLEARING THE AREA.
NICE WORK.
NO MORE FALSE FACES. YOU SAID YOU WANTED THE MANDARIN...
I AM THE MANDARIN!

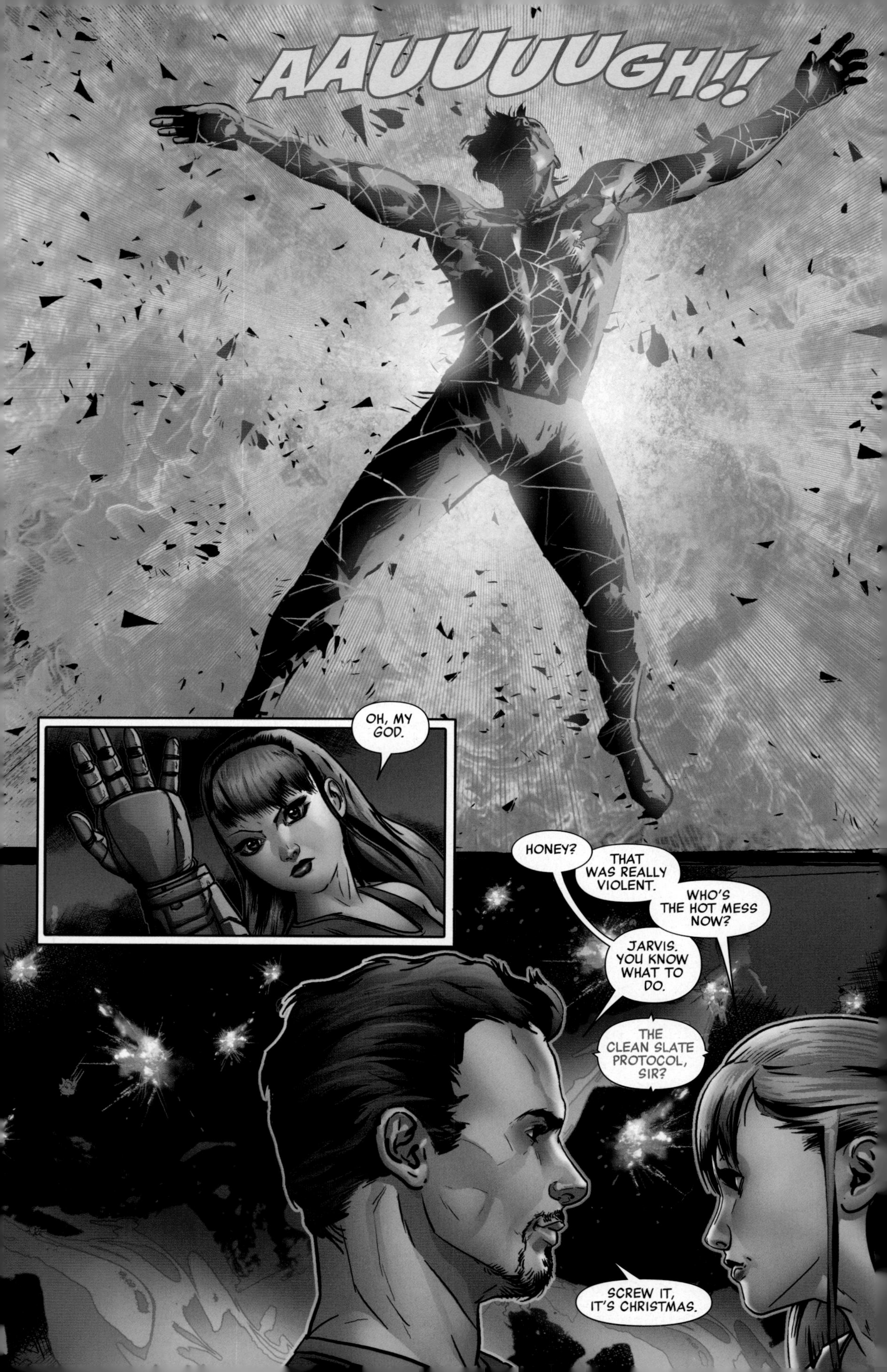
AAUUUUGH!!
OH, MY GOD.
HONEY?
THAT WAS REALLY VIOLENT.
WHO'S THE HOT MESS NOW?
JARVIS. YOU KNOW WHAT TO DO.
THE CLEAN SLATE PROTOCOL, SIR?
SCREW IT, IT'S CHRISTMAS.

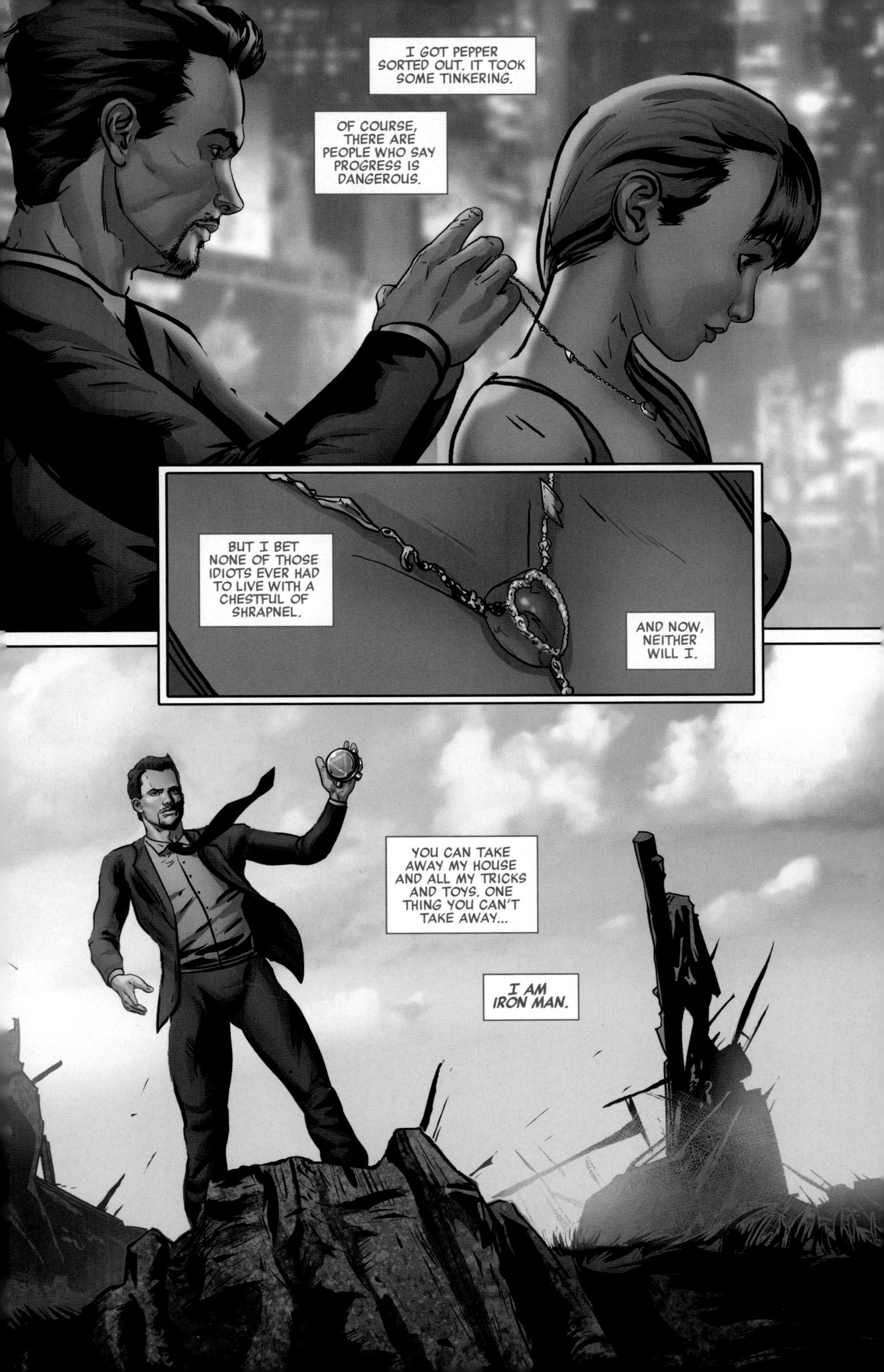
I GOT PEPPER SORTED OUT. IT TOOK SOME TINKERING.
OF COURSE, THERE ARE PEOPLE WHO SAY PROGRESS IS DANGEROUS.
BUT I BET NONE OF THOSE IDIOTS EVER HAD TO LIVE WITH A CHESTFUL OF SHRAPNEL.
AND NOW, NEITHER WILL I.
YOU CAN TAKE AWAY MY HOUSE AND ALL MY TRICKS AND TOYS. ONE THING YOU CAN'T TAKE AWAY...
I AM IRON MAN.

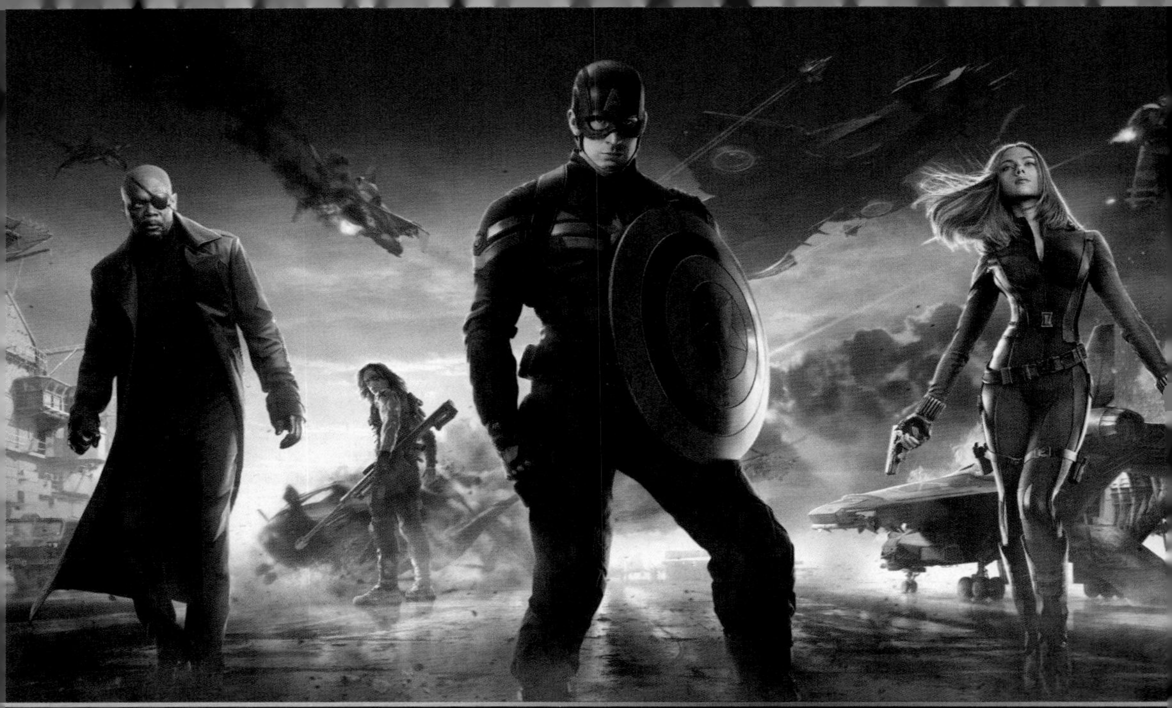

MARVEL'S CAPTAIN AMERICA: CIVIL WAR PRELUDE #3

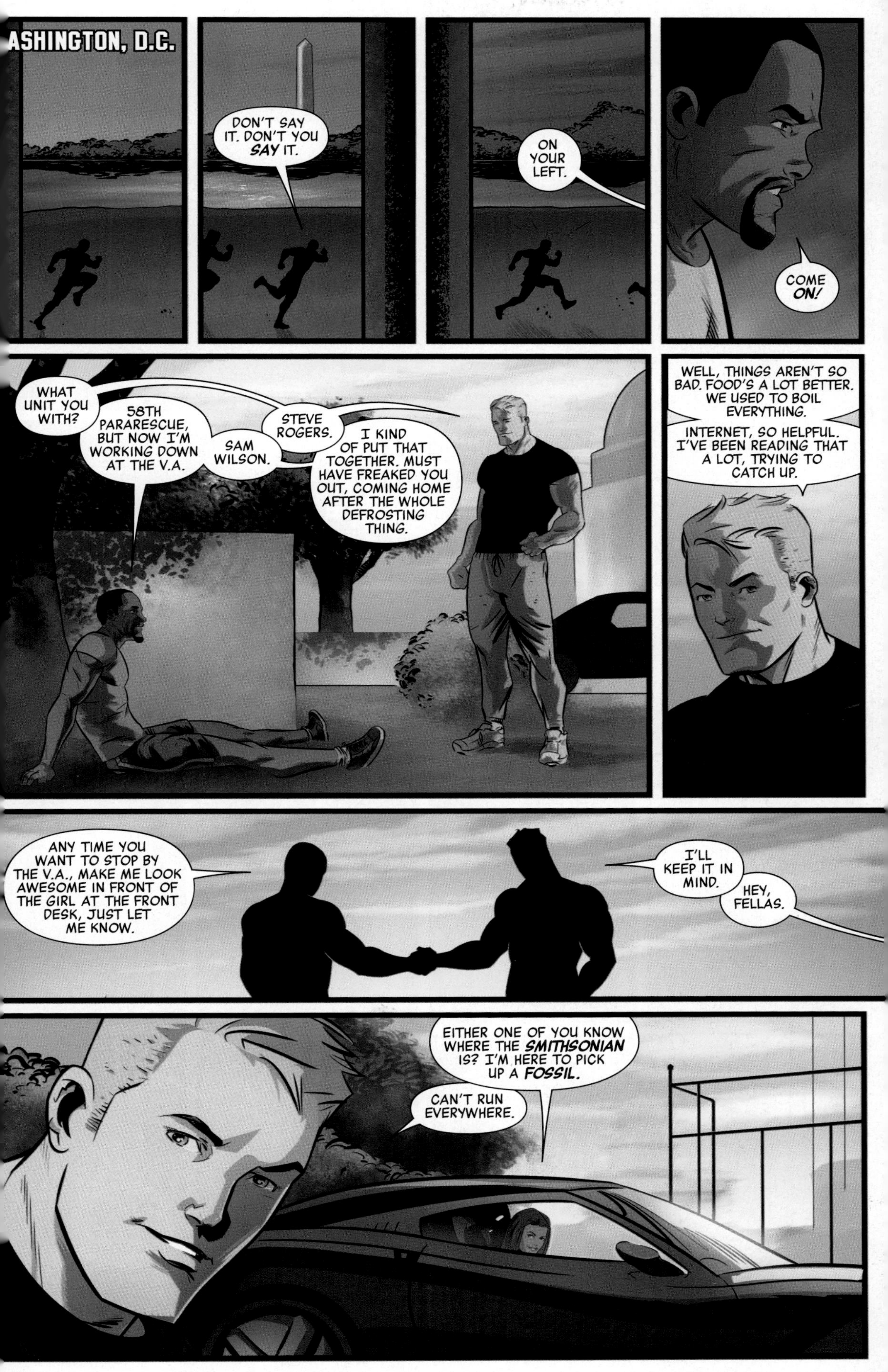
ASHINGTON, D.C.
DON'T SAY IT. DON'T YOU SAY IT.
ON YOUR LEFT.
COME ON!
WHAT UNIT YOU WITH?
58TH PARARESCUE, BUT NOW I'M WORKING DOWN AT THE V.A.
STEVE ROGERS.
SAM WILSON.
I KIND OF PUT THAT TOGETHER. MUST HAVE FREAKED YOU OUT, COMING HOME AFTER THE WHOLE DEFROSTING THING.
WELL, THINGS AREN'T SO BAD. FOOD'S A LOT BETTER. WE USED TO BOIL EVERYTHING.
INTERNET, SO HELPFUL. I'VE BEEN READING THAT A LOT, TRYING TO CATCH UP.
ANY TIME YOU WANT TO STOP BY THE V.A., MAKE ME LOOK AWESOME IN FRONT OF THE GIRL AT THE FRONT DESK, JUST LET ME KNOW.
I'LL KEEP IT IN MIND.
HEY, FELLAS.
EITHER ONE OF YOU KNOW WHERE THE SMITHSONIAN IS? I'M HERE TO PICK UP A FOSSIL.
CAN'T RUN EVERYWHERE.

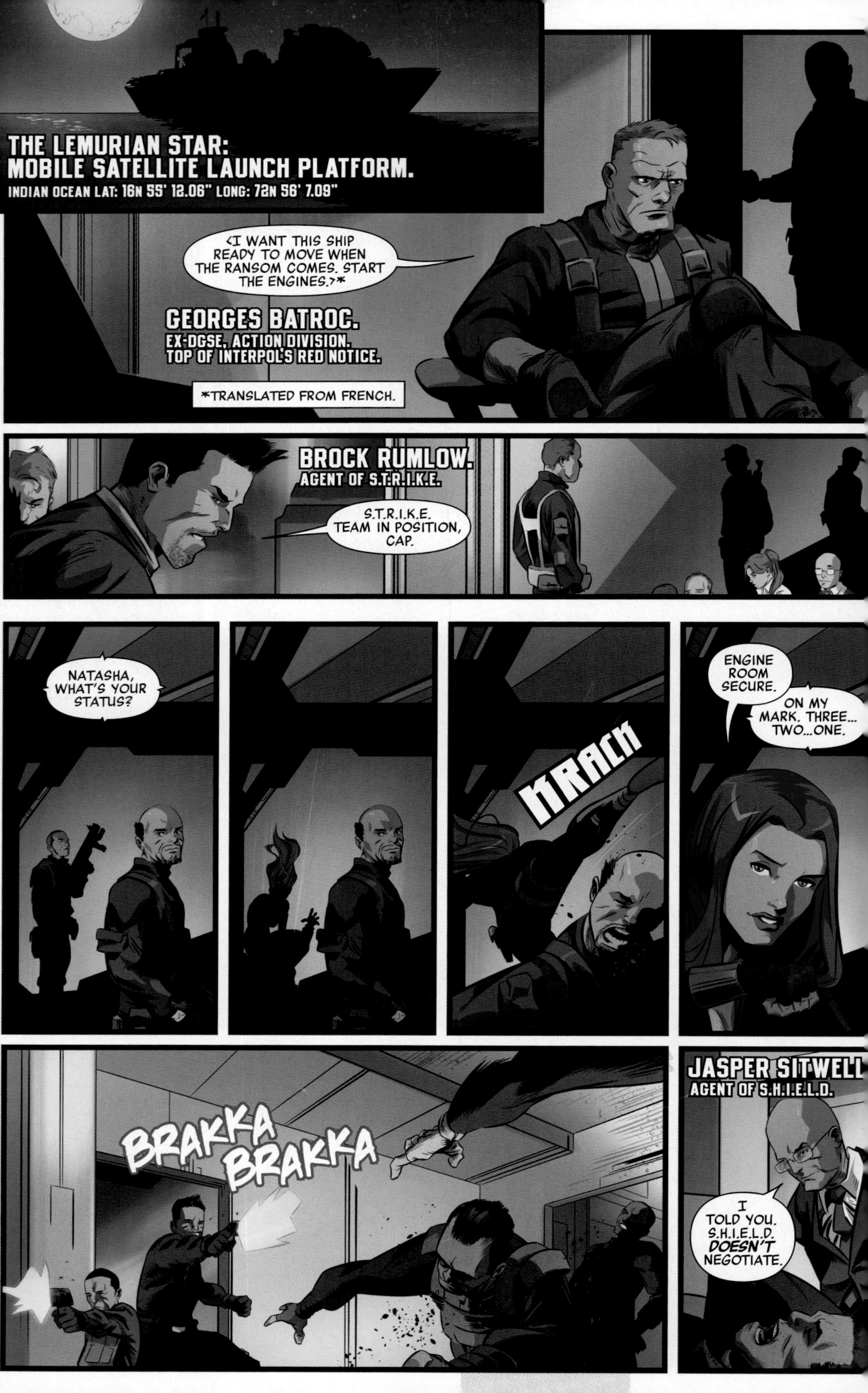
THE LEMURIAN STAR:
MOBILE SATELLITE LAUNCH PLATFORM.
INDIAN OCEAN LAT: 16N 55' 12.06" LONG: 72N 56' 7.09"
<I WANT THIS SHIP READY TO MOVE WHEN THE RANSOM COMES. START THE ENGINES.>*
GEORGES BATROC.
EX-DGSE, ACTION DIVISION. TOP OF INTERPOL'S RED NOTICE.
*TRANSLATED FROM FRENCH.
BROCK RUMLOW.
AGENT OF S.T.R.I.K.E.
S.T.R.I.K.E. TEAM IN POSITION, CAP.
NATASHA, WHAT'S YOUR STATUS?
KRACK
ENGINE ROOM SECURE.
ON MY MARK. THREE... TWO...ONE.
BRAKKA BRAKKA
JASPER SITWELL
AGENT OF S.H.I.E.L.D.
I TOLD YOU. S.H.I.E.L.D. DOESN'T NEGOTIATE.

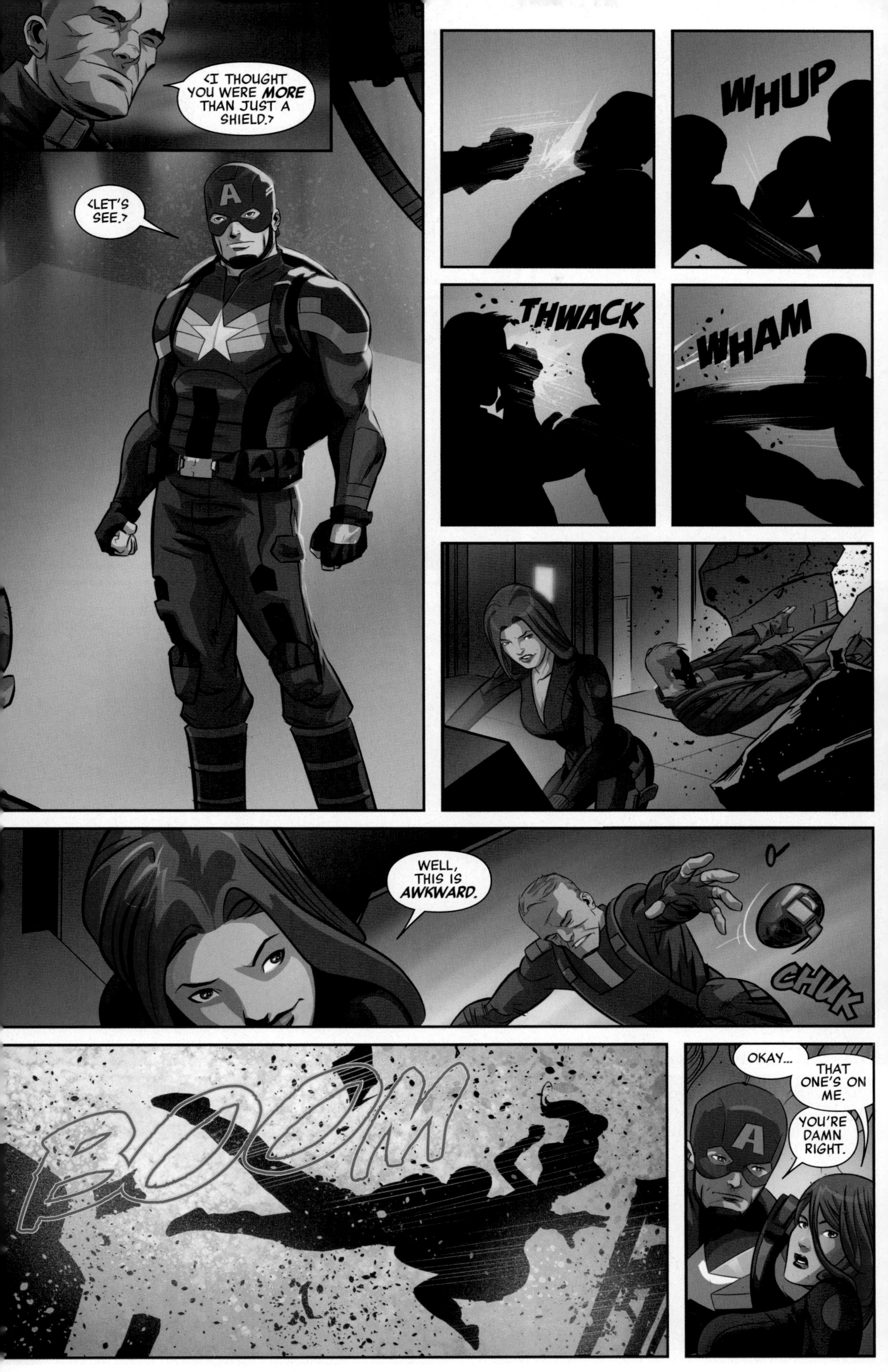

<I THOUGHT YOU WERE MORE THAN JUST A SHIELD.>
<LET'S SEE.>
WHUP
THWACK
WHAM
WELL, THIS IS AWKWARD.
CHUK
BOOM
OKAY...
THAT ONE'S ON ME.
YOU'RE DAMN RIGHT.

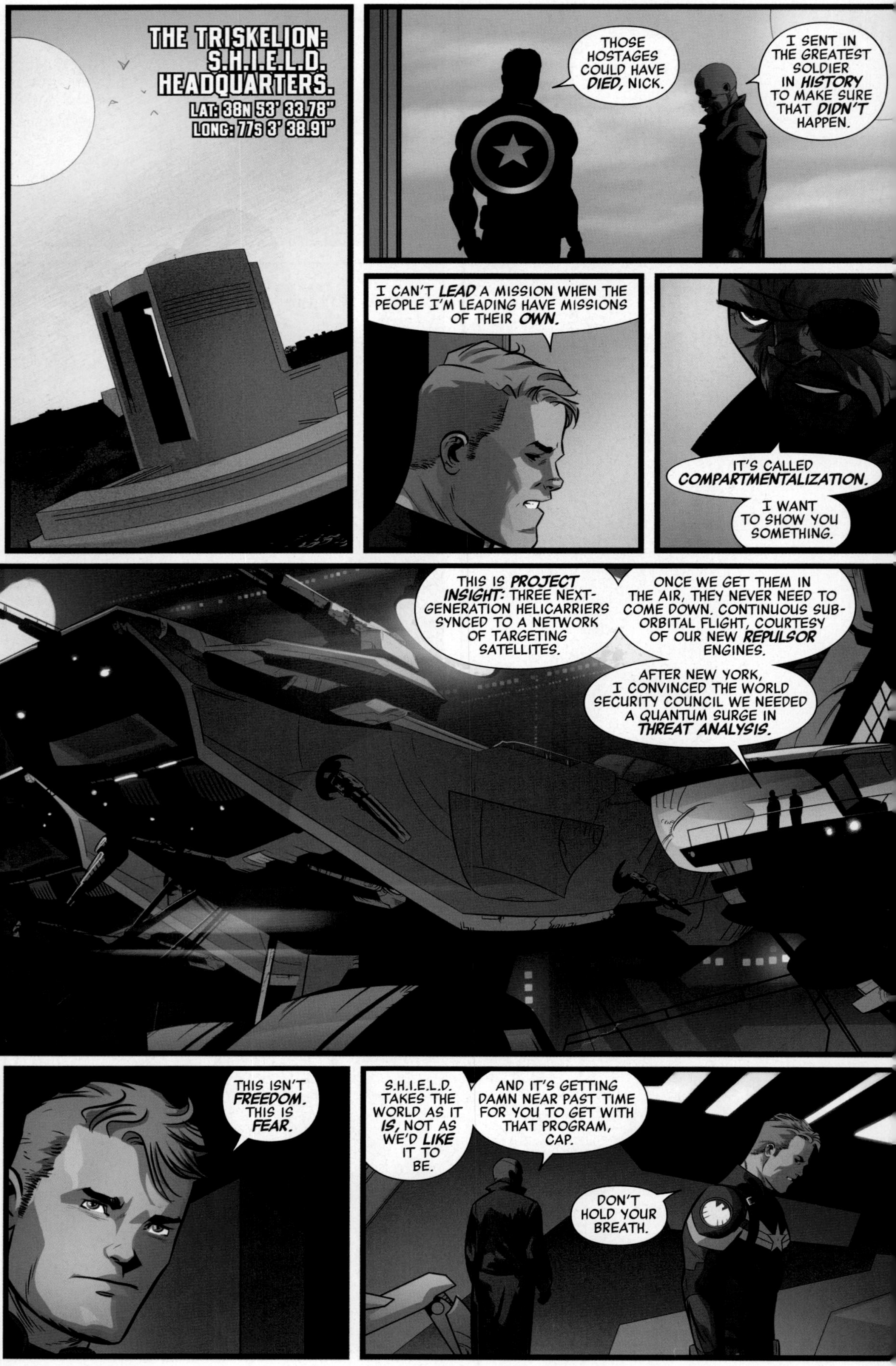
THE TRISKELION: S.H.I.E.L.D. HEADQUARTERS.
LAT: 38N 53' 33.78"
LONG: 77S 3' 38.91"
THOSE HOSTAGES COULD HAVE DIED, NICK.
I SENT IN THE GREATEST SOLDIER IN HISTORY TO MAKE SURE THAT DIDN'T HAPPEN.
I CAN'T LEAD A MISSION WHEN THE PEOPLE I'M LEADING HAVE MISSIONS OF THEIR OWN.
IT'S CALLED COMPARTMENTALIZATION.
I WANT TO SHOW YOU SOMETHING.
THIS IS PROJECT INSIGHT: THREE NEXT-GENERATION HELICARRIERS SYNCED TO A NETWORK OF TARGETING SATELLITES.
ONCE WE GET THEM IN THE AIR, THEY NEVER NEED TO COME DOWN. CONTINUOUS SUB-ORBITAL FLIGHT, COURTESY OF OUR NEW REPULSOR ENGINES.
AFTER NEW YORK, I CONVINCED THE WORLD SECURITY COUNCIL WE NEEDED A QUANTUM SURGE IN THREAT ANALYSIS.
THIS ISN'T FREEDOM. THIS IS FEAR.
S.H.I.E.L.D. TAKES THE WORLD AS IT IS, NOT AS WE'D LIKE IT TO BE.
AND IT'S GETTING DAMN NEAR PAST TIME FOR YOU TO GET WITH THAT PROGRAM, CAP.
DON'T HOLD YOUR BREATH.

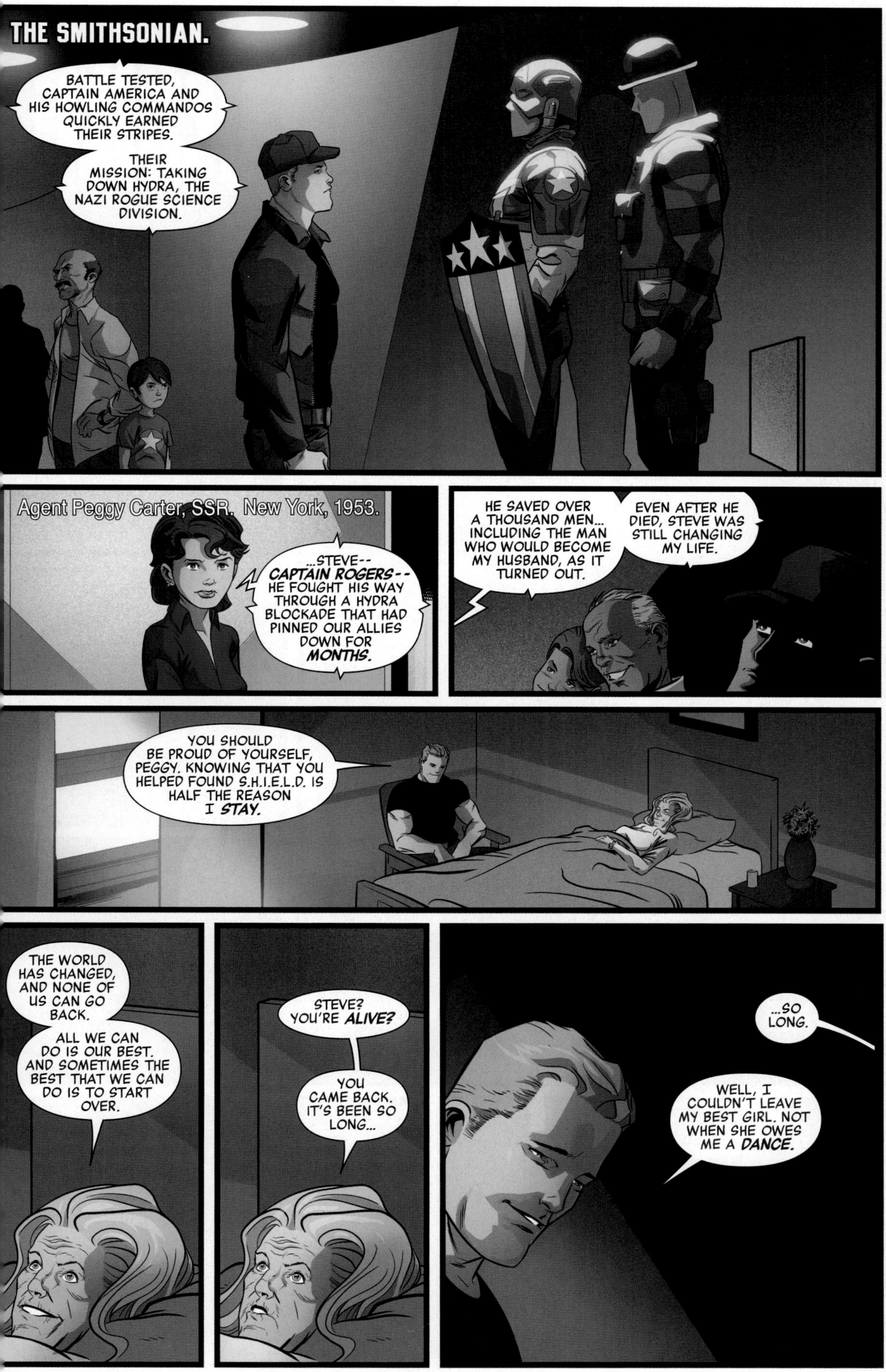
THE SMITHSONIAN.
BATTLE TESTED, CAPTAIN AMERICA AND HIS HOWLING COMMANDOS QUICKLY EARNED THEIR STRIPES.
THEIR MISSION: TAKING DOWN HYDRA, THE NAZI ROGUE SCIENCE DIVISION.
Agent Peggy Carter, SSR. New York, 1953.
...STEVE-- CAPTAIN ROGERS-- HE FOUGHT HIS WAY THROUGH A HYDRA BLOCKADE THAT HAD PINNED OUR ALLIES DOWN FOR MONTHS.
HE SAVED OVER A THOUSAND MEN... INCLUDING THE MAN WHO WOULD BECOME MY HUSBAND, AS IT TURNED OUT.
EVEN AFTER HE DIED, STEVE WAS STILL CHANGING MY LIFE.
YOU SHOULD BE PROUD OF YOURSELF, PEGGY. KNOWING THAT YOU HELPED FOUND S.H.I.E.L.D. IS HALF THE REASON I STAY.
THE WORLD HAS CHANGED, AND NONE OF US CAN GO BACK.
ALL WE CAN DO IS OUR BEST. AND SOMETIMES THE BEST THAT WE CAN DO IS TO START OVER.
STEVE? YOU'RE ALIVE?
YOU CAME BACK. IT'S BEEN SO LONG...
...SO LONG.
WELL, I COULDN'T LEAVE MY BEST GIRL. NOT WHEN SHE OWES ME A DANCE.

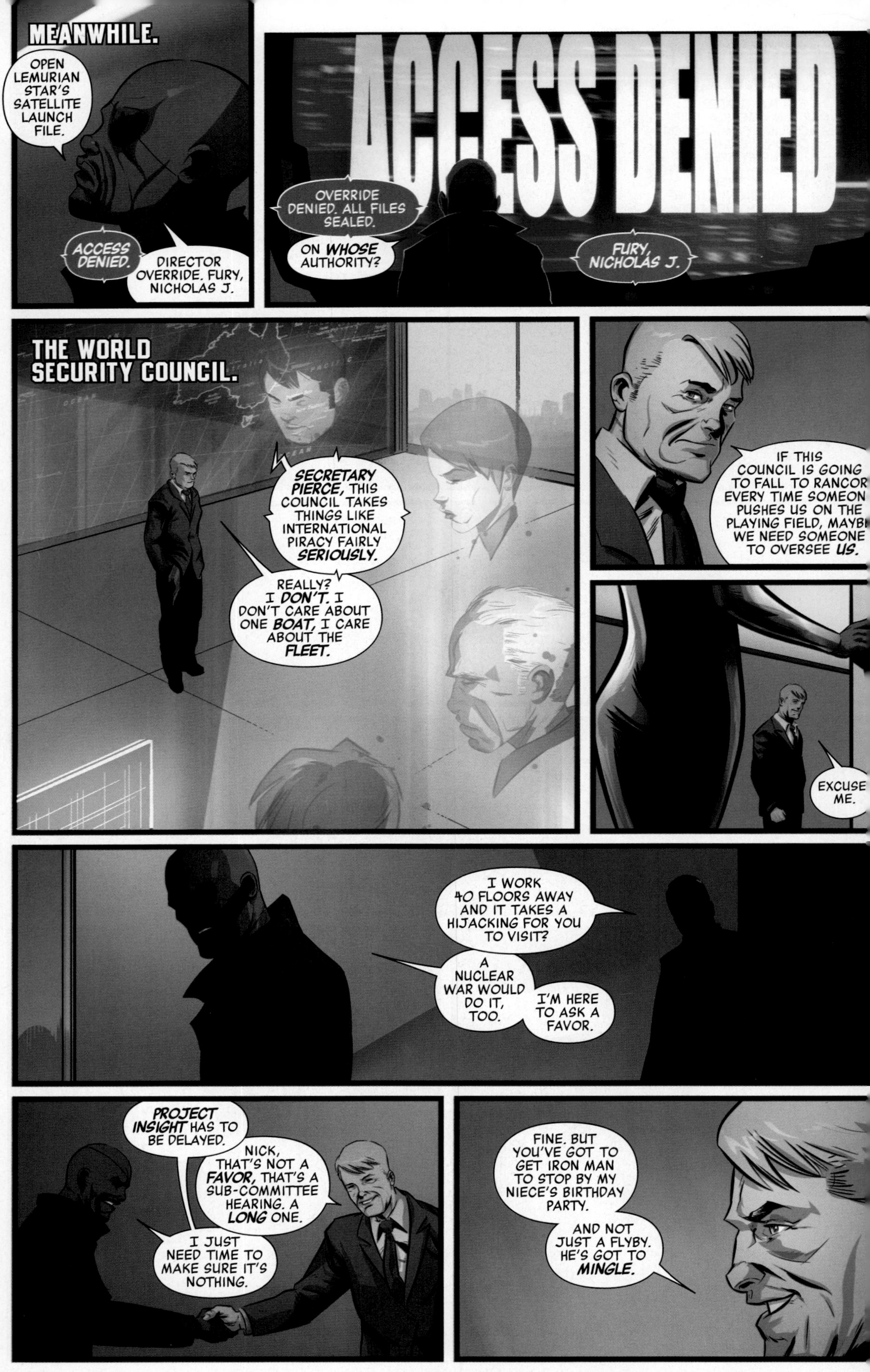
MEANWHILE.
OPEN LEMURIAN STAR'S SATELLITE LAUNCH FILE.
ACCESS DENIED.
DIRECTOR OVERRIDE. FURY, NICHOLAS J.
ACCESS DENIED
OVERRIDE DENIED. ALL FILES SEALED.
ON WHOSE AUTHORITY?
FURY, NICHOLAS J.
THE WORLD SECURITY COUNCIL.
SECRETARY PIERCE, THIS COUNCIL TAKES THINGS LIKE INTERNATIONAL PIRACY FAIRLY SERIOUSLY.
REALLY? I DON'T. I DON'T CARE ABOUT ONE BOAT, I CARE ABOUT THE FLEET.
IF THIS COUNCIL IS GOING TO FALL TO RANCOR EVERY TIME SOMEON PUSHES US ON THE PLAYING FIELD, MAYB WE NEED SOMEONE TO OVERSEE US.
EXCUSE ME.
I WORK 40 FLOORS AWAY AND IT TAKES A HIJACKING FOR YOU TO VISIT?
A NUCLEAR WAR WOULD DO IT, TOO.
I'M HERE TO ASK A FAVOR.
PROJECT INSIGHT HAS TO BE DELAYED.
NICK, THAT'S NOT A FAVOR, THAT'S A SUB-COMMITTEE HEARING. A LONG ONE.
I JUST NEED TIME TO MAKE SURE IT'S NOTHING.
FINE. BUT YOU'VE GOT TO GET IRON MAN TO STOP BY MY NIECE'S BIRTHDAY PARTY.
AND NOT JUST A FLYBY. HE'S GOT TO MINGLE.

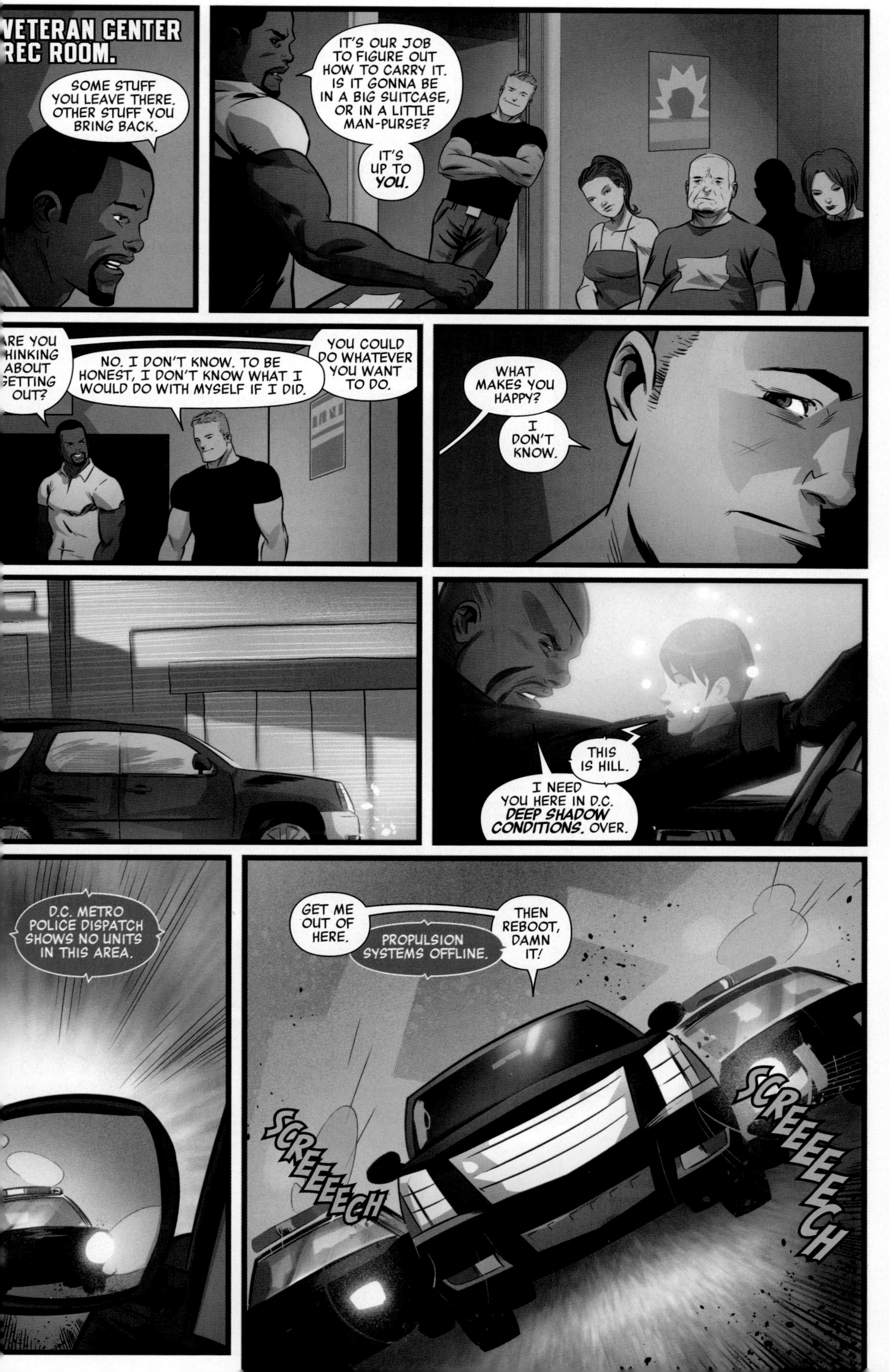

VETERAN CENTER REC ROOM.
SOME STUFF YOU LEAVE THERE. OTHER STUFF YOU BRING BACK.
IT'S OUR JOB TO FIGURE OUT HOW TO CARRY IT. IS IT GONNA BE IN A BIG SUITCASE, OR IN A LITTLE MAN-PURSE?
IT'S UP TO YOU.
ARE YOU THINKING ABOUT GETTING OUT?
NO. I DON'T KNOW. TO BE HONEST, I DON'T KNOW WHAT I WOULD DO WITH MYSELF IF I DID.
YOU COULD DO WHATEVER YOU WANT TO DO.
WHAT MAKES YOU HAPPY?
I DON'T KNOW.
THIS IS HILL.
I NEED YOU HERE IN D.C. DEEP SHADOW CONDITIONS. OVER.
D.C. METRO POLICE DISPATCH SHOWS NO UNITS IN THIS AREA.
GET ME OUT OF HERE.
PROPULSION SYSTEMS OFFLINE.
THEN REBOOT, DAMN IT!
SCREEEECH
SCREEEEECH

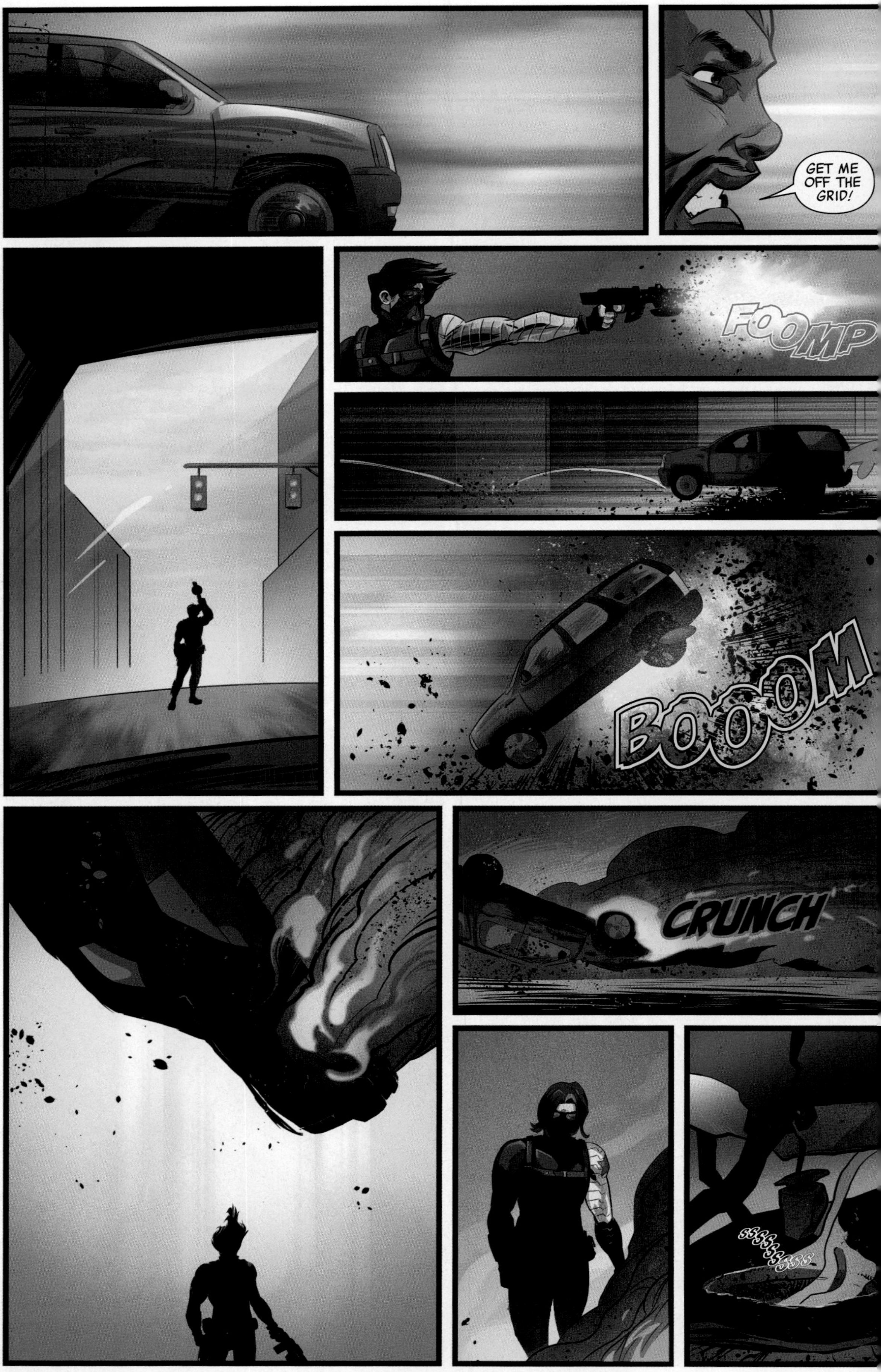
GET ME OFF THE GRID!
FOOMP
BOOOM
CRUNCH
SSSSSSSSS

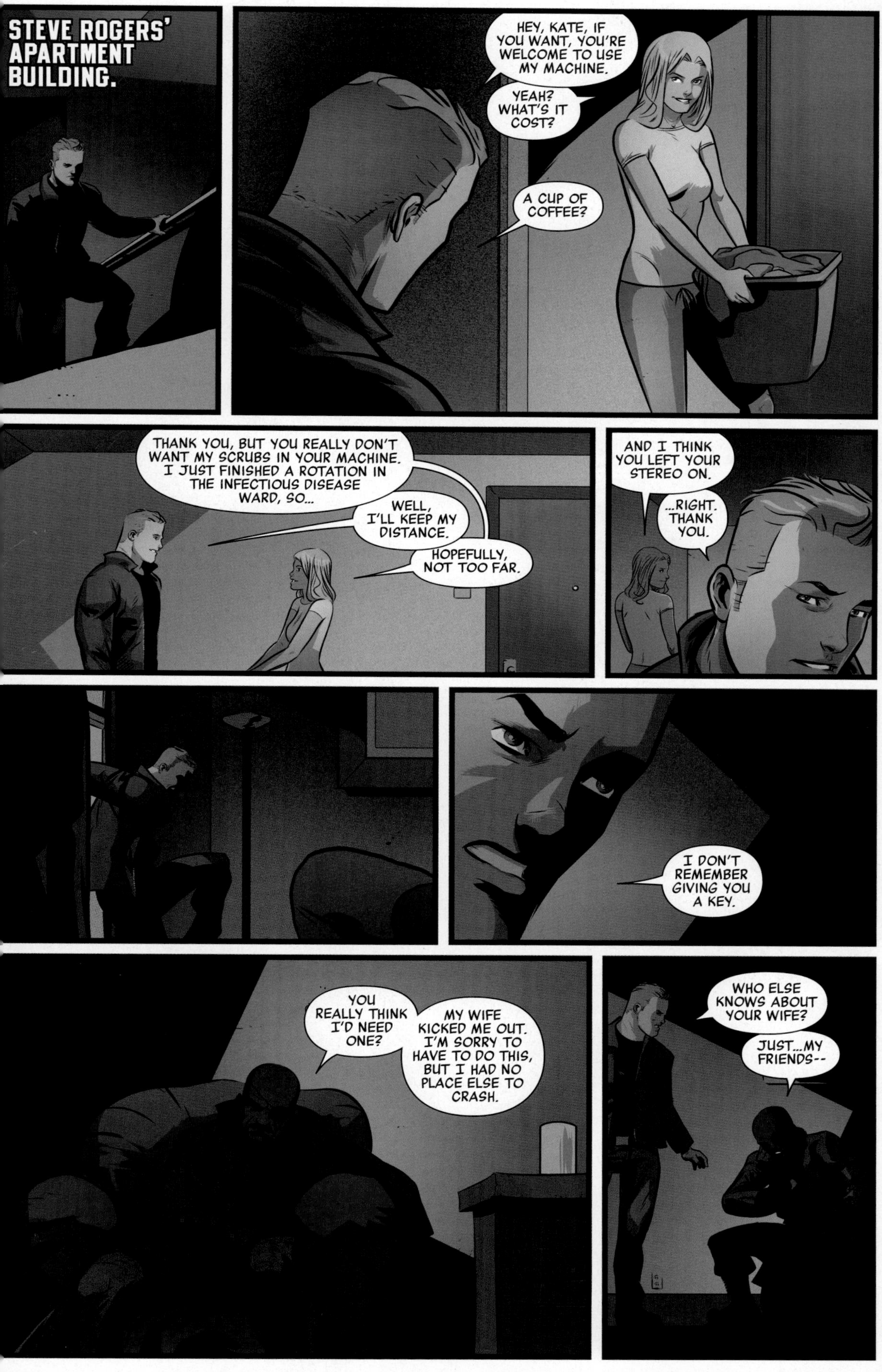
STEVE ROGERS' APARTMENT BUILDING.
HEY, KATE, IF YOU WANT, YOU'RE WELCOME TO USE MY MACHINE.
YEAH? WHAT'S IT COST?
A CUP OF COFFEE?
THANK YOU, BUT YOU REALLY DON'T WANT MY SCRUBS IN YOUR MACHINE. I JUST FINISHED A ROTATION IN THE INFECTIOUS DISEASE WARD, SO...
WELL, I'LL KEEP MY DISTANCE.
HOPEFULLY, NOT TOO FAR.
AND I THINK YOU LEFT YOUR STEREO ON.
...RIGHT. THANK YOU.
I DON'T REMEMBER GIVING YOU A KEY.
YOU REALLY THINK I'D NEED ONE?
MY WIFE KICKED ME OUT. I'M SORRY TO HAVE TO DO THIS, BUT I HAD NO PLACE ELSE TO CRASH.
WHO ELSE KNOWS ABOUT YOUR WIFE?
JUST...MY FRIENDS--

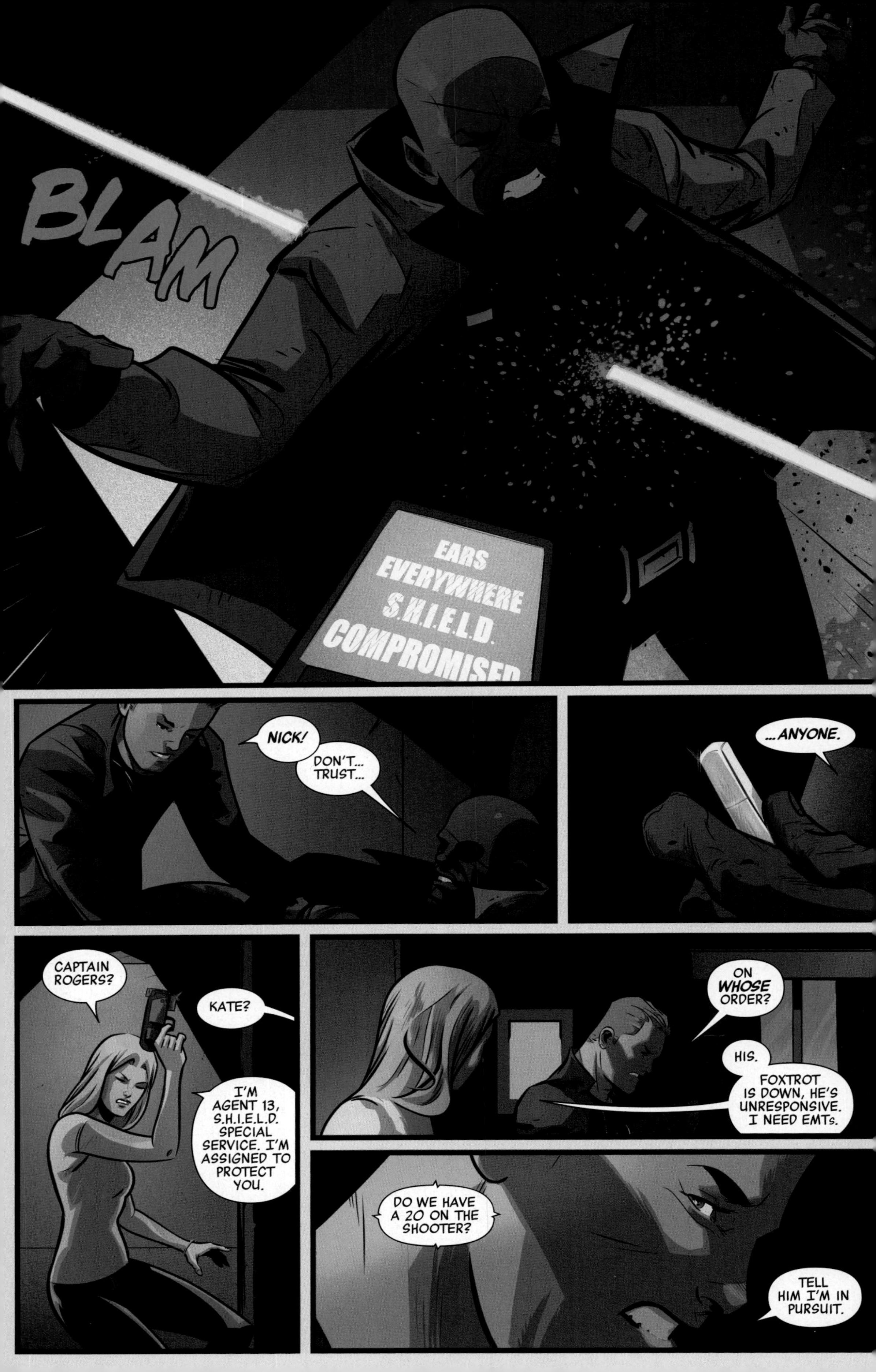
BLAM
EARS EVERYWHERE S.H.I.E.L.D. COMPROMISED
NICK!
DON'T... TRUST...
...ANYONE.
CAPTAIN ROGERS?
KATE?
I'M AGENT 13, S.H.I.E.L.D. SPECIAL SERVICE. I'M ASSIGNED TO PROTECT YOU.
ON WHOSE ORDER?
HIS.
FOXTROT IS DOWN, HE'S UNRESPONSIVE. I NEED EMTs.
DO WE HAVE A 20 ON THE SHOOTER?
TELL HIM I'M IN PURSUIT.

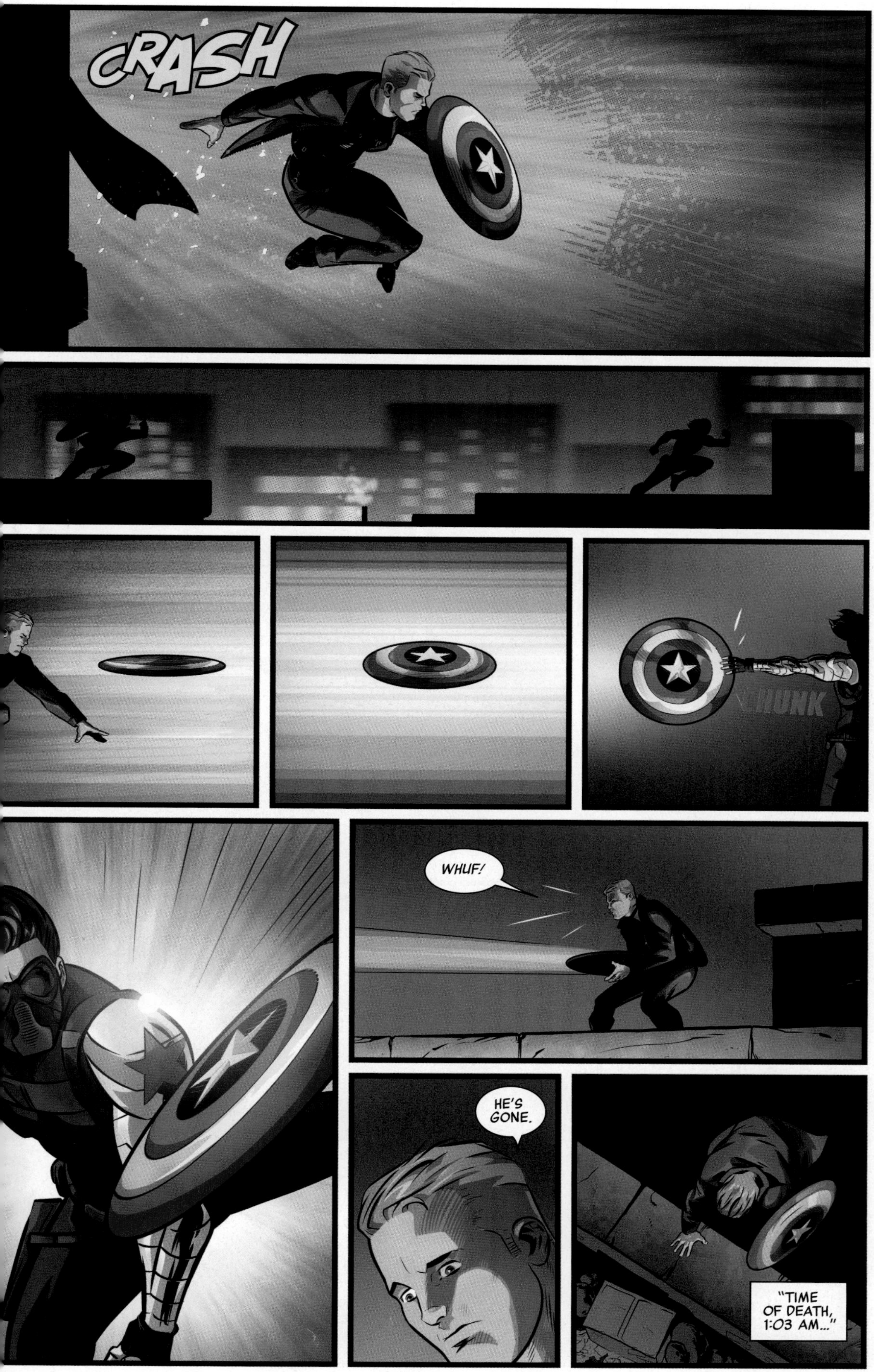
CRASH
CHUNK
WHUF!
HE'S GONE.
"TIME OF DEATH, 1:03 AM..."

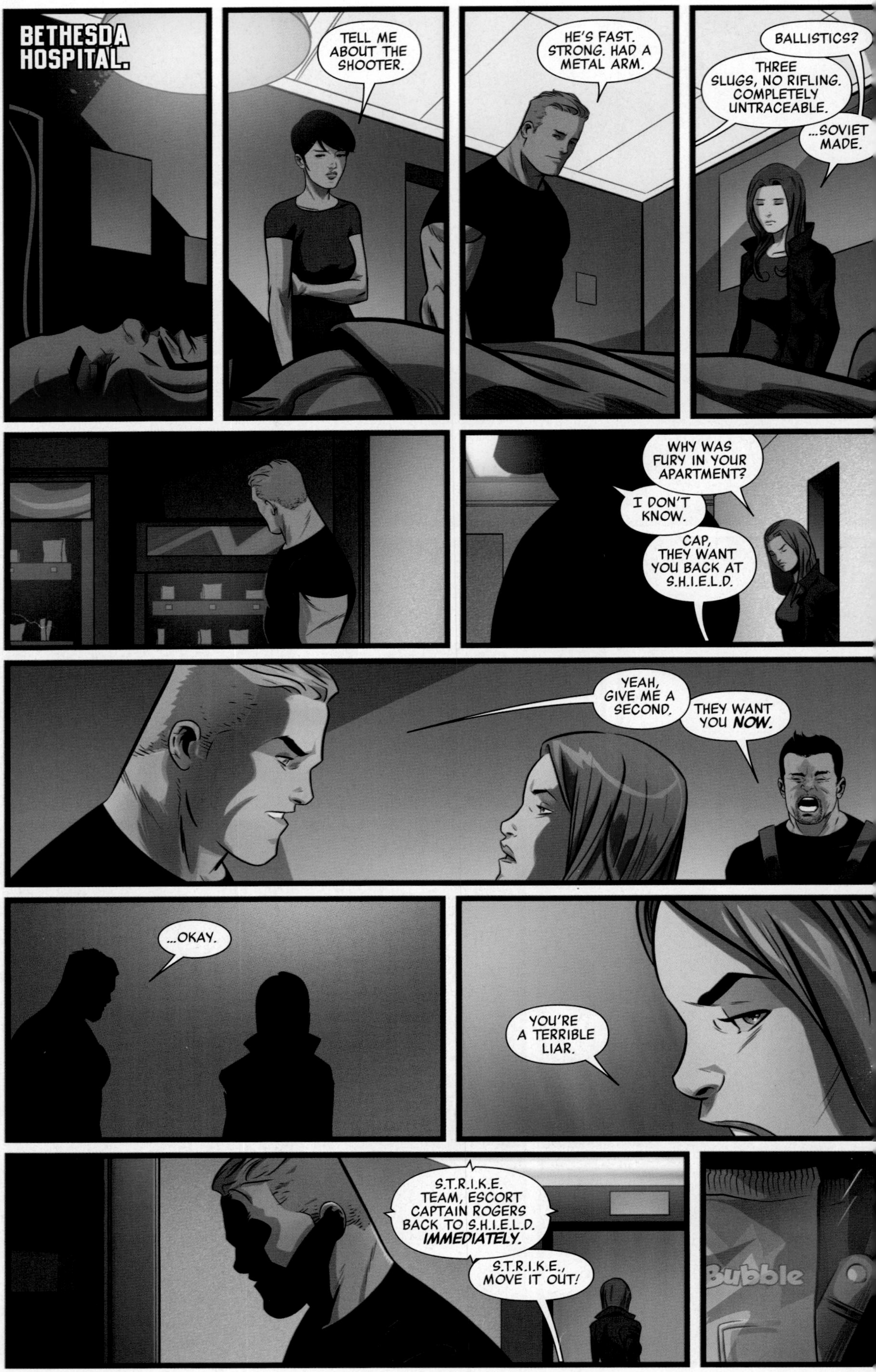

BETHESDA HOSPITAL.
TELL ME ABOUT THE SHOOTER.
HE'S FAST. STRONG. HAD A METAL ARM.
BALLISTICS?
THREE SLUGS, NO RIFLING. COMPLETELY UNTRACEABLE.
...SOVIET MADE.
WHY WAS FURY IN YOUR APARTMENT?
I DON'T KNOW.
CAP, THEY WANT YOU BACK AT S.H.I.E.L.D.
YEAH, GIVE ME A SECOND.
THEY WANT YOU *NOW.*
...OKAY.
YOU'RE A TERRIBLE LIAR.
S.T.R.I.K.E. TEAM, ESCORT CAPTAIN ROGERS BACK TO S.H.I.E.L.D. *IMMEDIATELY.*
S.T.R.I.K.E., MOVE IT OUT!
Bubble

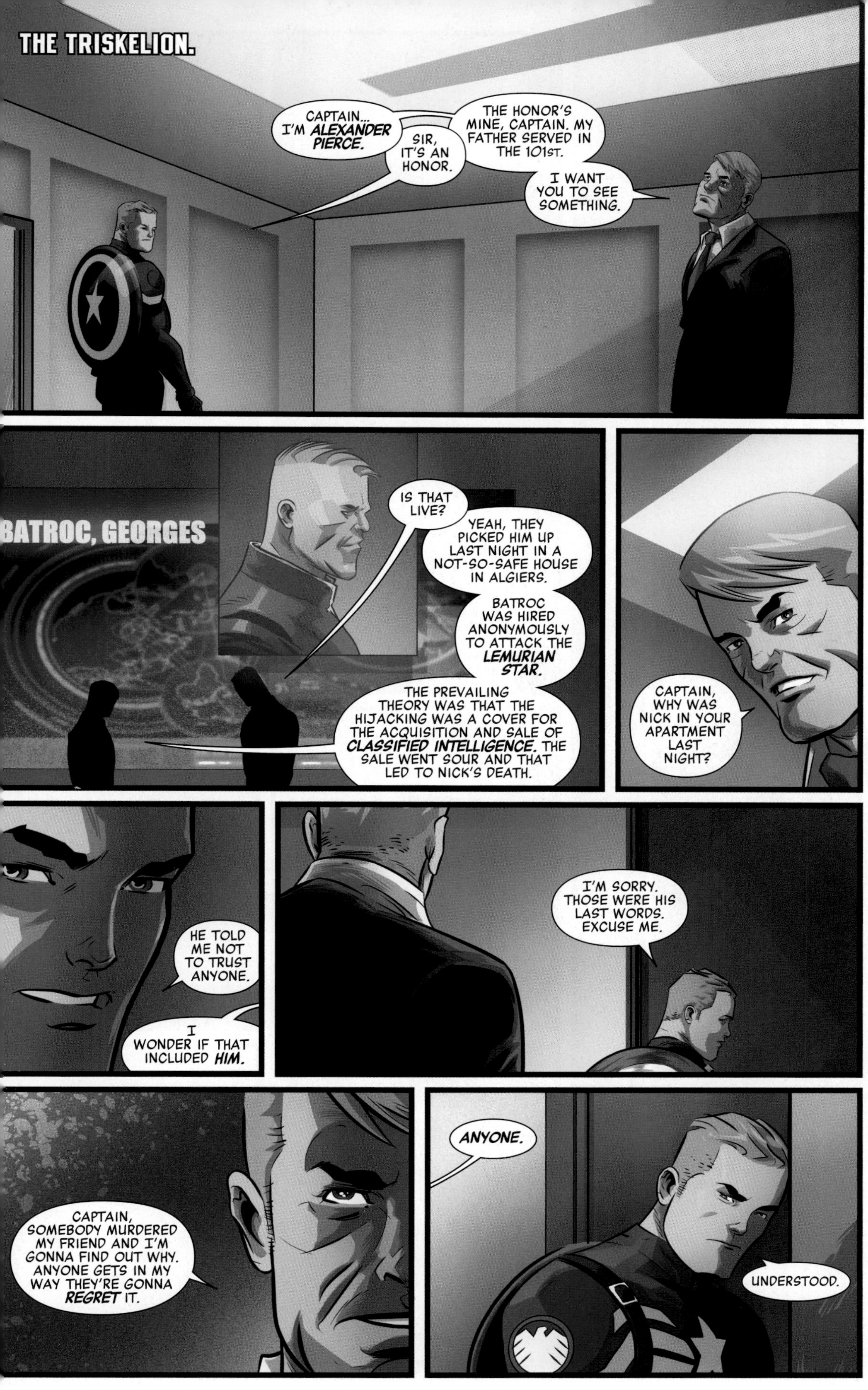
THE TRISKELION.
CAPTAIN... I'M ALEXANDER PIERCE.
SIR, IT'S AN HONOR.
THE HONOR'S MINE, CAPTAIN. MY FATHER SERVED IN THE 101ST.
I WANT YOU TO SEE SOMETHING.
BATROC, GEORGES
IS THAT LIVE?
YEAH, THEY PICKED HIM UP LAST NIGHT IN A NOT-SO-SAFE HOUSE IN ALGIERS.
BATROC WAS HIRED ANONYMOUSLY TO ATTACK THE LEMURIAN STAR.
THE PREVAILING THEORY WAS THAT THE HIJACKING WAS A COVER FOR THE ACQUISITION AND SALE OF CLASSIFIED INTELLIGENCE. THE SALE WENT SOUR AND THAT LED TO NICK'S DEATH.
CAPTAIN, WHY WAS NICK IN YOUR APARTMENT LAST NIGHT?
HE TOLD ME NOT TO TRUST ANYONE.
I WONDER IF THAT INCLUDED HIM.
I'M SORRY. THOSE WERE HIS LAST WORDS. EXCUSE ME.
CAPTAIN, SOMEBODY MURDERED MY FRIEND AND I'M GONNA FIND OUT WHY. ANYONE GETS IN MY WAY THEY'RE GONNA REGRET IT.
ANYONE.
UNDERSTOOD.

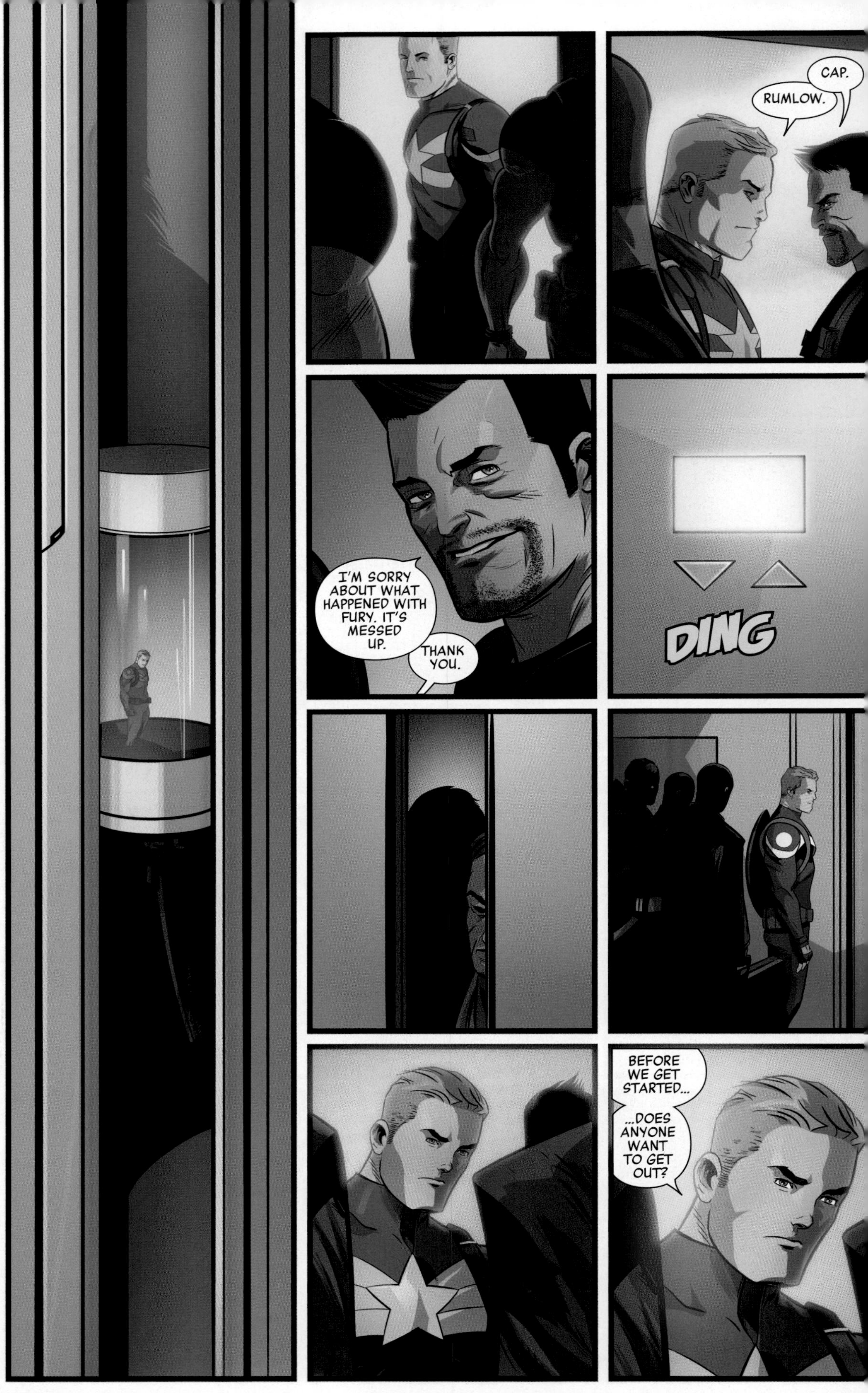

RUMLOW.
CAP.
I'M SORRY ABOUT WHAT HAPPENED WITH FURY. IT'S MESSED UP.
THANK YOU.
DING
BEFORE WE GET STARTED...
...DOES ANYONE WANT TO GET OUT?

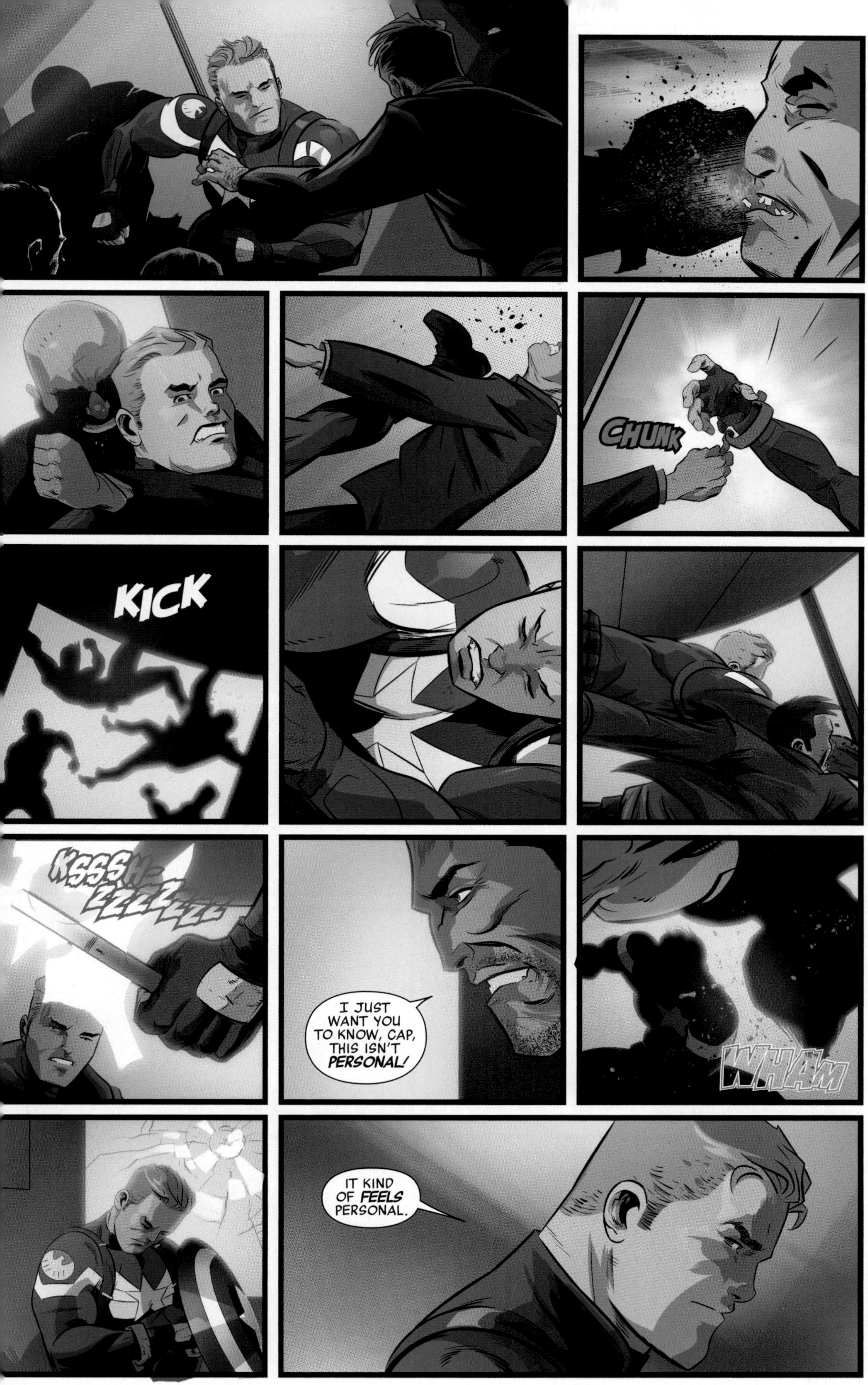
CHUNK
KICK
KSSSH-ZZZZZZZ
I JUST WANT YOU TO KNOW, CAP, THIS ISN'T *PERSONAL!*
WHAM
IT KIND OF *FEELS* PERSONAL.

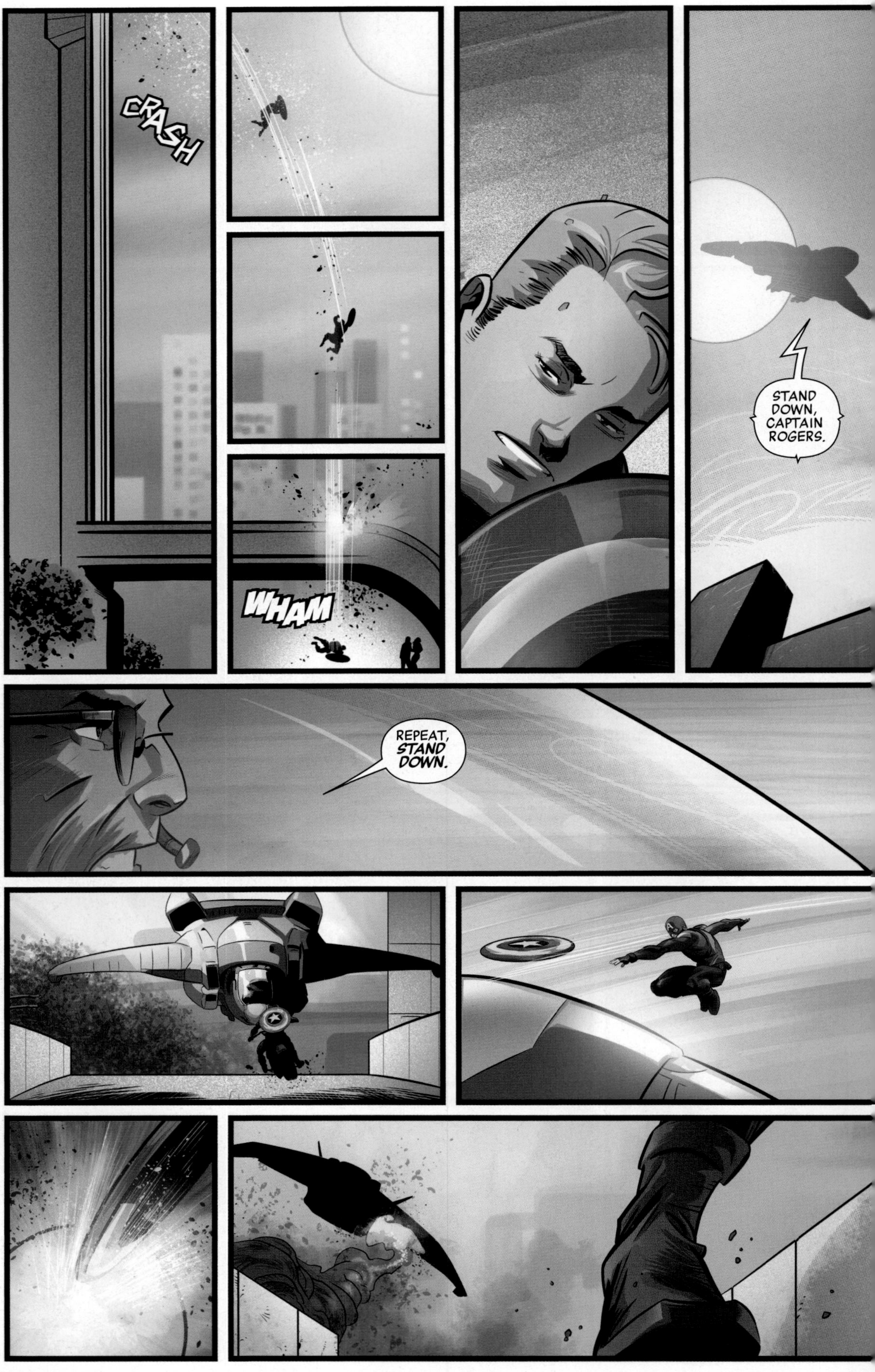
CRASH
WHAM
STAND DOWN, CAPTAIN ROGERS.
REPEAT, STAND DOWN.

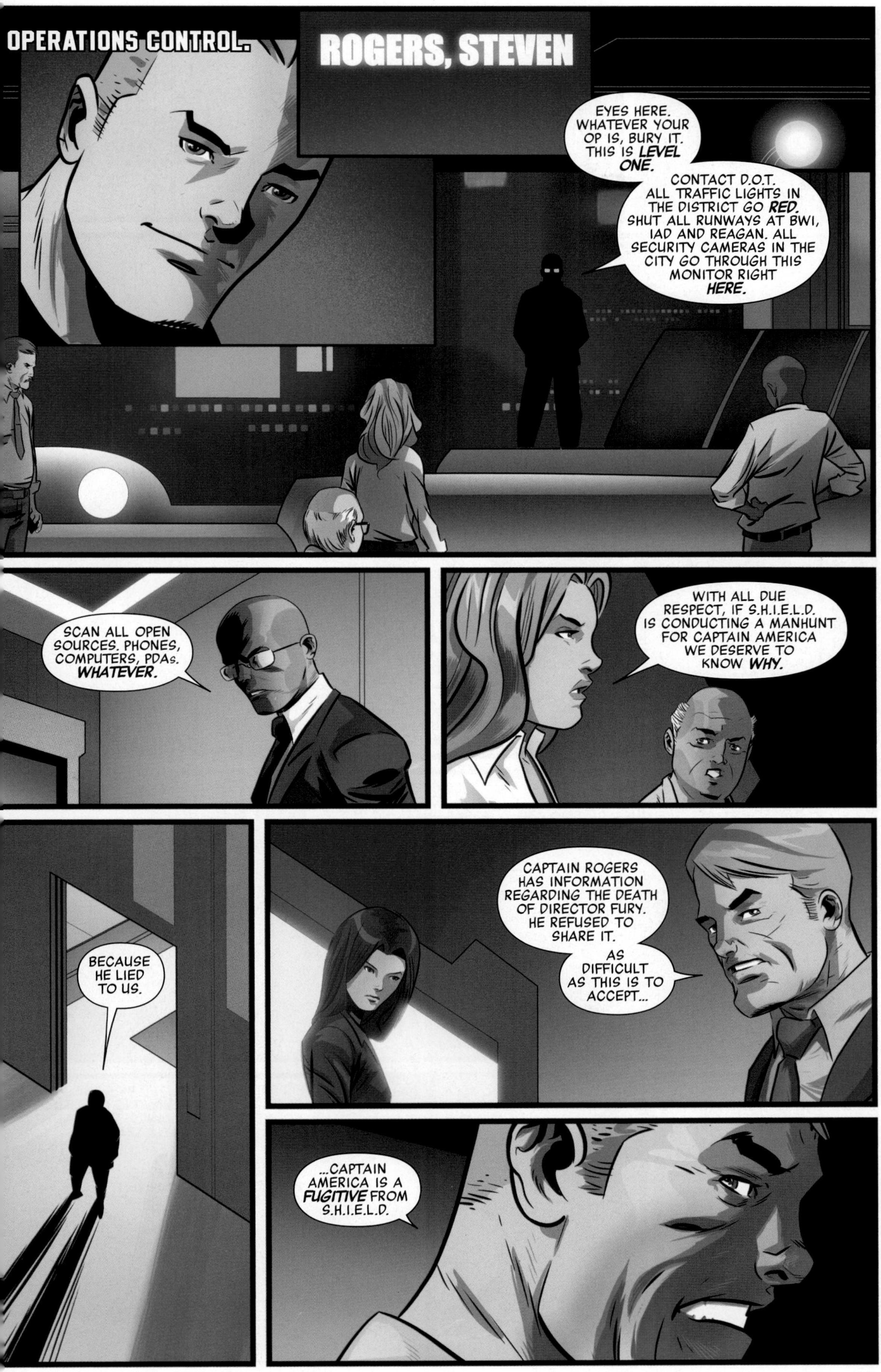
OPERATIONS CONTROL.
ROGERS, STEVEN
EYES HERE. WHATEVER YOUR OP IS, BURY IT. THIS IS LEVEL ONE.
CONTACT D.O.T. ALL TRAFFIC LIGHTS IN THE DISTRICT GO RED. SHUT ALL RUNWAYS AT BWI, IAD AND REAGAN. ALL SECURITY CAMERAS IN THE CITY GO THROUGH THIS MONITOR RIGHT HERE.
SCAN ALL OPEN SOURCES. PHONES, COMPUTERS, PDAs. WHATEVER.
WITH ALL DUE RESPECT, IF S.H.I.E.L.D. IS CONDUCTING A MANHUNT FOR CAPTAIN AMERICA WE DESERVE TO KNOW WHY.
BECAUSE HE LIED TO US.
CAPTAIN ROGERS HAS INFORMATION REGARDING THE DEATH OF DIRECTOR FURY. HE REFUSED TO SHARE IT.
AS DIFFICULT AS THIS IS TO ACCEPT...
...CAPTAIN AMERICA IS A FUGITIVE FROM S.H.I.E.L.D.

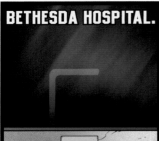

WHERE
IS IT?

POP

SAFE.

DO
BETTER.

FURY
GAVE IT
TO YOU.
WHY?

WHAT'S
ON IT?

I DON'T
KNOW...BUT
I KNOW WHO
KILLED FURY.

MOST OF THE INTELLIGENCE
COMMUNITY DOESN'T BELIEVE HE
EXISTS. THE ONES THAT DO CALL
HIM THE *WINTER SOLDIER.*

HE'S CREDITED WITH
OVER TWO DOZEN
ASSASSINATIONS IN THE
LAST *50 YEARS.* GOING
AFTER HIM IS A DEAD END.
I KNOW, I'VE TRIED.
HE'S A GHOST
STORY.

WELL, LET'S
FIND OUT WHAT THE
GHOST *WANTS.*

THIS DRIVE IS PROTECTED BY SOME SORT
OF A.I. IT KEEPS REWRITING ITSELF TO
COUNTER MY COMMANDS. I'M GONNA
TRY RUNNING A TRACER.

SO IF WE CAN'T
READ THE FILE MAYBE
WE CAN FIND OUT WHERE IT
CAME FROM...WHEATON, NJ.
YOU KNOW IT?

I USED
TO. LET'S GO.

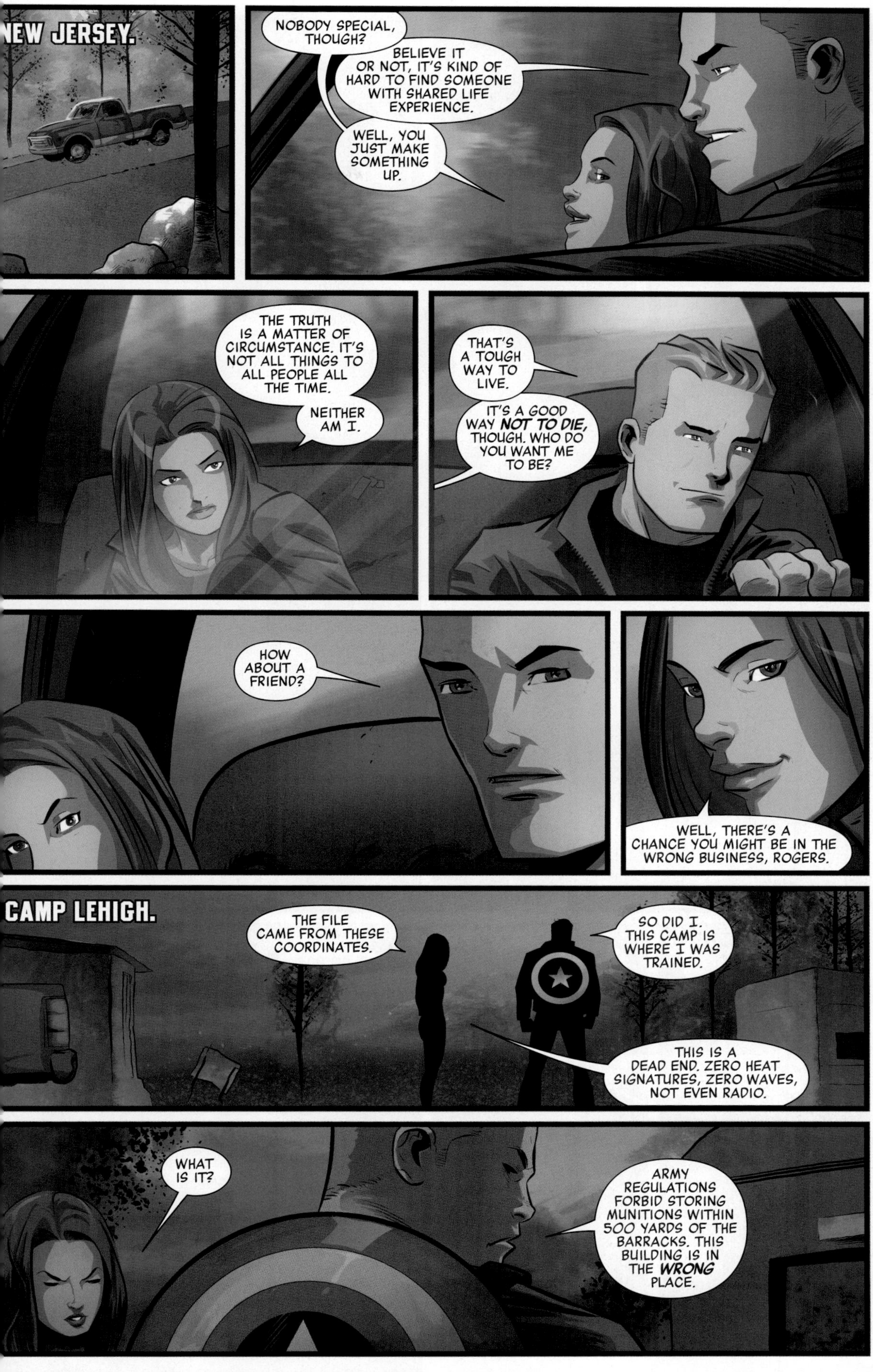
NEW JERSEY.
NOBODY SPECIAL, THOUGH?
BELIEVE IT OR NOT, IT'S KIND OF HARD TO FIND SOMEONE WITH SHARED LIFE EXPERIENCE.
WELL, YOU JUST MAKE SOMETHING UP.
THE TRUTH IS A MATTER OF CIRCUMSTANCE. IT'S NOT ALL THINGS TO ALL PEOPLE ALL THE TIME.
NEITHER AM I.
THAT'S A TOUGH WAY TO LIVE.
IT'S A GOOD WAY NOT TO DIE, THOUGH. WHO DO YOU WANT ME TO BE?
HOW ABOUT A FRIEND?
WELL, THERE'S A CHANCE YOU MIGHT BE IN THE WRONG BUSINESS, ROGERS.
CAMP LEHIGH.
THE FILE CAME FROM THESE COORDINATES.
SO DID I. THIS CAMP IS WHERE I WAS TRAINED.
THIS IS A DEAD END. ZERO HEAT SIGNATURES, ZERO WAVES, NOT EVEN RADIO.
WHAT IS IT?
ARMY REGULATIONS FORBID STORING MUNITIONS WITHIN 500 YARDS OF THE BARRACKS. THIS BUILDING IS IN THE WRONG PLACE.

THIS IS S.H.I.E.L.D.

MAYBE WHERE IT *STARTED*.

IF YOU'RE ALREADY WORKING IN A SECRET OFFICE... WHY DO YOU NEED TO *HIDE* THE ELEVATOR?

THIS CAN'T BE THE DATA POINT. THIS TECHNOLOGY IS *ANCIENT*.

INITIATE SYSTEM...

ROGERS, STEVEN: BORN 1918.

ROMANOFF, NATALIA ALIANOVNA: BORN 1984.

IT'S SOME KIND OF RECORDING.

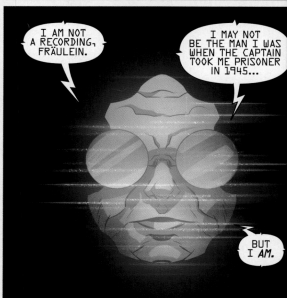

I AM NOT A RECORDING, FRÄULEIN.

I MAY NOT BE THE MAN I WAS WHEN THE CAPTAIN TOOK ME PRISONER IN 1945...

BUT I *AM*.

MARVEL'S CAPTAIN AMERICA: CIVIL WAR PRELUDE #4

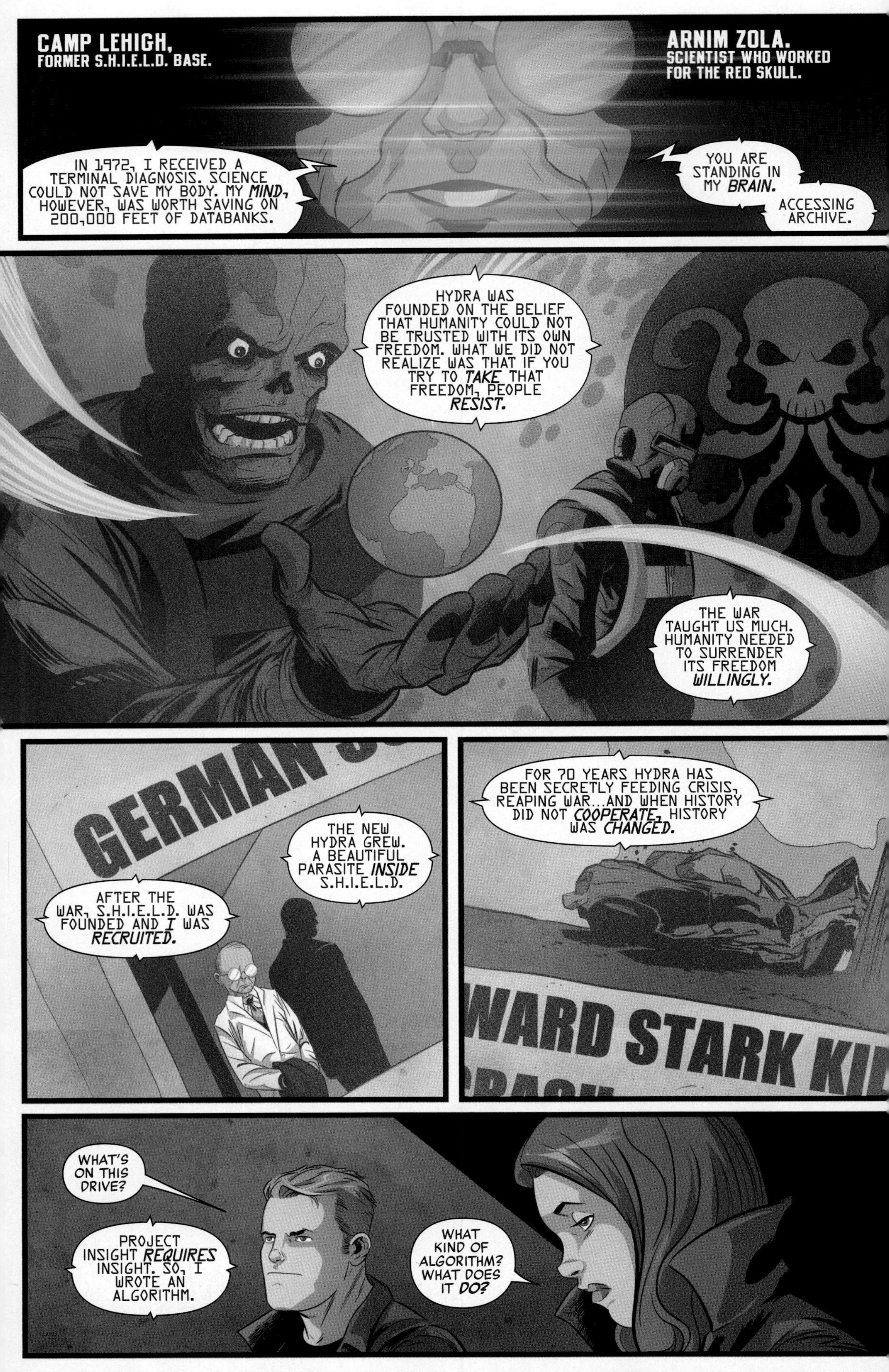
CAMP LEHIGH, FORMER S.H.I.E.L.D. BASE.
ARNIM ZOLA. SCIENTIST WHO WORKED FOR THE RED SKULL.
IN 1972, I RECEIVED A TERMINAL DIAGNOSIS. SCIENCE COULD NOT SAVE MY BODY. MY MIND, HOWEVER, WAS WORTH SAVING ON 200,000 FEET OF DATABANKS.
YOU ARE STANDING IN MY BRAIN.
ACCESSING ARCHIVE.
HYDRA WAS FOUNDED ON THE BELIEF THAT HUMANITY COULD NOT BE TRUSTED WITH ITS OWN FREEDOM. WHAT WE DID NOT REALIZE WAS THAT IF YOU TRY TO TAKE THAT FREEDOM, PEOPLE RESIST.
THE WAR TAUGHT US MUCH. HUMANITY NEEDED TO SURRENDER ITS FREEDOM WILLINGLY.
GERMAN
AFTER THE WAR, S.H.I.E.L.D. WAS FOUNDED AND I WAS RECRUITED.
THE NEW HYDRA GREW. A BEAUTIFUL PARASITE INSIDE S.H.I.E.L.D.
FOR 70 YEARS HYDRA HAS BEEN SECRETLY FEEDING CRISIS, REAPING WAR...AND WHEN HISTORY DID NOT COOPERATE, HISTORY WAS CHANGED.
WARD STARK KI
WHAT'S ON THIS DRIVE?
PROJECT INSIGHT REQUIRES INSIGHT. SO, I WROTE AN ALGORITHM.
WHAT KIND OF ALGORITHM? WHAT DOES IT DO?

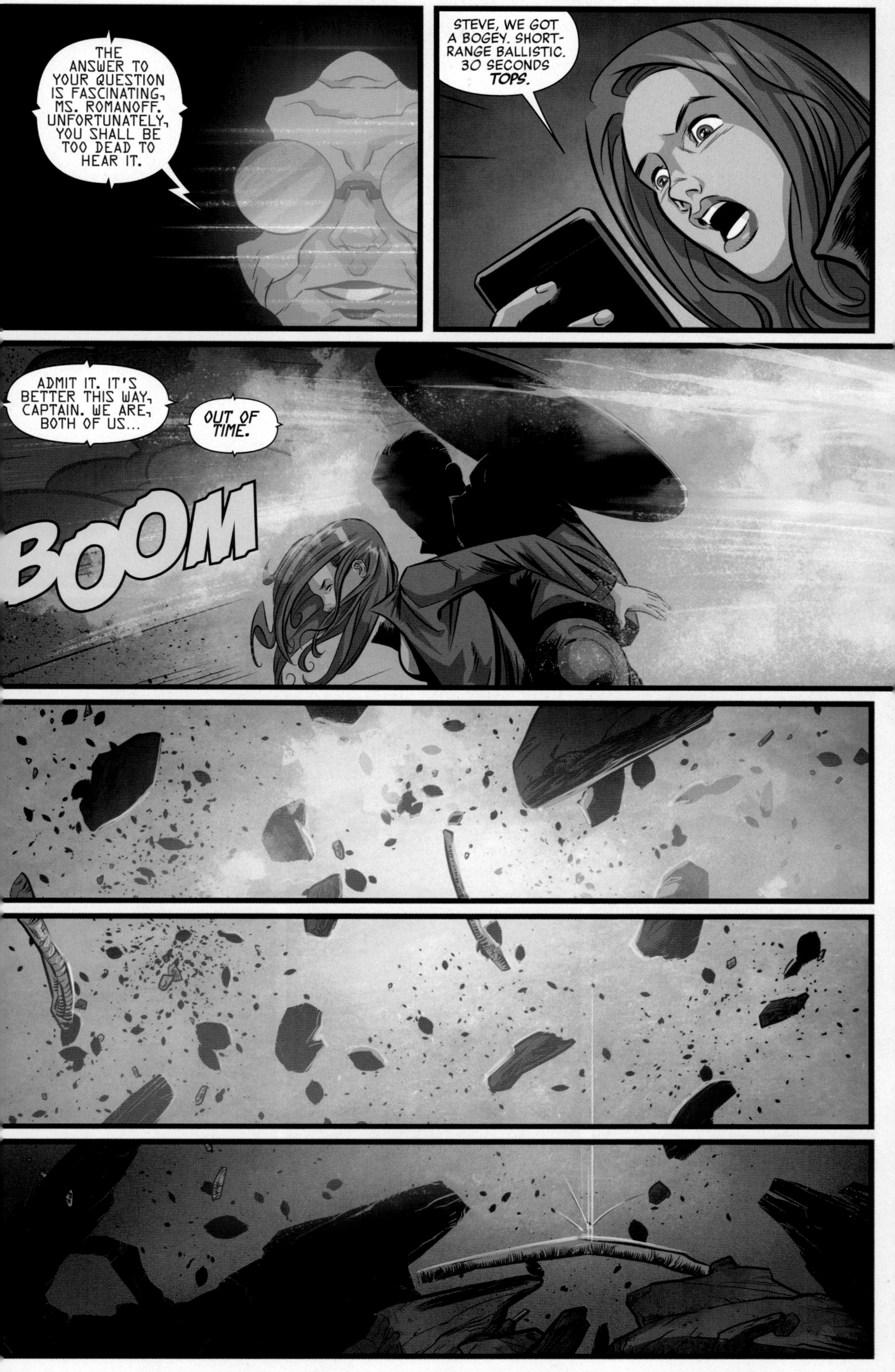
THE ANSWER TO YOUR QUESTION IS FASCINATING, MS. ROMANOFF. UNFORTUNATELY, YOU SHALL BE TOO DEAD TO HEAR IT.
STEVE, WE GOT A BOGEY. SHORT-RANGE BALLISTIC. 30 SECONDS TOPS.
ADMIT IT. IT'S BETTER THIS WAY, CAPTAIN. WE ARE, BOTH OF US...
OUT OF TIME.
BOOM

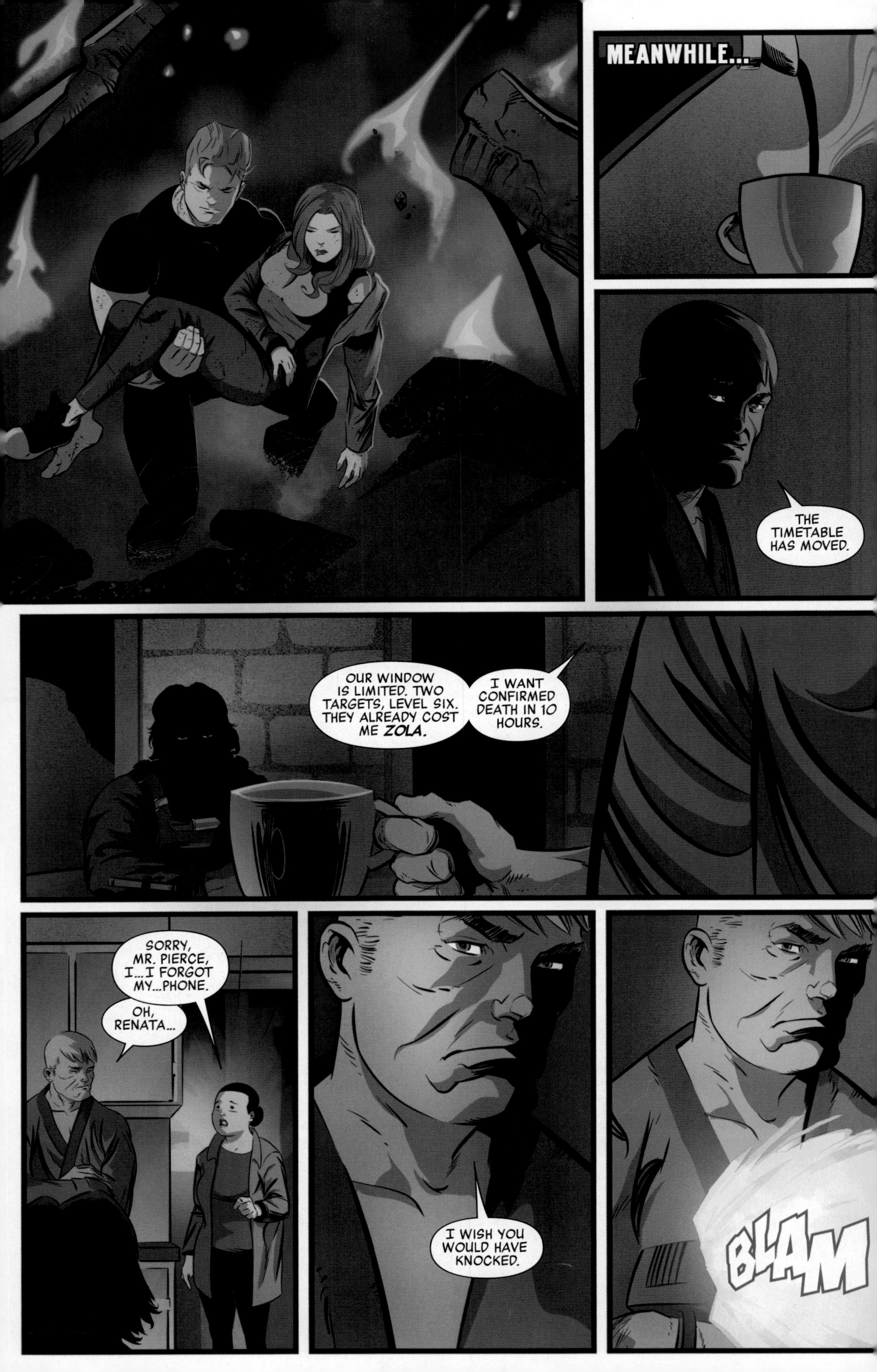
MEANWHILE...
THE TIMETABLE HAS MOVED.
OUR WINDOW IS LIMITED. TWO TARGETS, LEVEL SIX. THEY ALREADY COST ME ZOLA.
I WANT CONFIRMED DEATH IN 10 HOURS.
SORRY, MR. PIERCE, I...I FORGOT MY...PHONE.
OH, RENATA...
I WISH YOU WOULD HAVE KNOCKED.
BLAM

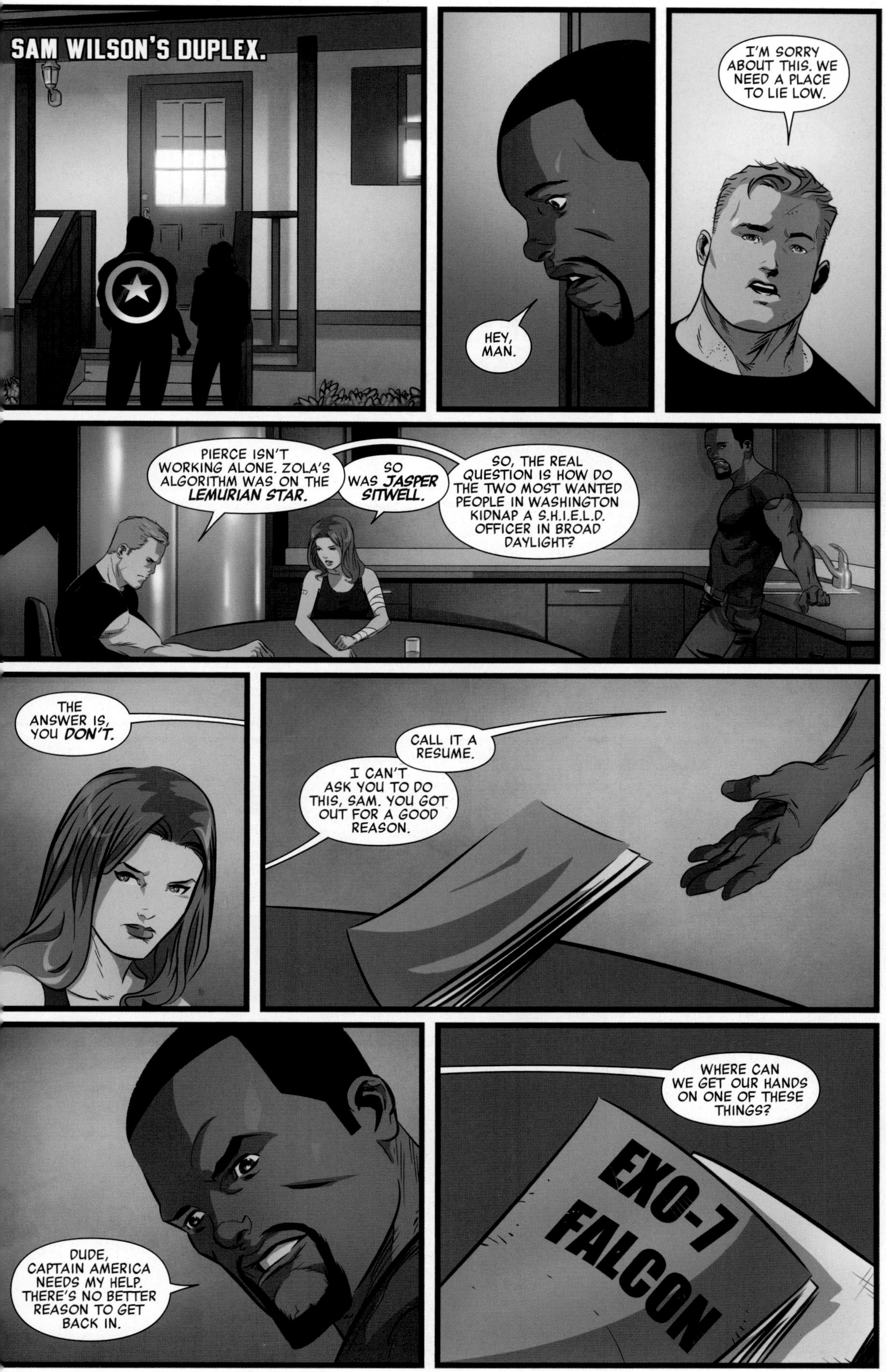
SAM WILSON'S DUPLEX.
HEY, MAN.
I'M SORRY ABOUT THIS. WE NEED A PLACE TO LIE LOW.
PIERCE ISN'T WORKING ALONE. ZOLA'S ALGORITHM WAS ON THE LEMURIAN STAR.
SO WAS JASPER SITWELL.
SO, THE REAL QUESTION IS HOW DO THE TWO MOST WANTED PEOPLE IN WASHINGTON KIDNAP A S.H.I.E.L.D. OFFICER IN BROAD DAYLIGHT?
THE ANSWER IS, YOU DON'T.
CALL IT A RESUME.
I CAN'T ASK YOU TO DO THIS, SAM. YOU GOT OUT FOR A GOOD REASON.
DUDE, CAPTAIN AMERICA NEEDS MY HELP. THERE'S NO BETTER REASON TO GET BACK IN.
WHERE CAN WE GET OUR HANDS ON ONE OF THESE THINGS?
EXO-7 FALCON

LATER...

WAIT. WHAT ABOUT THAT GIRL FROM ACCOUNTING, LAURA--

LILLIAN. LIP PIERCING, RIGHT?

YEAH, SHE'S CUTE.

YEAH. I'M NOT READY FOR THAT.

BWAAAAA!

HUFF! HUFF!

HELLO, SITWELL...

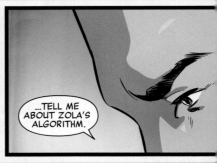

...TELL ME ABOUT ZOLA'S ALGORITHM.

IT'S A PROGRAM FOR CHOOSING INSIGHT'S TARGETS. THE 21ST CENTURY IS A DIGITAL BOOK. ZOLA TAUGHT HYDRA HOW TO *READ* IT.

IT EVALUATES PEOPLE'S *PASTS* TO PREDICT THEIR *FUTURES.* THEN THE INSIGHT HELICARRIERS CREATE A LIST OF POTENTIAL THREATS TO HYDRA, AND SCRATCH PEOPLE OFF THE LIST...A FEW *MILLION* AT A TIME.

LATER...ON THE HIGHWAY...

INSIGHT LAUNCHES IN 16 HOURS. WE'RE CUTTING IT CLOSE HERE, STEVE.

I KNOW. WE'LL USE SITWELL TO BYPASS THE DNA SCANS AND ACCESS THE HELICARRIERS DIRECTLY.

WHAT?! ARE YOU *CRAZY?* THAT IS A TERRIBLE, *TERRIBLE* IDEA.

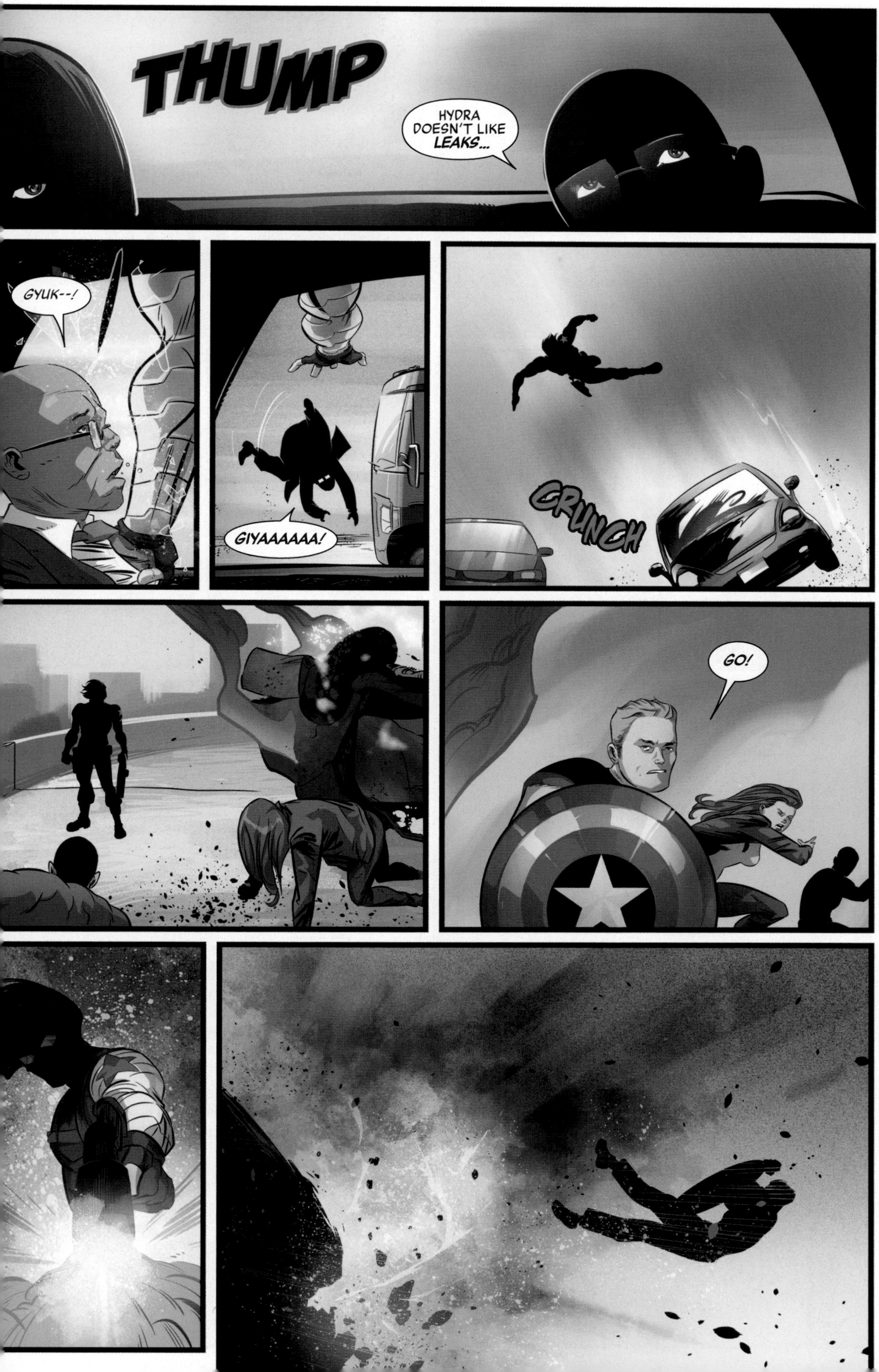
THUMP
HYDRA DOESN'T LIKE LEAKS...
GYUK--!
GIYAAAAAA!
CRUNCH
GO!

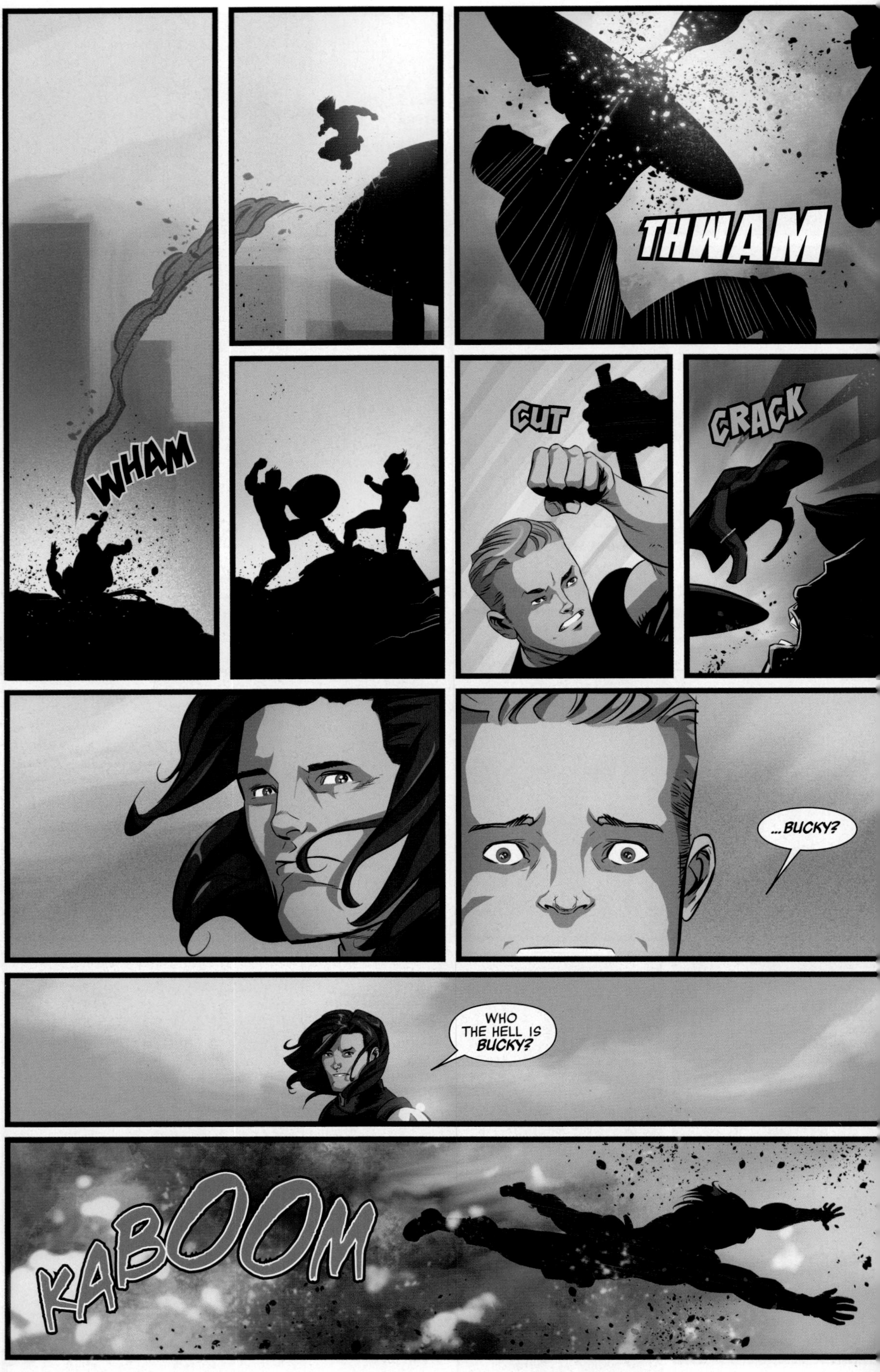
WHAM
THWAM
CUT
CRACK
...BUCKY?
WHO THE HELL IS BUCKY?
KABOOM

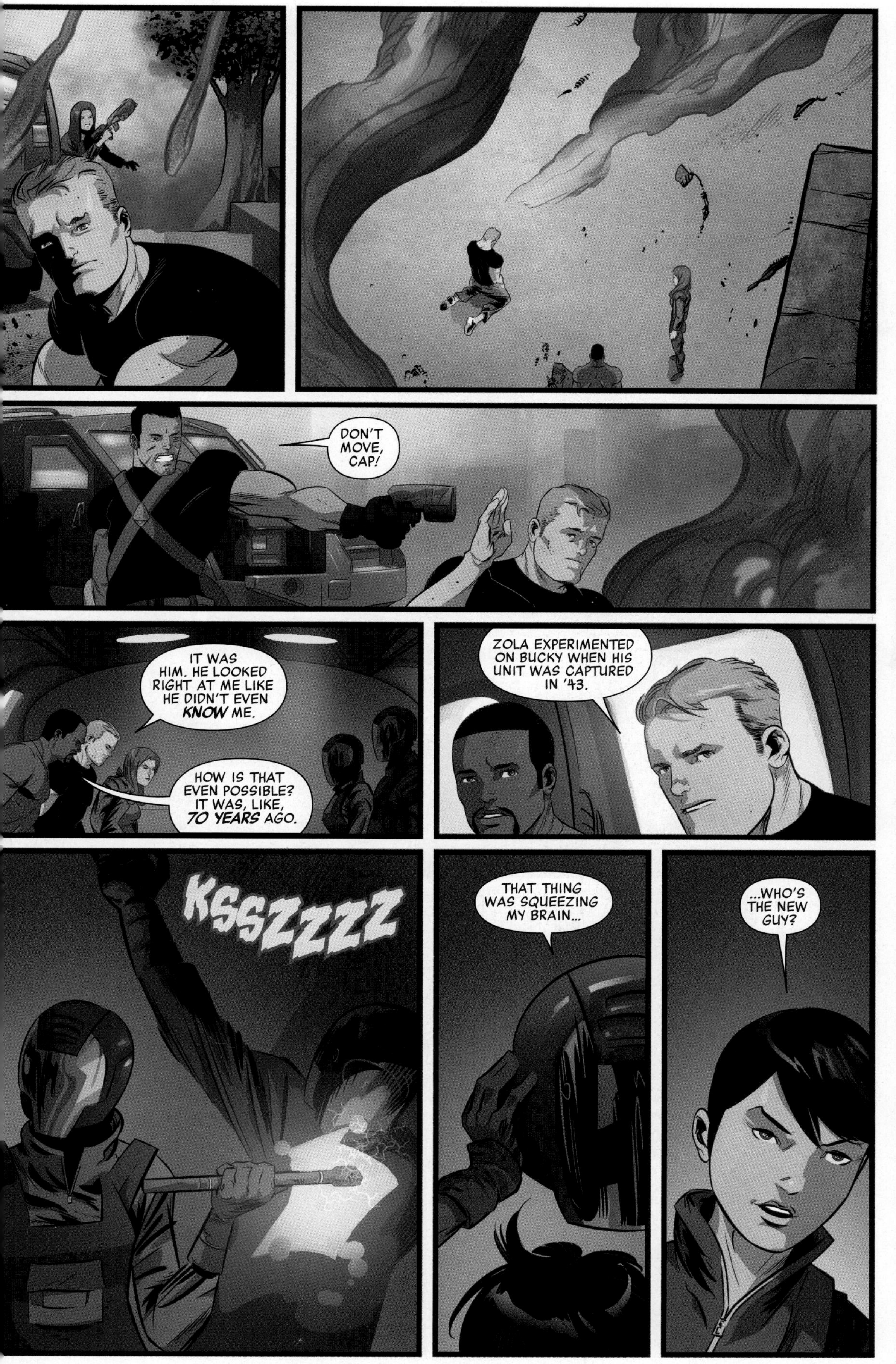
DON'T MOVE, CAP!
IT WAS HIM. HE LOOKED RIGHT AT ME LIKE HE DIDN'T EVEN KNOW ME.
HOW IS THAT EVEN POSSIBLE? IT WAS, LIKE, 70 YEARS AGO.
ZOLA EXPERIMENTED ON BUCKY WHEN HIS UNIT WAS CAPTURED IN '43.
KSSZZZZ
THAT THING WAS SQUEEZING MY BRAIN...
...WHO'S THE NEW GUY?

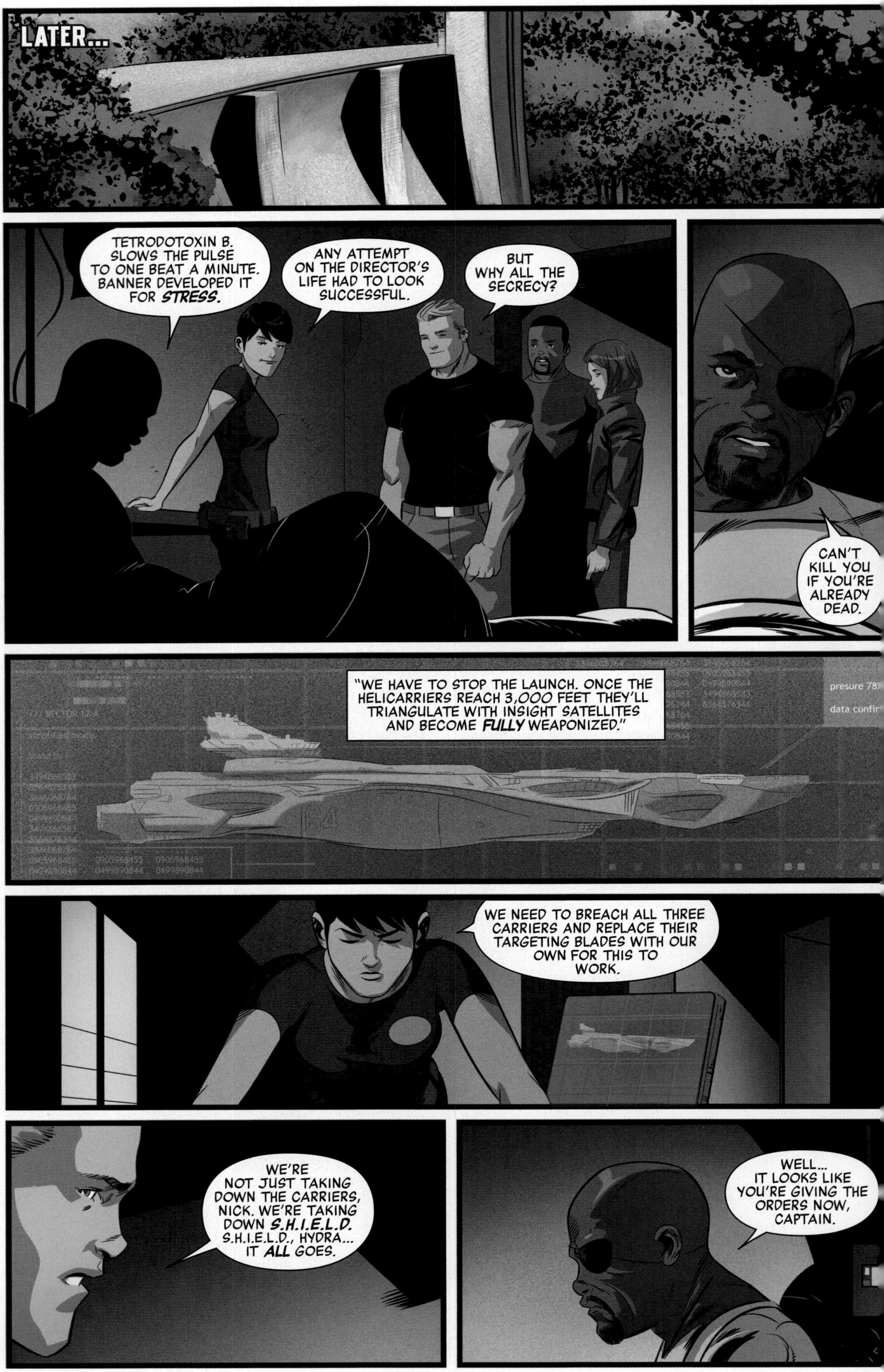
LATER...
TETRODOTOXIN B. SLOWS THE PULSE TO ONE BEAT A MINUTE. BANNER DEVELOPED IT FOR STRESS.
ANY ATTEMPT ON THE DIRECTOR'S LIFE HAD TO LOOK SUCCESSFUL.
BUT WHY ALL THE SECRECY?
CAN'T KILL YOU IF YOU'RE ALREADY DEAD.
"WE HAVE TO STOP THE LAUNCH. ONCE THE HELICARRIERS REACH 3,000 FEET THEY'LL TRIANGULATE WITH INSIGHT SATELLITES AND BECOME FULLY WEAPONIZED."
WE NEED TO BREACH ALL THREE CARRIERS AND REPLACE THEIR TARGETING BLADES WITH OUR OWN FOR THIS TO WORK.
WE'RE NOT JUST TAKING DOWN THE CARRIERS, NICK. WE'RE TAKING DOWN S.H.I.E.L.D. S.H.I.E.L.D., HYDRA... IT ALL GOES.
WELL... IT LOOKS LIKE YOU'RE GIVING THE ORDERS NOW, CAPTAIN.

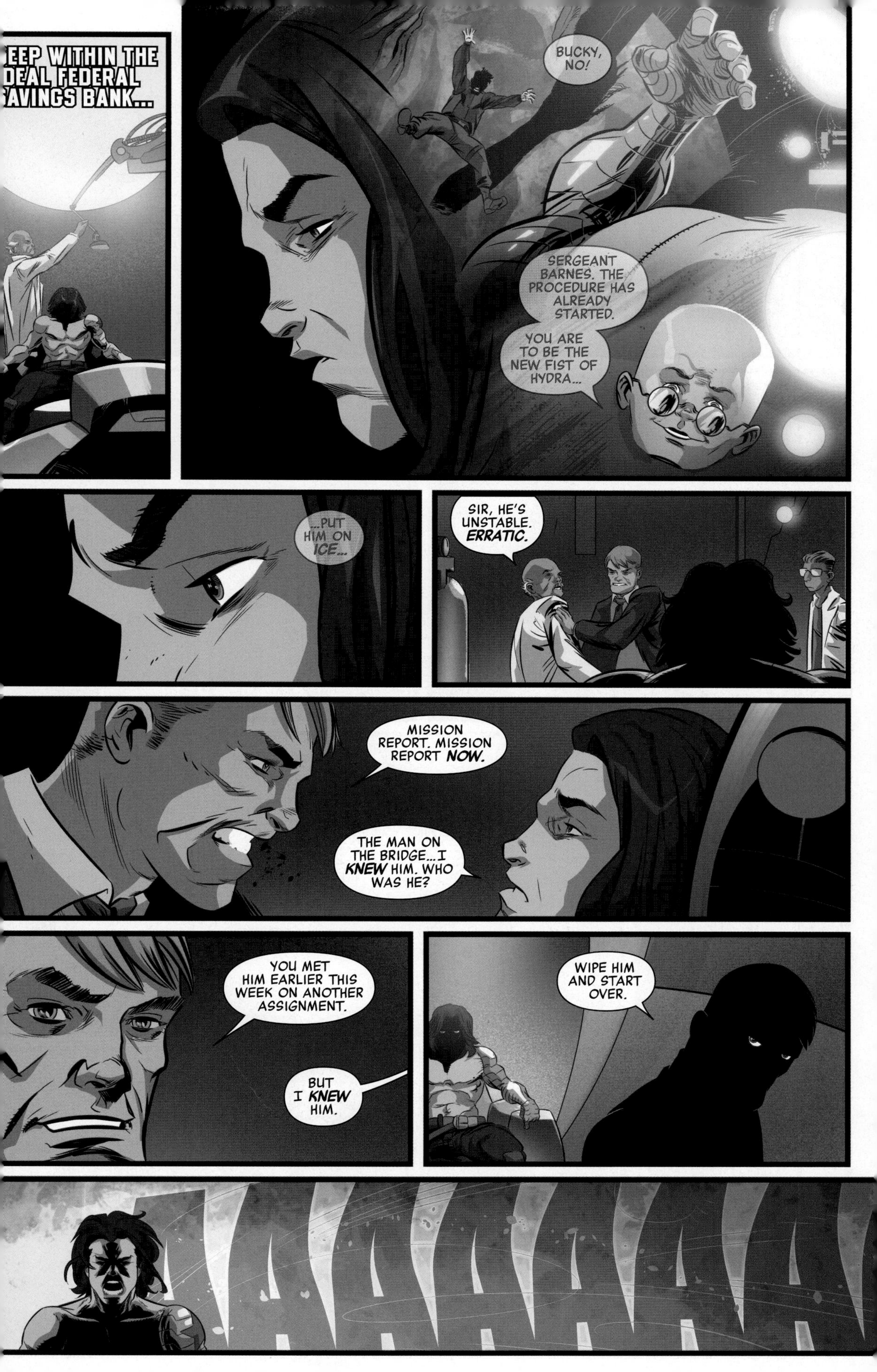

EEP WITHIN THE
DEAL FEDERAL
SAVINGS BANK...
BUCKY, NO!
SERGEANT BARNES. THE PROCEDURE HAS ALREADY STARTED.
YOU ARE TO BE THE NEW FIST OF HYDRA...
...PUT HIM ON ICE...
SIR, HE'S UNSTABLE. ERRATIC.
MISSION REPORT. MISSION REPORT NOW.
THE MAN ON THE BRIDGE...I KNEW HIM. WHO WAS HE?
YOU MET HIM EARLIER THIS WEEK ON ANOTHER ASSIGNMENT.
BUT I KNEW HIM.
WIPE HIM AND START OVER.

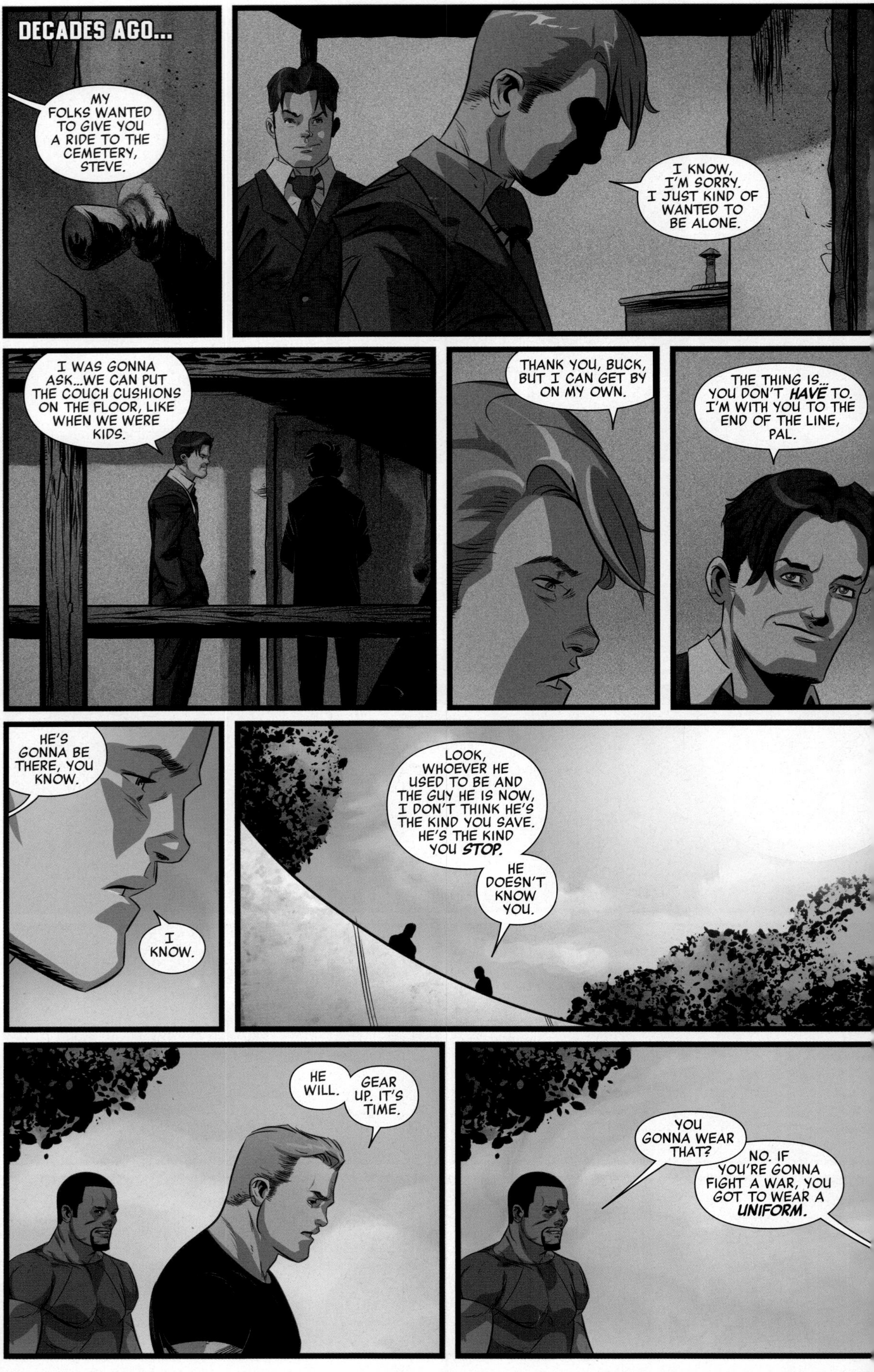
DECADES AGO...
MY FOLKS WANTED TO GIVE YOU A RIDE TO THE CEMETERY, STEVE.
I KNOW, I'M SORRY. I JUST KIND OF WANTED TO BE ALONE.
I WAS GONNA ASK...WE CAN PUT THE COUCH CUSHIONS ON THE FLOOR, LIKE WHEN WE WERE KIDS.
THANK YOU, BUCK, BUT I CAN GET BY ON MY OWN.
THE THING IS... YOU DON'T HAVE TO. I'M WITH YOU TO THE END OF THE LINE, PAL.
HE'S GONNA BE THERE, YOU KNOW.
I KNOW.
LOOK, WHOEVER HE USED TO BE AND THE GUY HE IS NOW, I DON'T THINK HE'S THE KIND YOU SAVE. HE'S THE KIND YOU STOP.
HE DOESN'T KNOW YOU.
HE WILL.
GEAR UP. IT'S TIME.
YOU GONNA WEAR THAT?
NO. IF YOU'RE GONNA FIGHT A WAR, YOU GOT TO WEAR A UNIFORM.

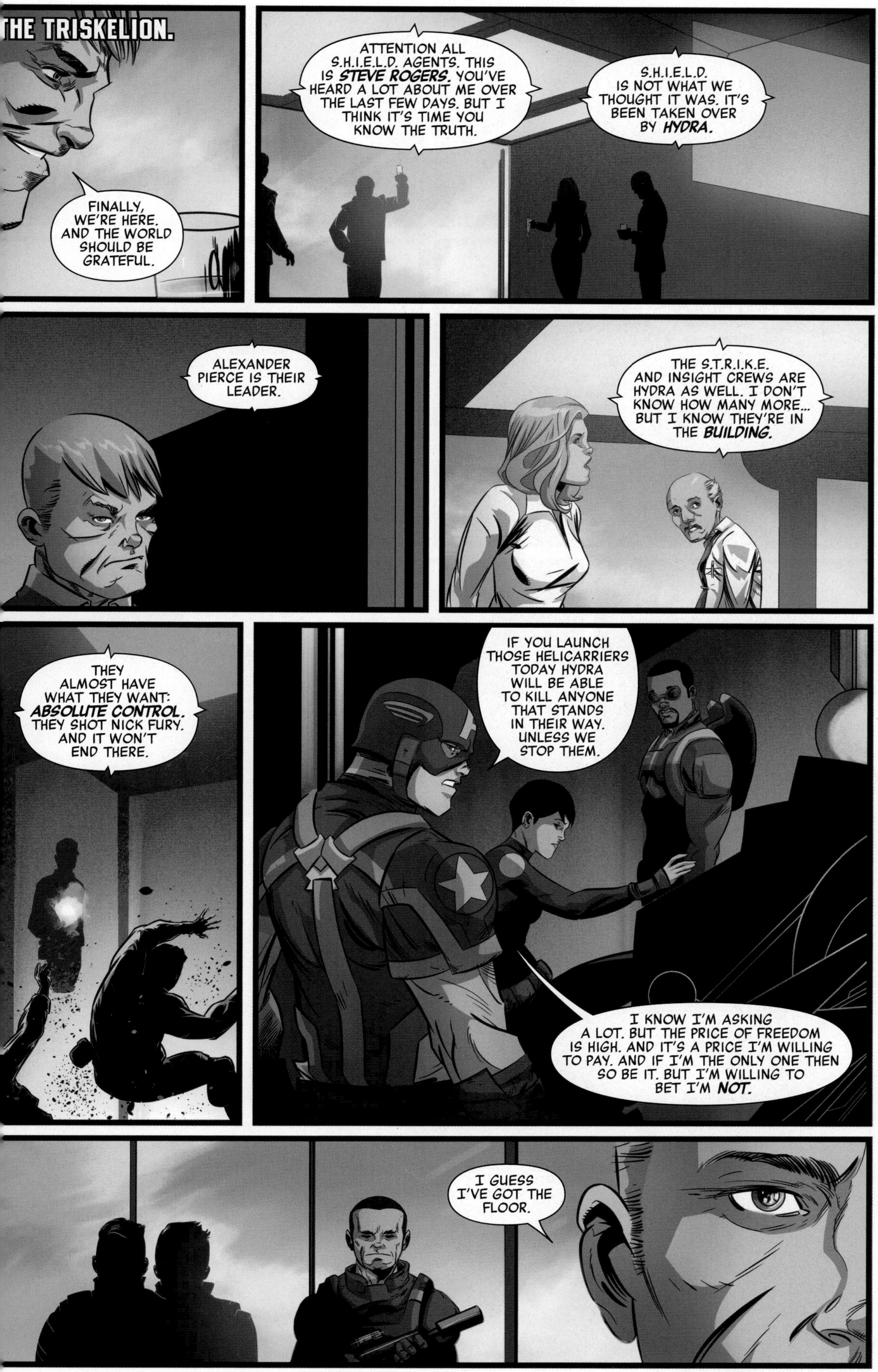
THE TRISKELION.
FINALLY, WE'RE HERE. AND THE WORLD SHOULD BE GRATEFUL.
ATTENTION ALL S.H.I.E.L.D. AGENTS. THIS IS STEVE ROGERS. YOU'VE HEARD A LOT ABOUT ME OVER THE LAST FEW DAYS. BUT I THINK IT'S TIME YOU KNOW THE TRUTH.
S.H.I.E.L.D. IS NOT WHAT WE THOUGHT IT WAS. IT'S BEEN TAKEN OVER BY HYDRA.
ALEXANDER PIERCE IS THEIR LEADER.
THE S.T.R.I.K.E. AND INSIGHT CREWS ARE HYDRA AS WELL. I DON'T KNOW HOW MANY MORE... BUT I KNOW THEY'RE IN THE BUILDING.
THEY ALMOST HAVE WHAT THEY WANT: ABSOLUTE CONTROL. THEY SHOT NICK FURY. AND IT WON'T END THERE.
IF YOU LAUNCH THOSE HELICARRIERS TODAY HYDRA WILL BE ABLE TO KILL ANYONE THAT STANDS IN THEIR WAY. UNLESS WE STOP THEM.
I KNOW I'M ASKING A LOT. BUT THE PRICE OF FREEDOM IS HIGH. AND IT'S A PRICE I'M WILLING TO PAY. AND IF I'M THE ONLY ONE THEN SO BE IT. BUT I'M WILLING TO BET I'M NOT.
I GUESS I'VE GOT THE FLOOR.

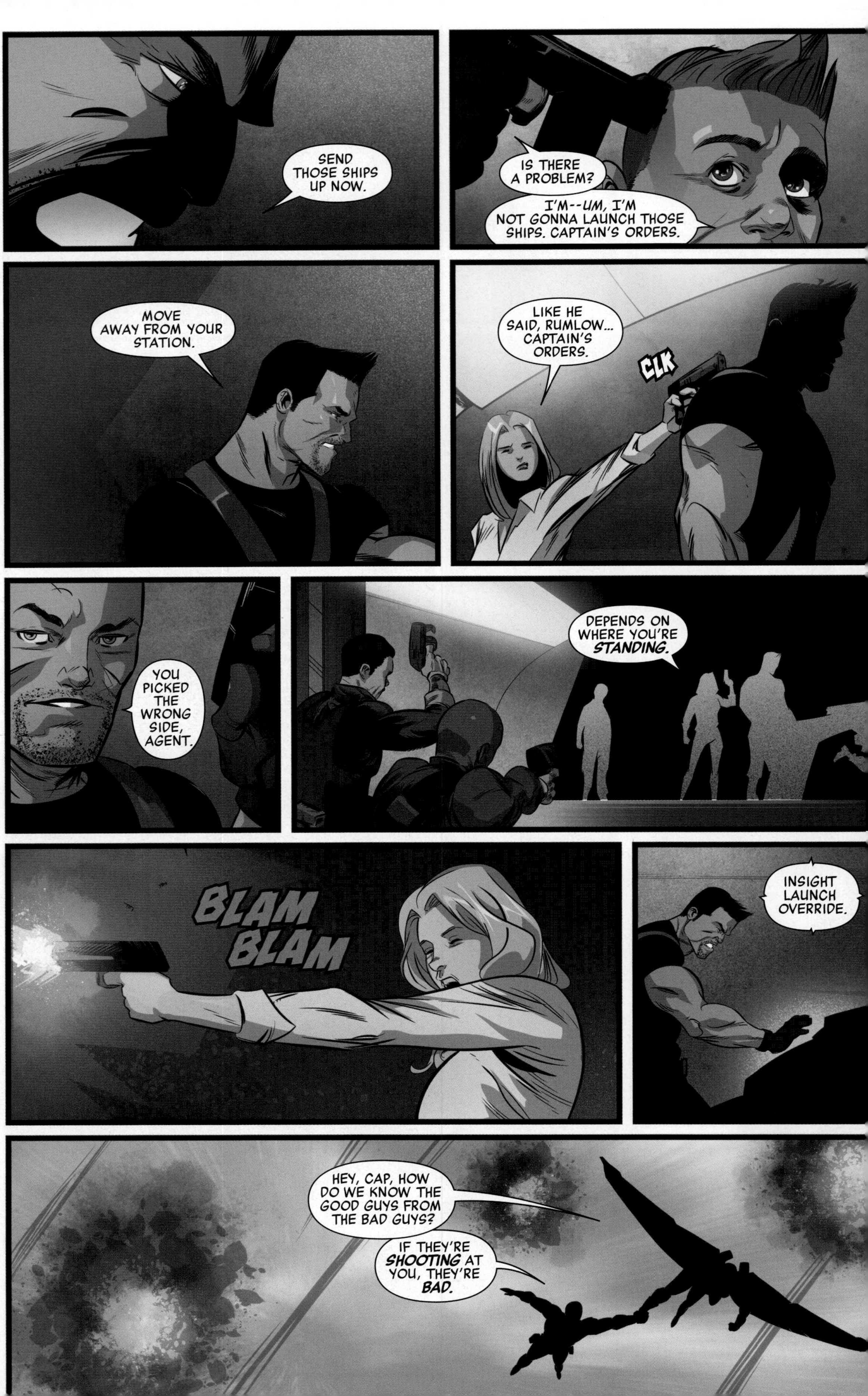
SEND THOSE SHIPS UP NOW.
IS THERE A PROBLEM?
I'M--UM, I'M NOT GONNA LAUNCH THOSE SHIPS. CAPTAIN'S ORDERS.
MOVE AWAY FROM YOUR STATION.
LIKE HE SAID, RUMLOW... CAPTAIN'S ORDERS.
CLK
YOU PICKED THE WRONG SIDE, AGENT.
DEPENDS ON WHERE YOU'RE STANDING.
BLAM BLAM
INSIGHT LAUNCH OVERRIDE.
HEY, CAP, HOW DO WE KNOW THE GOOD GUYS FROM THE BAD GUYS?
IF THEY'RE SHOOTING AT YOU, THEY'RE BAD.

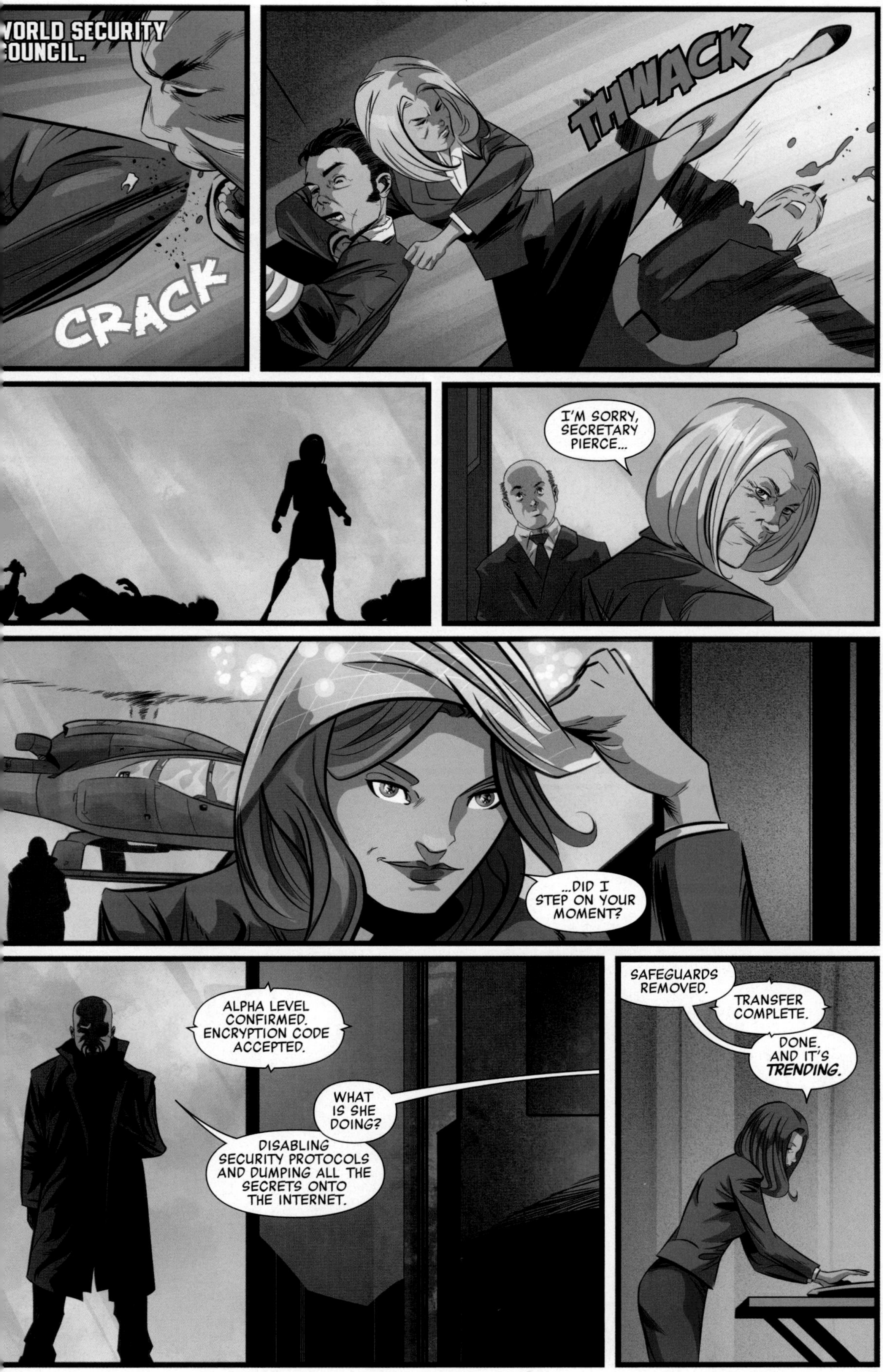
WORLD SECURITY COUNCIL.
CRACK
THWACK
I'M SORRY, SECRETARY PIERCE...
...DID I STEP ON YOUR MOMENT?
ALPHA LEVEL CONFIRMED. ENCRYPTION CODE ACCEPTED.
WHAT IS SHE DOING?
DISABLING SECURITY PROTOCOLS AND DUMPING ALL THE SECRETS ONTO THE INTERNET.
SAFEGUARDS REMOVED.
TRANSFER COMPLETE.
DONE. AND IT'S *TRENDING*.

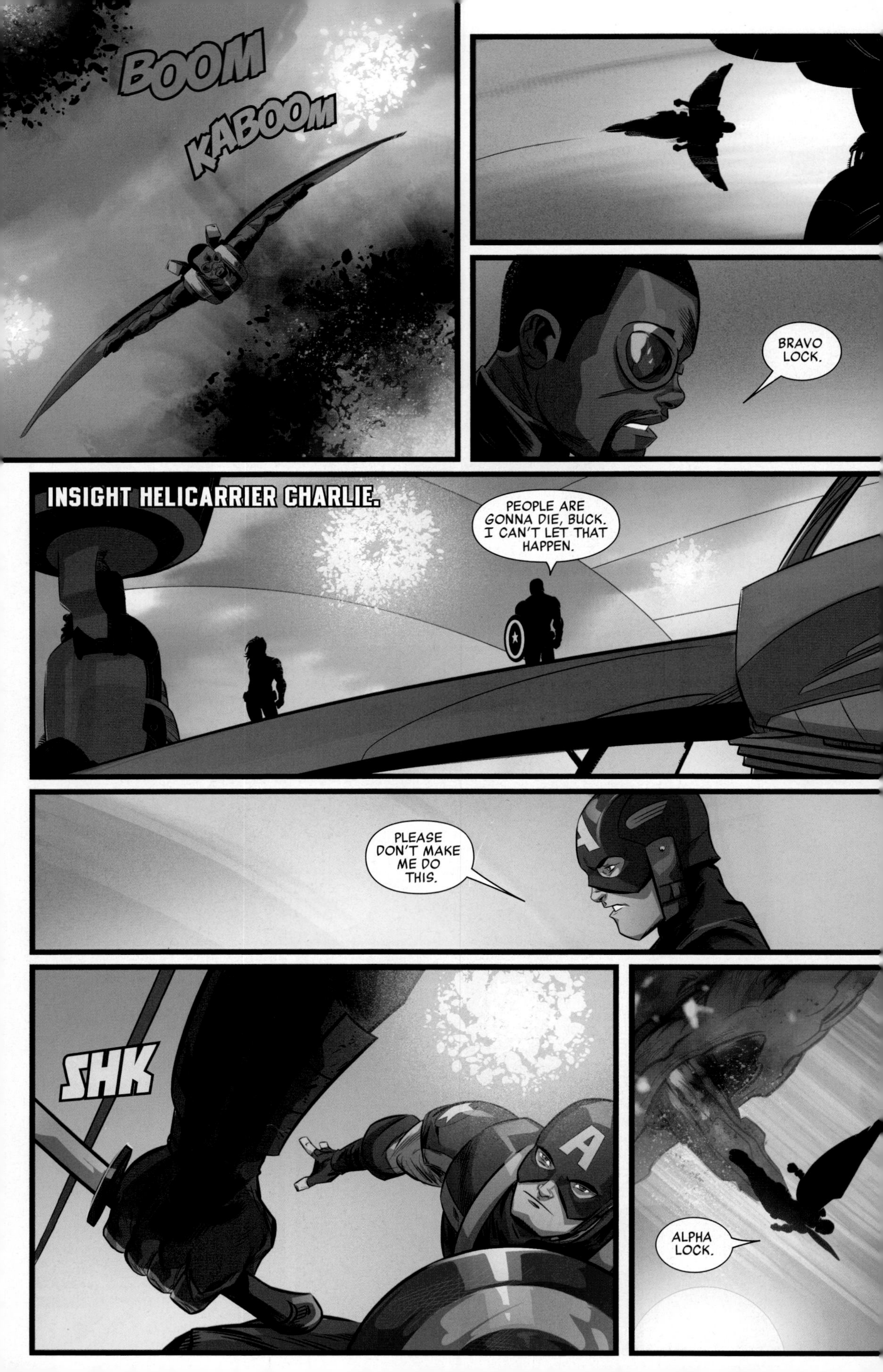
BOOM
KABOOM
BRAVO LOCK.
INSIGHT HELICARRIER CHARLIE.
PEOPLE ARE GONNA DIE, BUCK. I CAN'T LET THAT HAPPEN.
PLEASE DON'T MAKE ME DO THIS.
SHK
ALPHA LOCK.

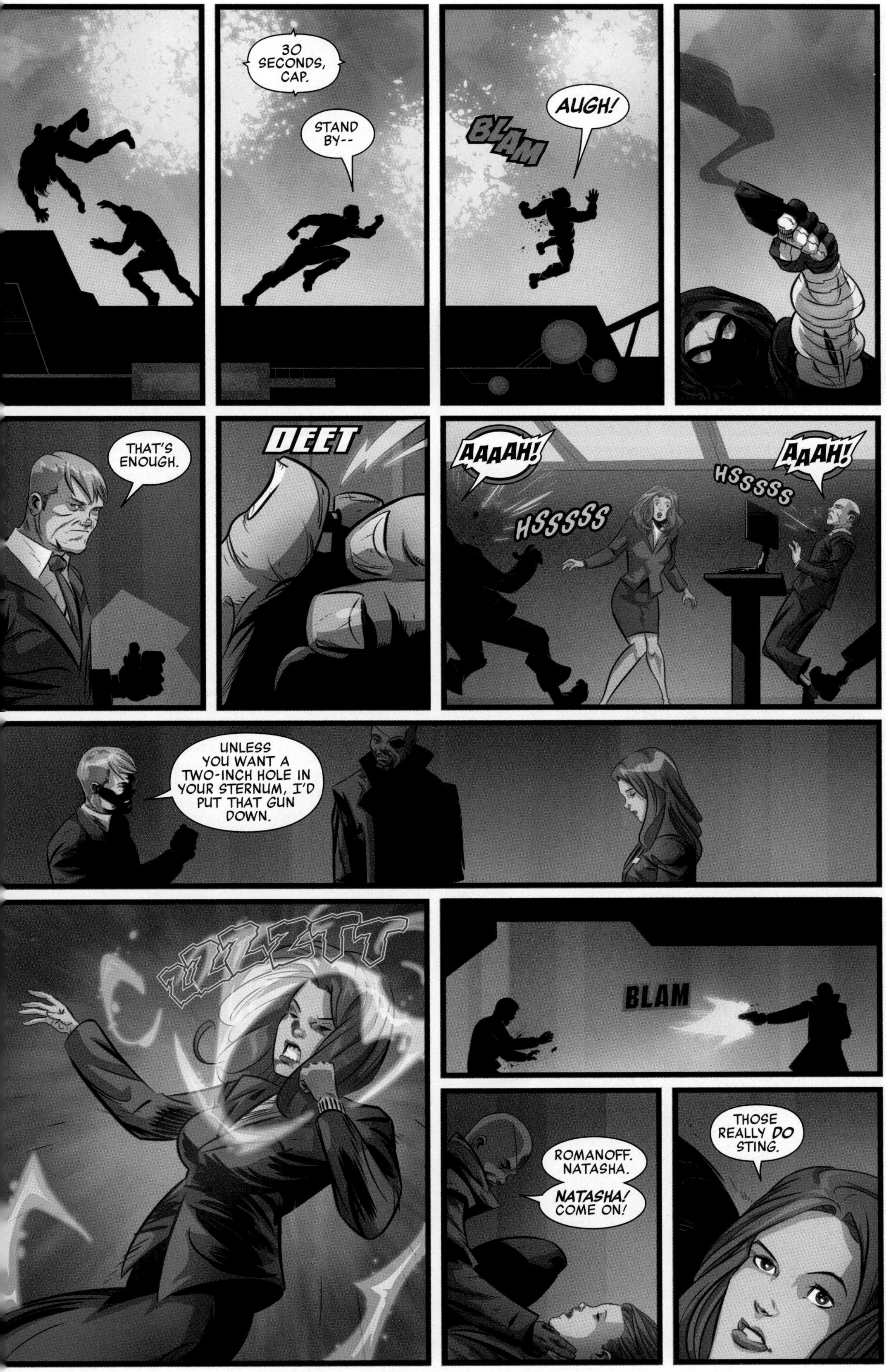
30 SECONDS, CAP.
STAND BY--
BLAM
AUGH!
THAT'S ENOUGH.
DEET
AAAAH!
HSSSSS
HSSSSS
AAAH!
UNLESS YOU WANT A TWO-INCH HOLE IN YOUR STERNUM, I'D PUT THAT GUN DOWN.
ZZZZTTT
BLAM
ROMANOFF. NATASHA.
NATASHA! COME ON!
THOSE REALLY DO STING.

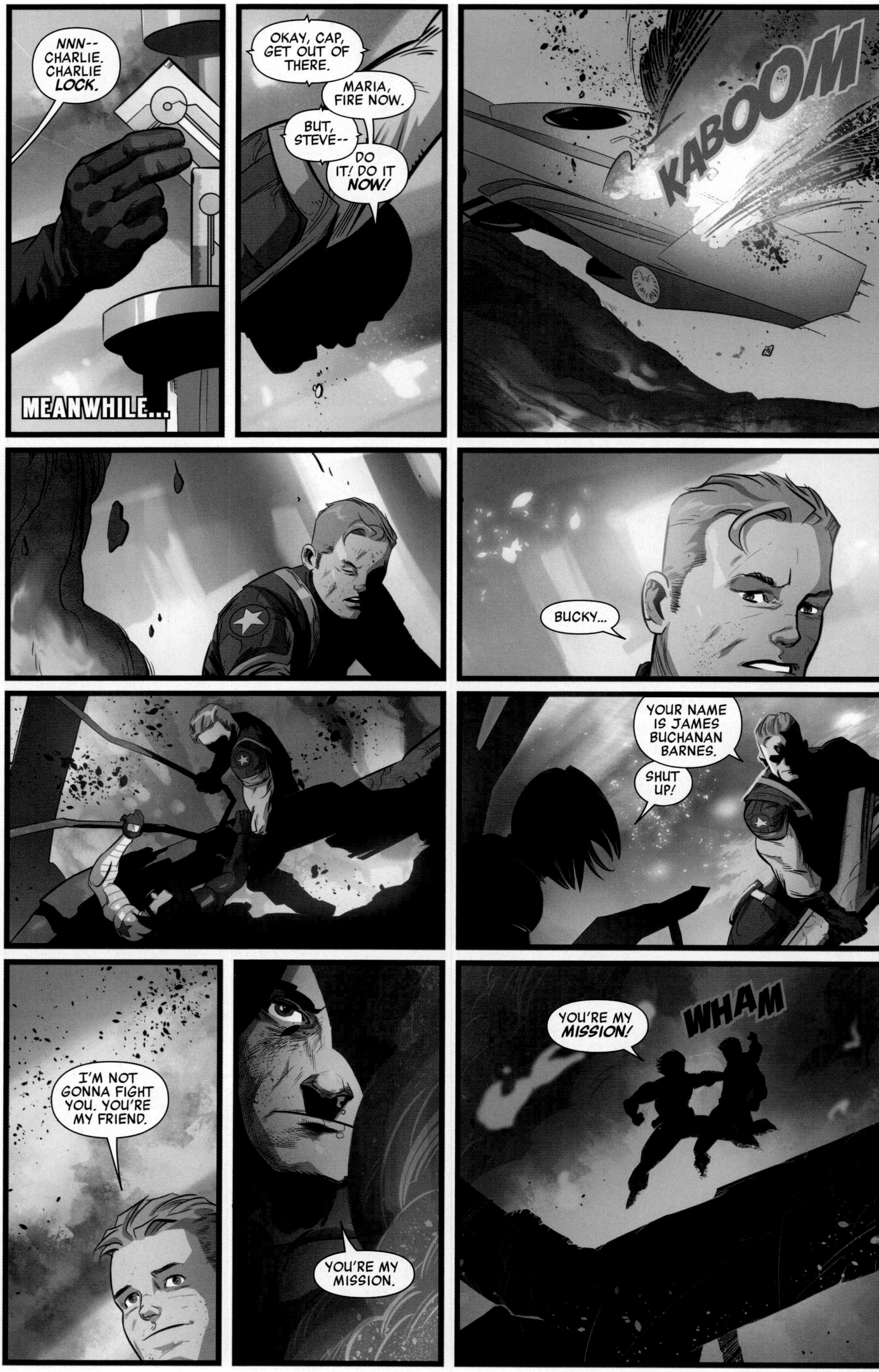
NNN--
CHARLIE. CHARLIE LOCK.
MEANWHILE...
OKAY, CAP, GET OUT OF THERE.
MARIA, FIRE NOW.
BUT, STEVE--
DO IT! DO IT NOW!
KABOOM
BUCKY...
YOUR NAME IS JAMES BUCHANAN BARNES.
SHUT UP!
I'M NOT GONNA FIGHT YOU. YOU'RE MY FRIEND.
YOU'RE MY MISSION.
YOU'RE MY MISSION!
WHAM

THEN *FINISH* T. 'CAUSE I'M WITH YOU...TO THE END OF THE LINE.

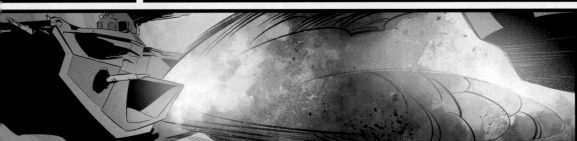

SPLASH

=HYAK! HYAK!=

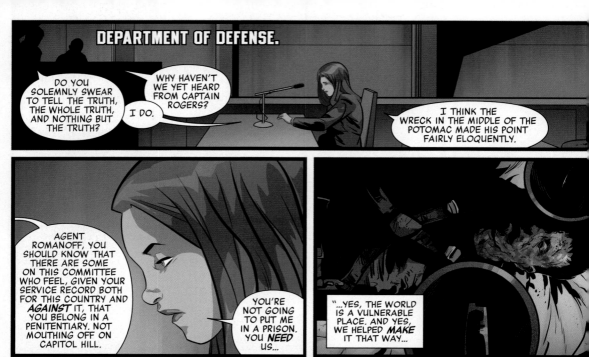

DEPARTMENT OF DEFENSE.

DO YOU SOLEMNLY SWEAR TO TELL THE TRUTH, THE WHOLE TRUTH, AND NOTHING BUT THE TRUTH?

I DO.

WHY HAVEN'T WE YET HEARD FROM CAPTAIN ROGERS?

I THINK THE WRECK IN THE MIDDLE OF THE POTOMAC MADE HIS POINT FAIRLY ELOQUENTLY.

AGENT ROMANOFF, YOU SHOULD KNOW THAT THERE ARE SOME ON THIS COMMITTEE WHO FEEL, GIVEN YOUR SERVICE RECORD BOTH FOR THIS COUNTRY AND *AGAINST* IT, THAT YOU BELONG IN A PENITENTIARY. NOT MOUTHING OFF ON CAPITOL HILL.

YOU'RE NOT GOING TO PUT ME IN A PRISON. YOU *NEED* US...

"...YES, THE WORLD IS A VULNERABLE PLACE. AND YES, WE HELPED *MAKE* IT THAT WAY..."

"...BUT WE'RE ALSO THE ONES BEST QUALIFIED TO *DEFEND* IT..."

"SO, IF YOU WANT TO ARREST ME, ARREST ME."

YOU'LL KNOW WHERE TO FIND ME.

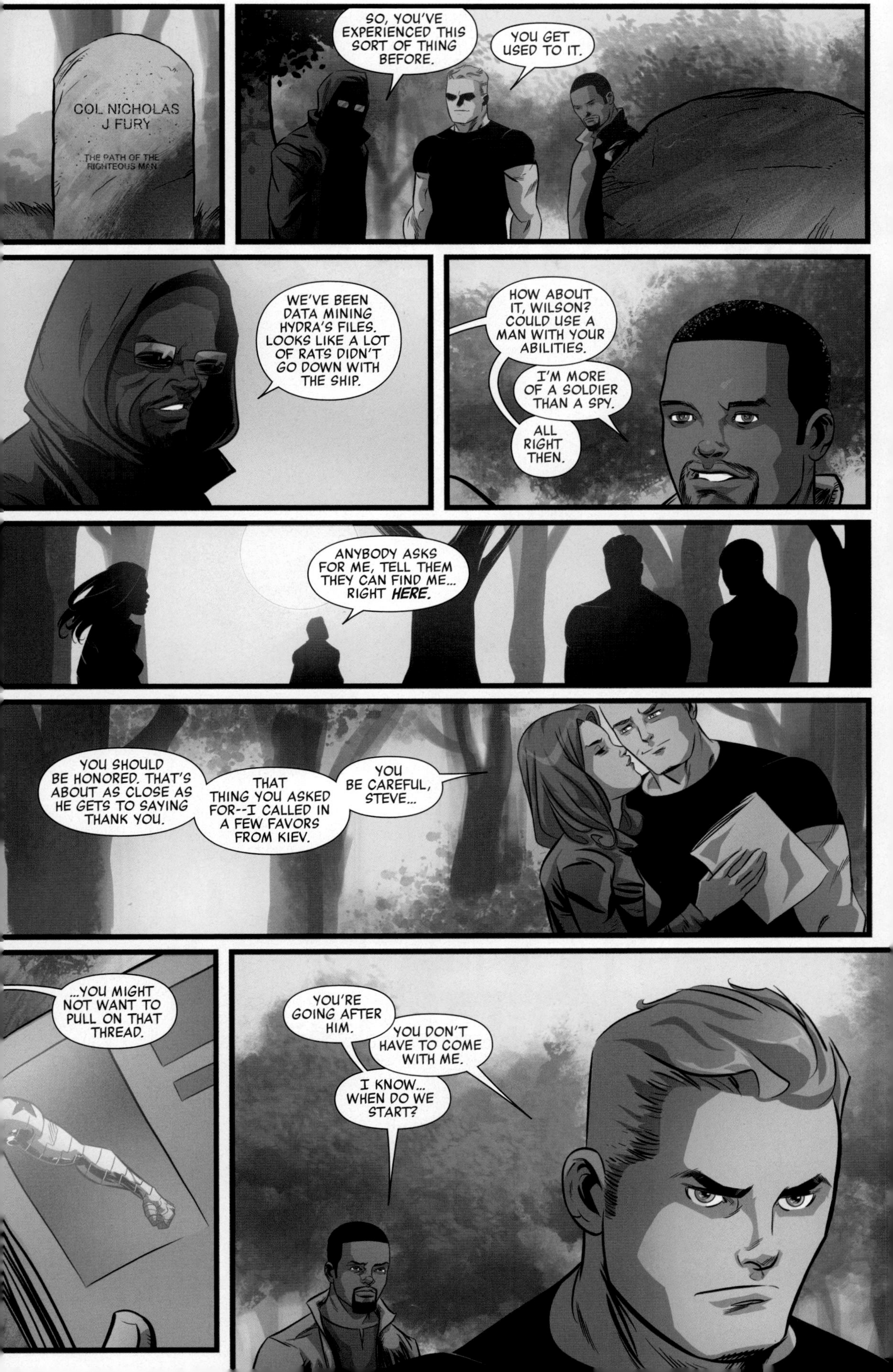
COL NICHOLAS J FURY
THE PATH OF THE RIGHTEOUS MAN
SO, YOU'VE EXPERIENCED THIS SORT OF THING BEFORE.
YOU GET USED TO IT.
WE'VE BEEN DATA MINING HYDRA'S FILES. LOOKS LIKE A LOT OF RATS DIDN'T GO DOWN WITH THE SHIP.
HOW ABOUT IT, WILSON? COULD USE A MAN WITH YOUR ABILITIES.
I'M MORE OF A SOLDIER THAN A SPY.
ALL RIGHT THEN.
ANYBODY ASKS FOR ME, TELL THEM THEY CAN FIND ME... RIGHT HERE.
YOU SHOULD BE HONORED. THAT'S ABOUT AS CLOSE AS HE GETS TO SAYING THANK YOU.
THAT THING YOU ASKED FOR--I CALLED IN A FEW FAVORS FROM KIEV.
YOU BE CAREFUL, STEVE...
...YOU MIGHT NOT WANT TO PULL ON THAT THREAD.
YOU'RE GOING AFTER HIM.
YOU DON'T HAVE TO COME WITH ME.
I KNOW... WHEN DO WE START?

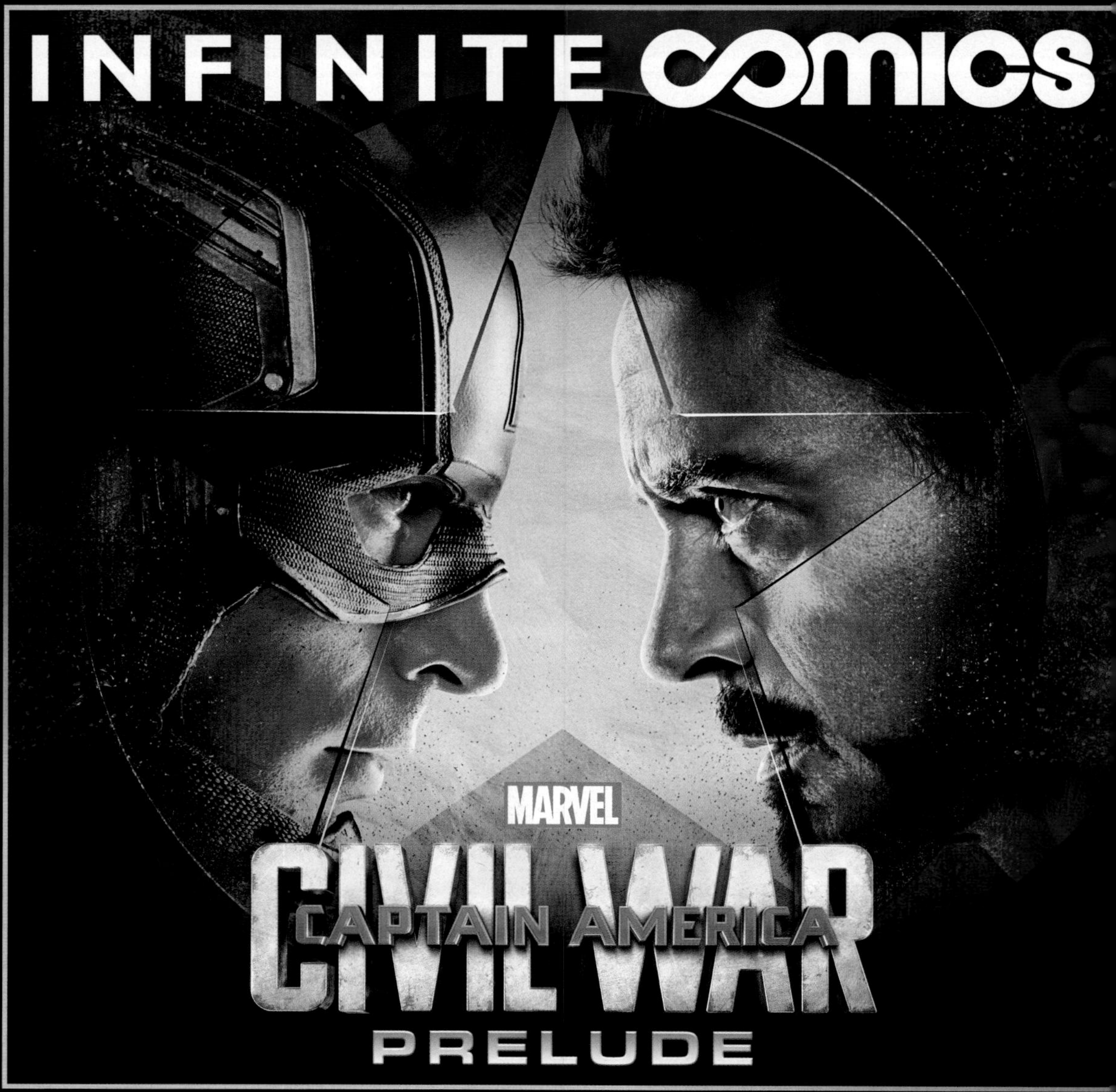
INFINITE COMICS
MARVEL
CAPTAIN AMERICA
CIVIL WAR
PRELUDE

MARVEL'S CAPTAIN AMERICA: CIVIL WAR PRELUDE INFINITE COMIC

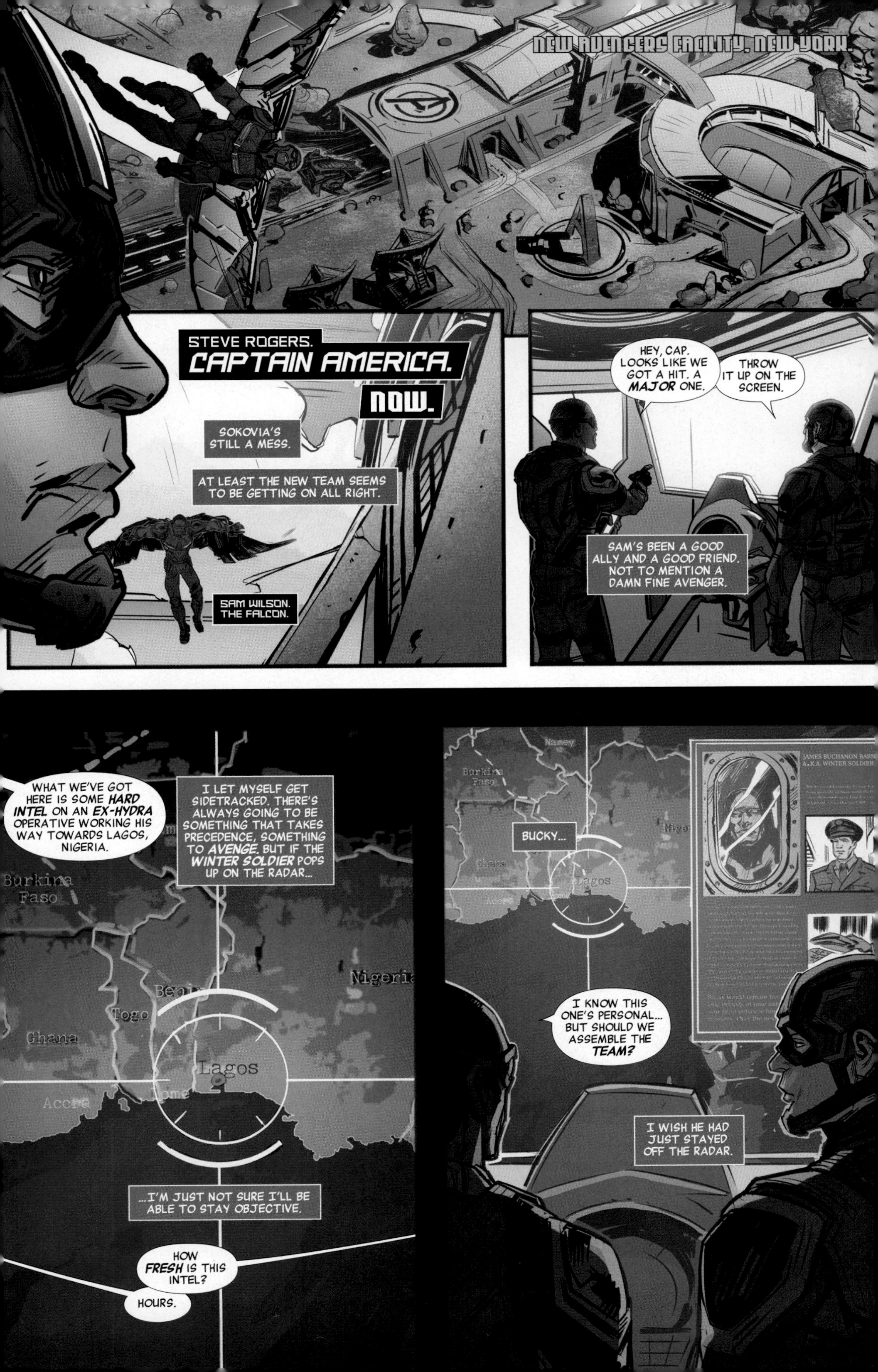
NEW AVENGERS FACILITY, NEW YORK.
STEVE ROGERS.
CAPTAIN AMERICA.
NOW.
SOKOVIA'S STILL A MESS.
AT LEAST THE NEW TEAM SEEMS TO BE GETTING ON ALL RIGHT.
SAM WILSON. THE FALCON.
HEY, CAP. LOOKS LIKE WE GOT A HIT. A MAJOR ONE.
THROW IT UP ON THE SCREEN.
SAM'S BEEN A GOOD ALLY AND A GOOD FRIEND. NOT TO MENTION A DAMN FINE AVENGER.
WHAT WE'VE GOT HERE IS SOME HARD INTEL ON AN EX-HYDRA OPERATIVE WORKING HIS WAY TOWARDS LAGOS, NIGERIA.
I LET MYSELF GET SIDETRACKED. THERE'S ALWAYS GOING TO BE SOMETHING THAT TAKES PRECEDENCE, SOMETHING TO AVENGE. BUT IF THE WINTER SOLDIER POPS UP ON THE RADAR...
Burkina Faso
Nigeria
Benin
Togo
Ghana
Lagos
Lome
Accra
...I'M JUST NOT SURE I'LL BE ABLE TO STAY OBJECTIVE.
HOW FRESH IS THIS INTEL?
HOURS.
Niamey
Burkina Faso
JAMES BUCHANON BARNES
A.K.A. WINTER SOLDIER
BUCKY...
Lagos
I KNOW THIS ONE'S PERSONAL... BUT SHOULD WE ASSEMBLE THE TEAM?
I WISH HE HAD JUST STAYED OFF THE RADAR.

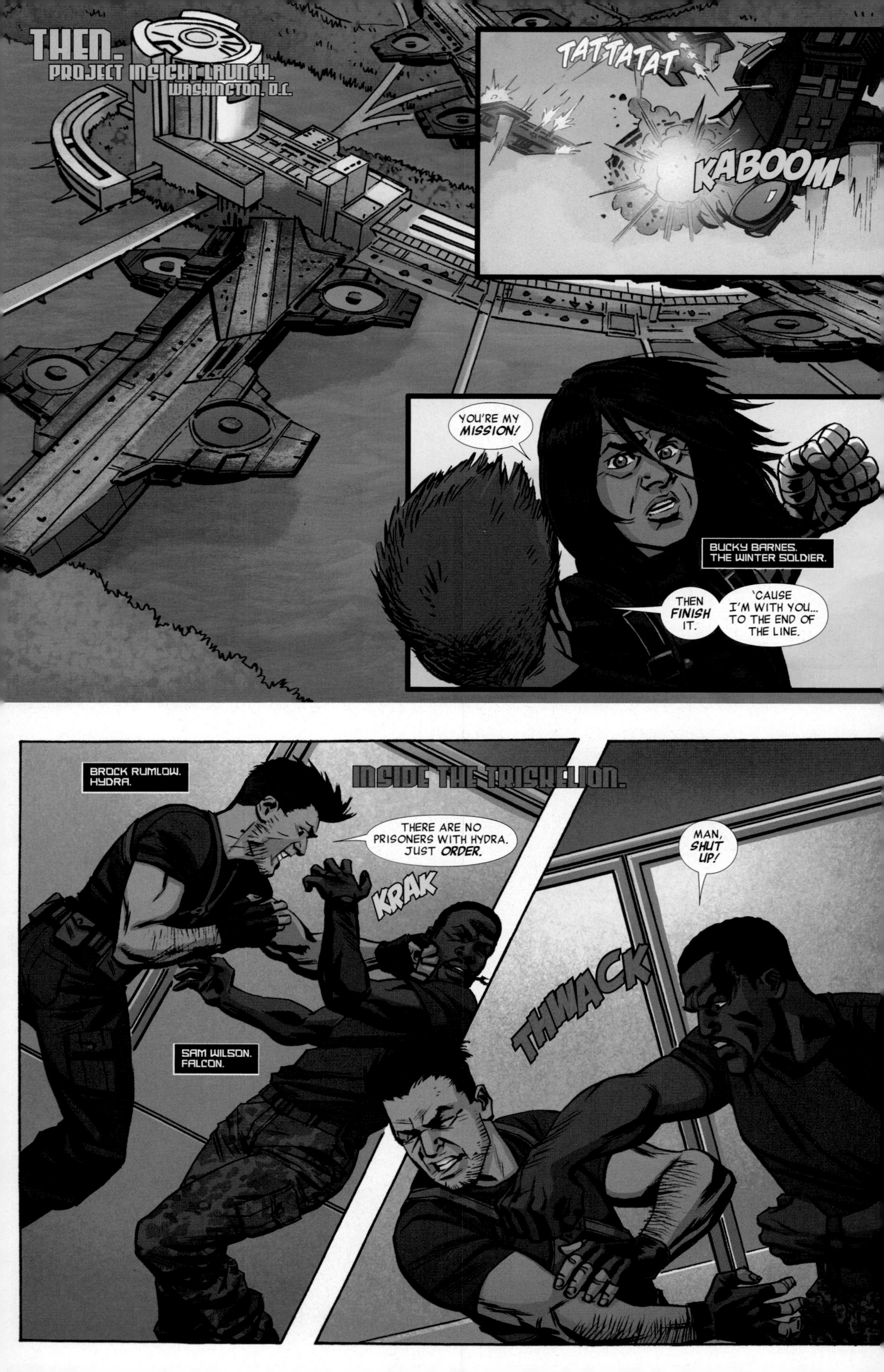
THEN.
PROJECT INSIGHT LAUNCH.
WASHINGTON, D.C.
TATTATAT
KABOOM
YOU'RE MY MISSION!
BUCKY BARNES. THE WINTER SOLDIER.
THEN FINISH IT.
'CAUSE I'M WITH YOU... TO THE END OF THE LINE.
BROCK RUMLOW. HYDRA.
INSIDE THE TRISKELION.
THERE ARE NO PRISONERS WITH HYDRA. JUST ORDER.
KRAK
SAM WILSON. FALCON.
MAN, SHUT UP!
THWACK

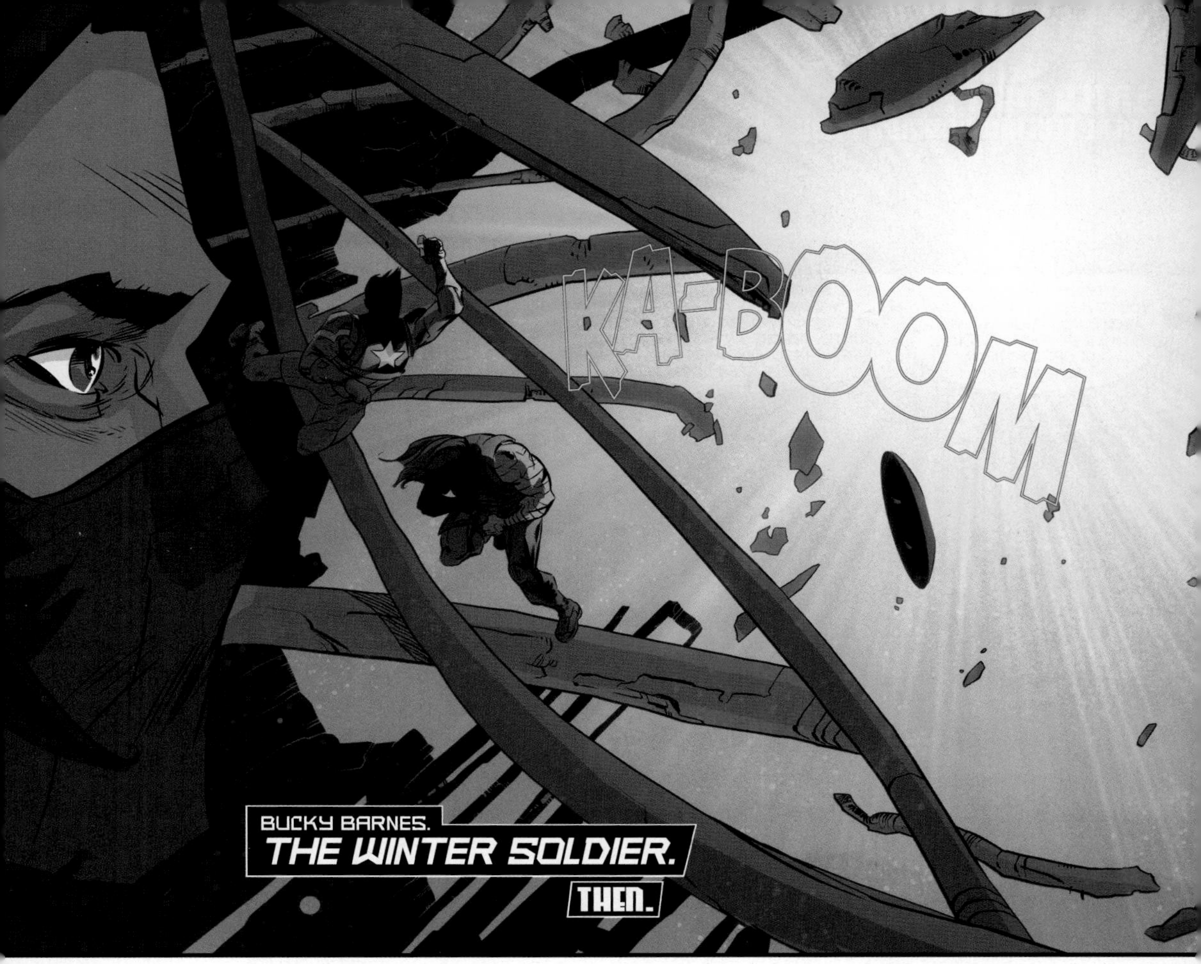
KA-BOOM
BUCKY BARNES.
THE WINTER SOLDIER.
THEN.

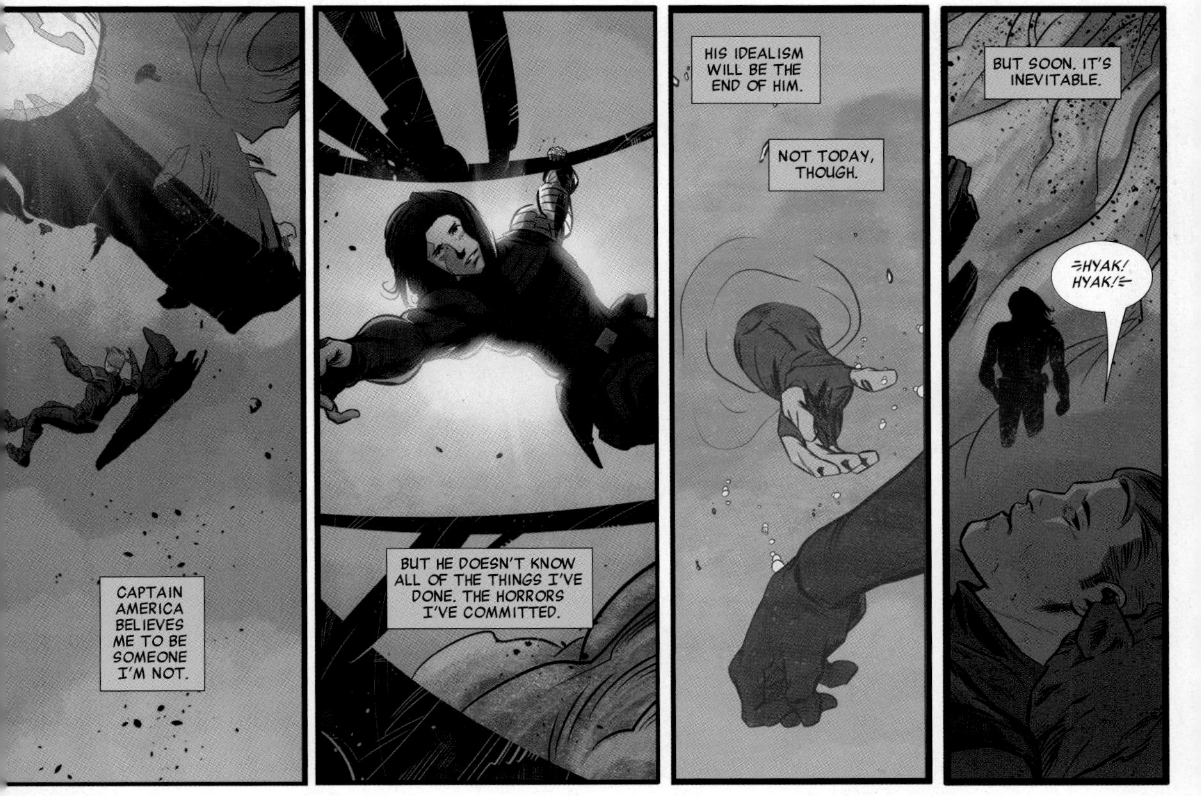
CAPTAIN AMERICA BELIEVES ME TO BE SOMEONE I'M NOT.
BUT HE DOESN'T KNOW ALL OF THE THINGS I'VE DONE. THE HORRORS I'VE COMMITTED.
HIS IDEALISM WILL BE THE END OF HIM.
NOT TODAY, THOUGH.
BUT SOON. IT'S INEVITABLE.
=HYAK! HYAK!=

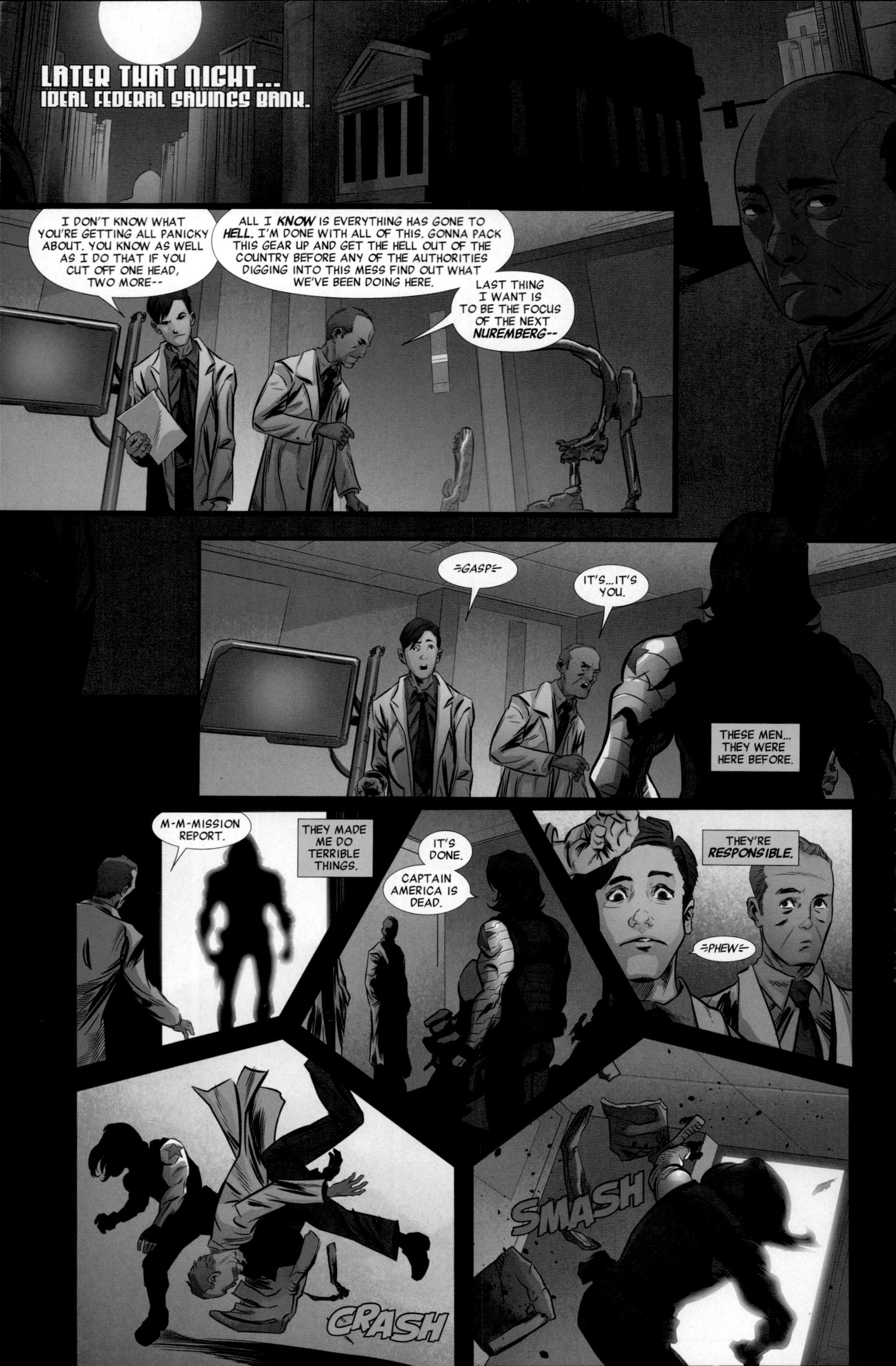

LATER THAT NIGHT...
IDEAL FEDERAL SAVINGS BANK.
I DON'T KNOW WHAT YOU'RE GETTING ALL PANICKY ABOUT. YOU KNOW AS WELL AS I DO THAT IF YOU CUT OFF ONE HEAD, TWO MORE--
ALL I KNOW IS EVERYTHING HAS GONE TO HELL. I'M DONE WITH ALL OF THIS. GONNA PACK THIS GEAR UP AND GET THE HELL OUT OF THE COUNTRY BEFORE ANY OF THE AUTHORITIES DIGGING INTO THIS MESS FIND OUT WHAT WE'VE BEEN DOING HERE.
LAST THING I WANT IS TO BE THE FOCUS OF THE NEXT NUREMBERG--
GASP
IT'S...IT'S YOU.
THESE MEN... THEY WERE HERE BEFORE.
M-M-MISSION REPORT.
THEY MADE ME DO TERRIBLE THINGS.
IT'S DONE.
CAPTAIN AMERICA IS DEAD.
THEY'RE RESPONSIBLE.
PHEW
CRASH
SMASH

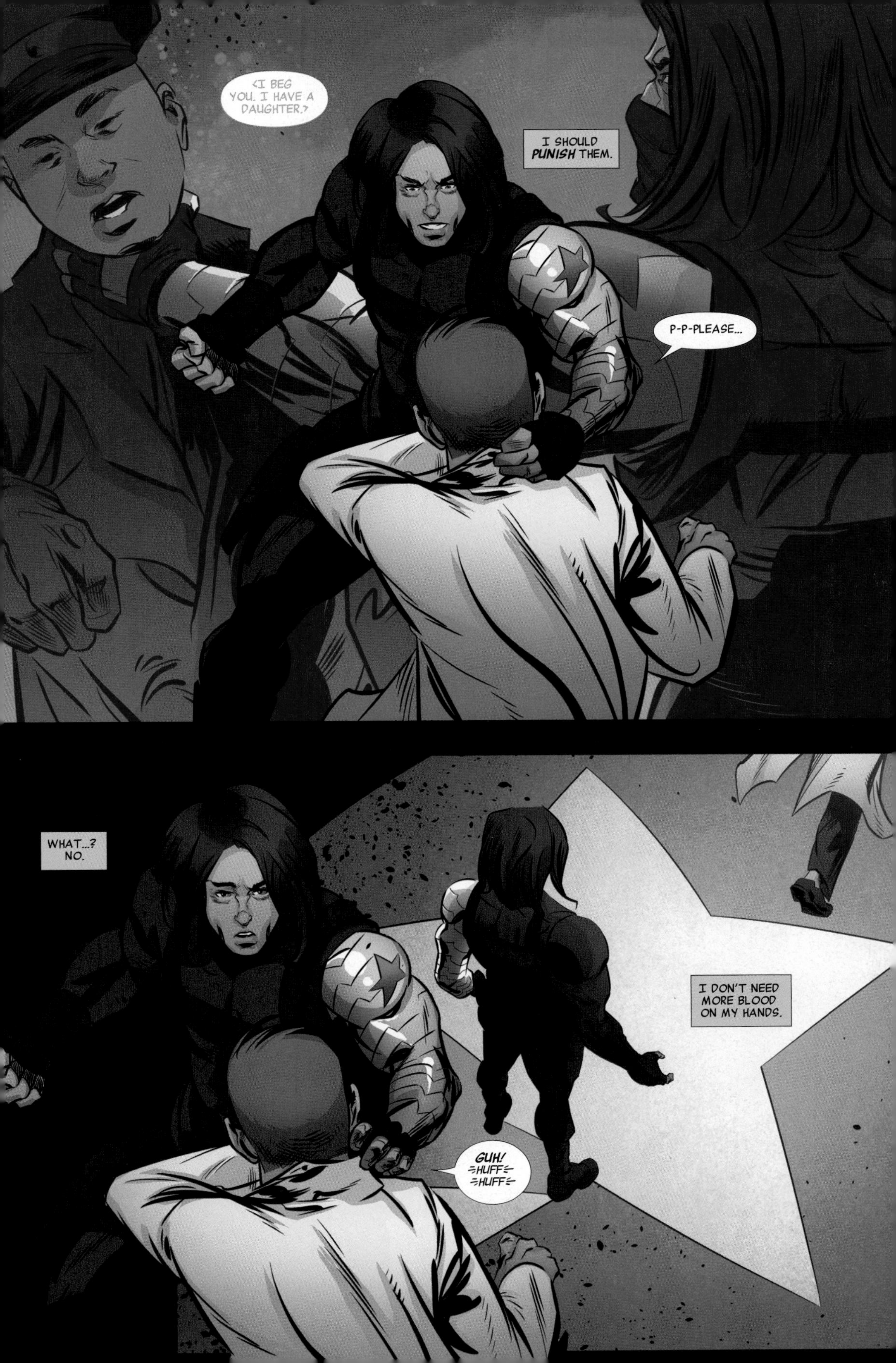
<I BEG YOU. I HAVE A DAUGHTER.>
I SHOULD PUNISH THEM.
P-P-PLEASE...
WHAT...? NO.
I DON'T NEED MORE BLOOD ON MY HANDS.
GUH! HUFF HUFF

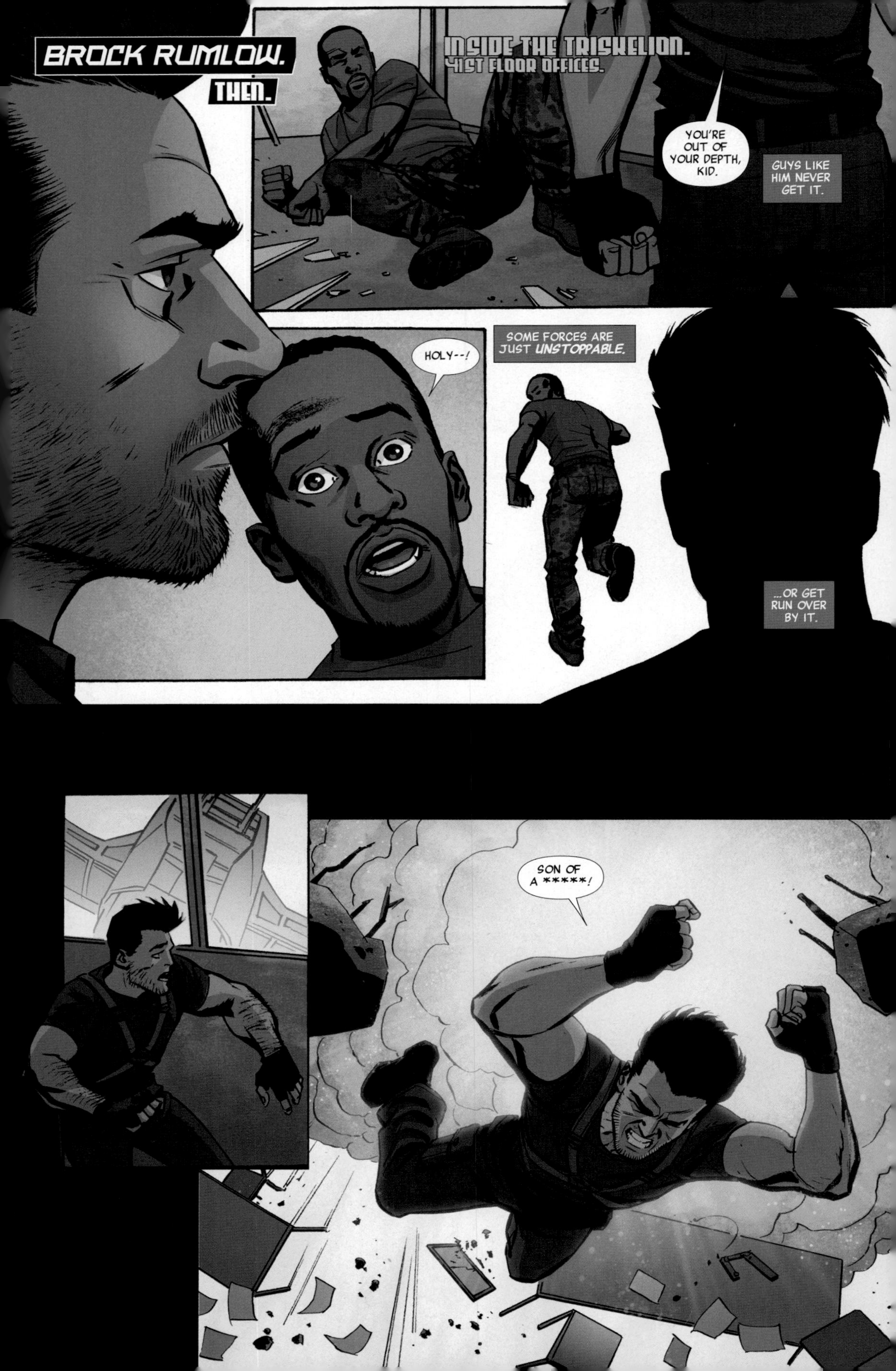
BROCK RUMLOW.
THEN.
INSIDE THE TRISKELION.
41ST FLOOR OFFICES.
YOU'RE OUT OF YOUR DEPTH, KID.
GUYS LIKE HIM NEVER GET IT.
HOLY--!
SOME FORCES ARE JUST UNSTOPPABLE.
...OR GET RUN OVER BY IT.
SON OF A *****!

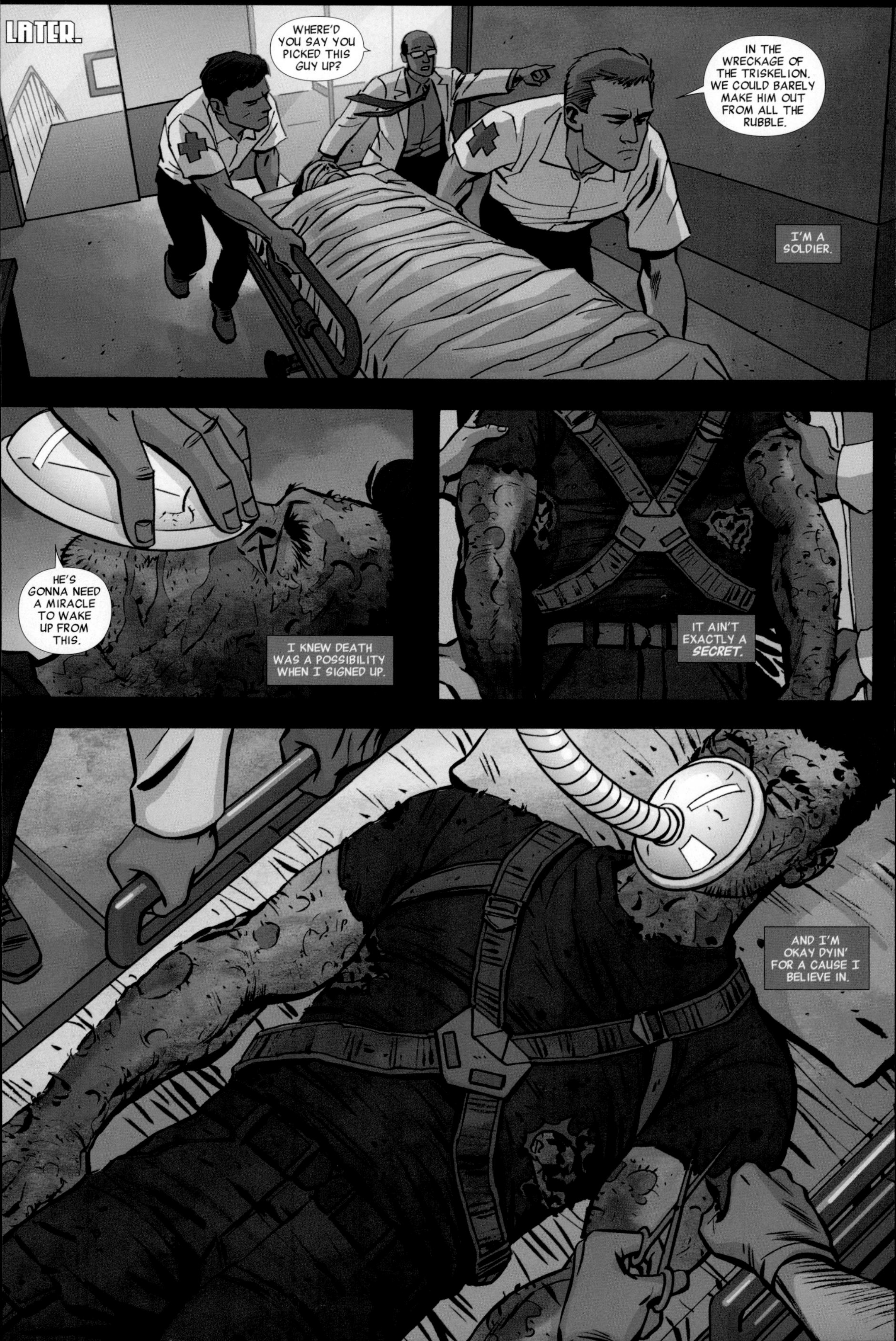
LATER.
WHERE'D YOU SAY YOU PICKED THIS GUY UP?
IN THE WRECKAGE OF THE TRISKELION. WE COULD BARELY MAKE HIM OUT FROM ALL THE RUBBLE.
I'M A SOLDIER.
HE'S GONNA NEED A MIRACLE TO WAKE UP FROM THIS.
I KNEW DEATH WAS A POSSIBILITY WHEN I SIGNED UP.
IT AIN'T EXACTLY A SECRET.
AND I'M OKAY DYIN' FOR A CAUSE I BELIEVE IN.

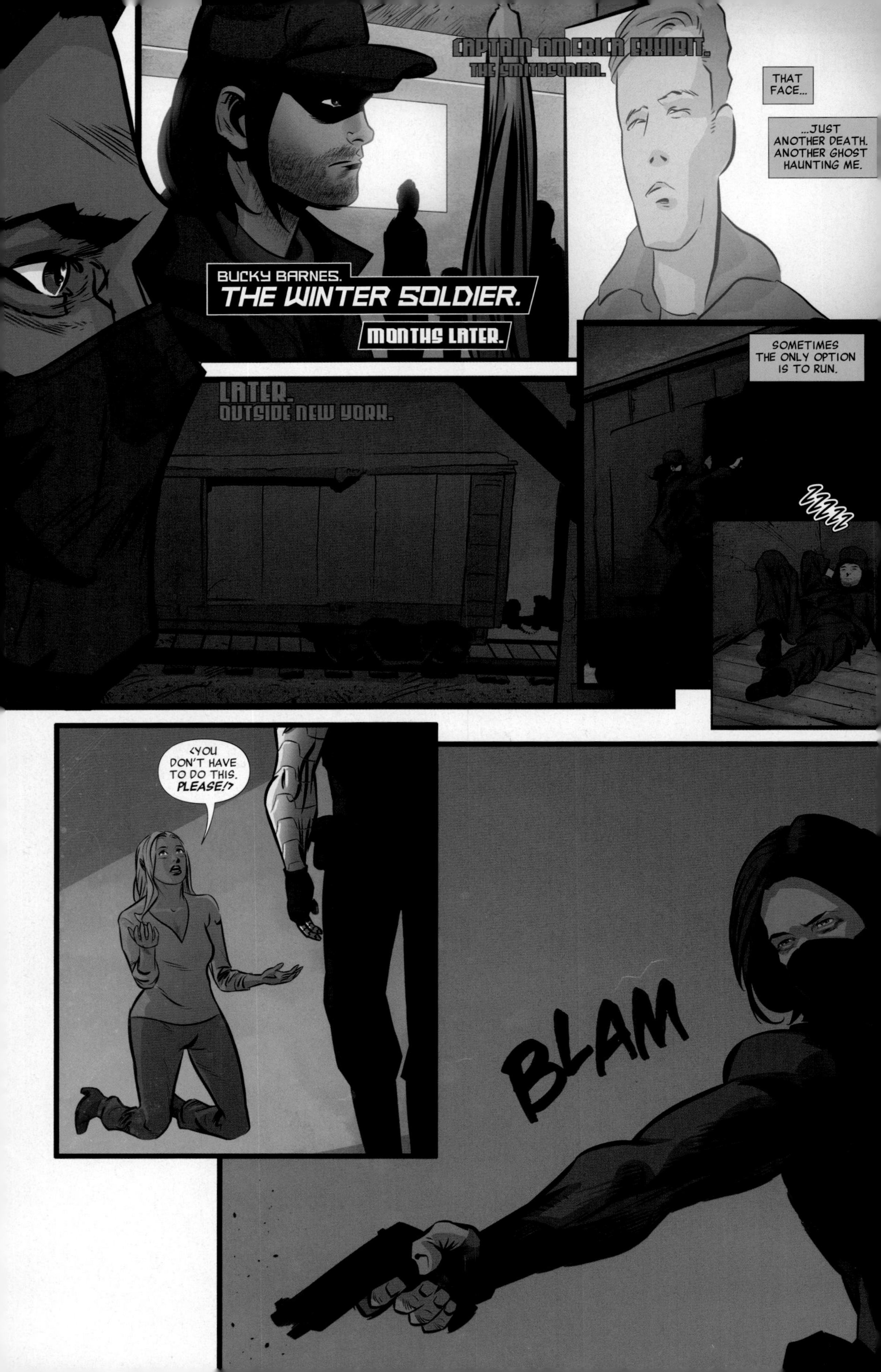

CAPTAIN AMERICA EXHIBIT.
THE SMITHSONIAN.
THAT FACE...
...JUST ANOTHER DEATH. ANOTHER GHOST HAUNTING ME.
BUCKY BARNES.
THE WINTER SOLDIER.
MONTHS LATER.
LATER.
OUTSIDE NEW YORK.
SOMETIMES THE ONLY OPTION IS TO RUN.
ZZZZZ
<YOU DON'T HAVE TO DO THIS. PLEASE!>
BLAM

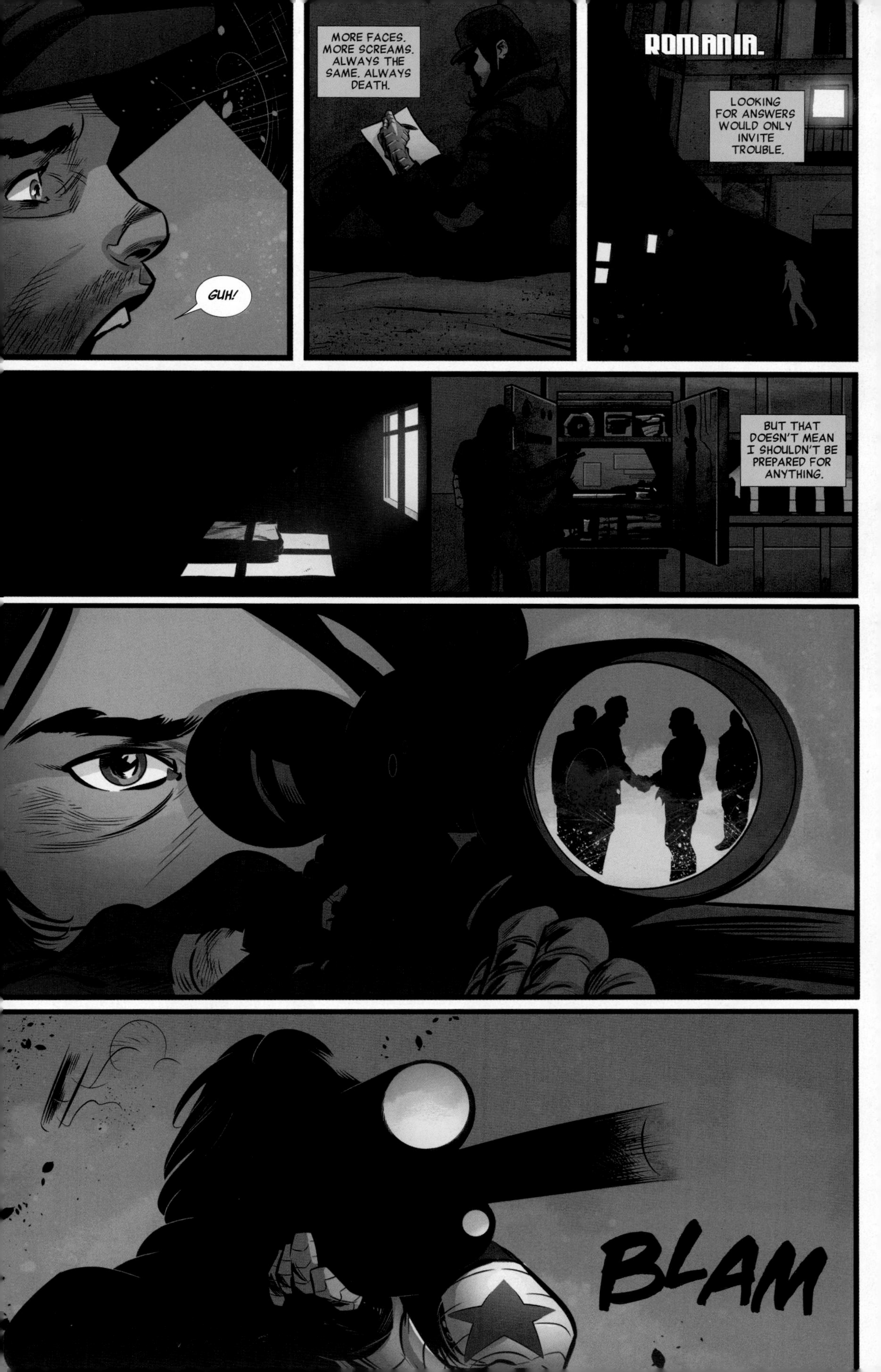
GUH!
MORE FACES. MORE SCREAMS. ALWAYS THE SAME. ALWAYS DEATH.
ROMANIA.
LOOKING FOR ANSWERS WOULD ONLY INVITE TROUBLE.
BUT THAT DOESN'T MEAN I SHOULDN'T BE PREPARED FOR ANYTHING.
BLAM

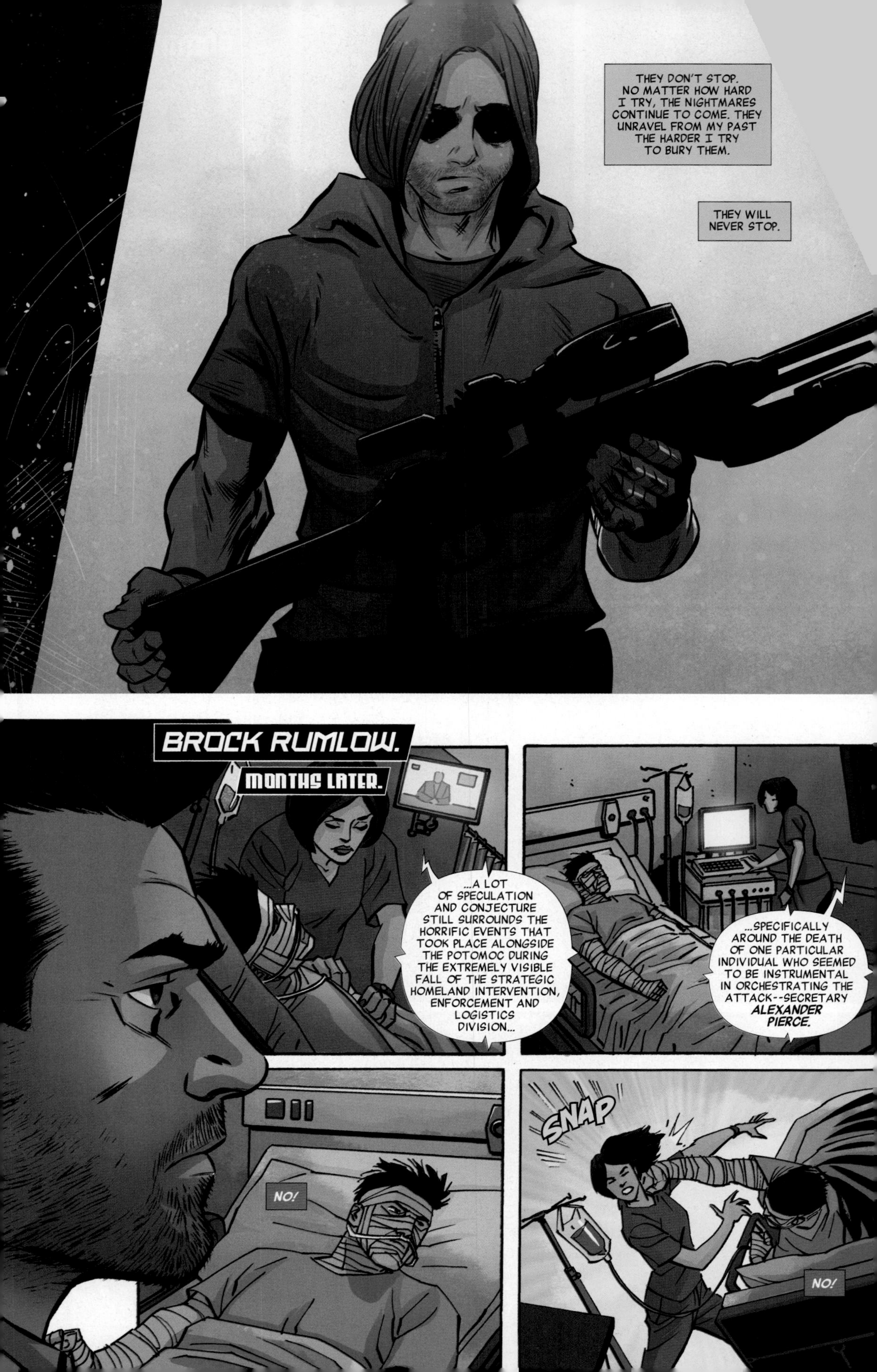
THEY DON'T STOP. NO MATTER HOW HARD I TRY, THE NIGHTMARES CONTINUE TO COME. THEY UNRAVEL FROM MY PAST THE HARDER I TRY TO BURY THEM.
THEY WILL NEVER STOP.
BROCK RUMLOW.
MONTHS LATER.
...A LOT OF SPECULATION AND CONJECTURE STILL SURROUNDS THE HORRIFIC EVENTS THAT TOOK PLACE ALONGSIDE THE POTOMOC DURING THE EXTREMELY VISIBLE FALL OF THE STRATEGIC HOMELAND INTERVENTION, ENFORCEMENT AND LOGISTICS DIVISION...
...SPECIFICALLY AROUND THE DEATH OF ONE PARTICULAR INDIVIDUAL WHO SEEMED TO BE INSTRUMENTAL IN ORCHESTRATING THE ATTACK--SECRETARY ALEXANDER PIERCE.
NO!
SNAP
NO!

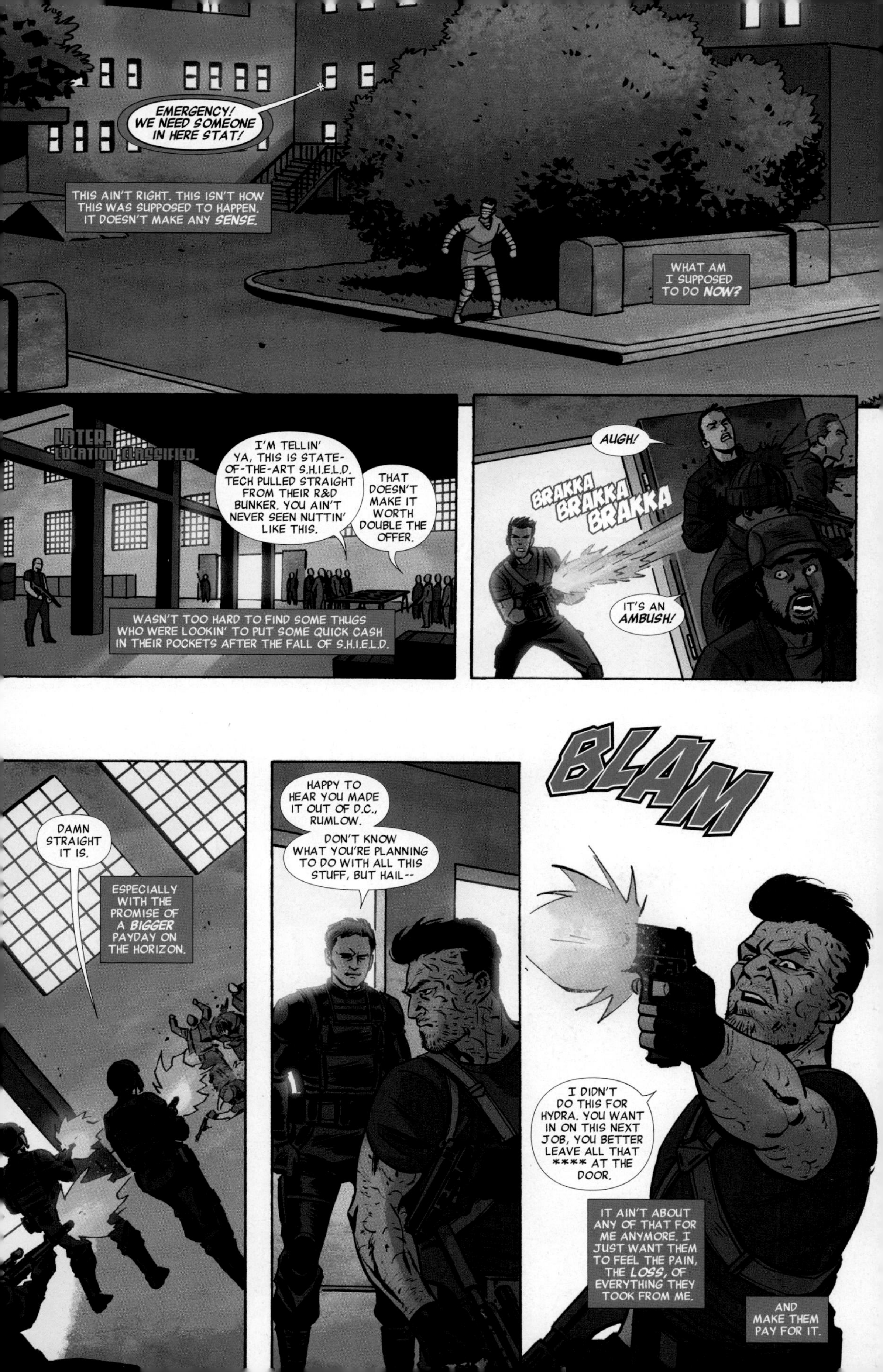
EMERGENCY! WE NEED SOMEONE IN HERE STAT!
THIS AIN'T RIGHT. THIS ISN'T HOW THIS WAS SUPPOSED TO HAPPEN. IT DOESN'T MAKE ANY SENSE.
WHAT AM I SUPPOSED TO DO NOW?
LATER. LOCATION CLASSIFIED.
I'M TELLIN' YA, THIS IS STATE-OF-THE-ART S.H.I.E.L.D. TECH PULLED STRAIGHT FROM THEIR R&D BUNKER. YOU AIN'T NEVER SEEN NUTTIN' LIKE THIS.
THAT DOESN'T MAKE IT WORTH DOUBLE THE OFFER.
WASN'T TOO HARD TO FIND SOME THUGS WHO WERE LOOKIN' TO PUT SOME QUICK CASH IN THEIR POCKETS AFTER THE FALL OF S.H.I.E.L.D.
AUGH!
BRAKKA BRAKKA BRAKKA
IT'S AN AMBUSH!
DAMN STRAIGHT IT IS.
ESPECIALLY WITH THE PROMISE OF A BIGGER PAYDAY ON THE HORIZON.
HAPPY TO HEAR YOU MADE IT OUT OF D.C., RUMLOW.
DON'T KNOW WHAT YOU'RE PLANNING TO DO WITH ALL THIS STUFF, BUT HAIL--
BLAM
I DIDN'T DO THIS FOR HYDRA. YOU WANT IN ON THIS NEXT JOB, YOU BETTER LEAVE ALL THAT **** AT THE DOOR.
IT AIN'T ABOUT ANY OF THAT FOR ME ANYMORE. I JUST WANT THEM TO FEEL THE PAIN, THE LOSS, OF EVERYTHING THEY TOOK FROM ME.
AND MAKE THEM PAY FOR IT.

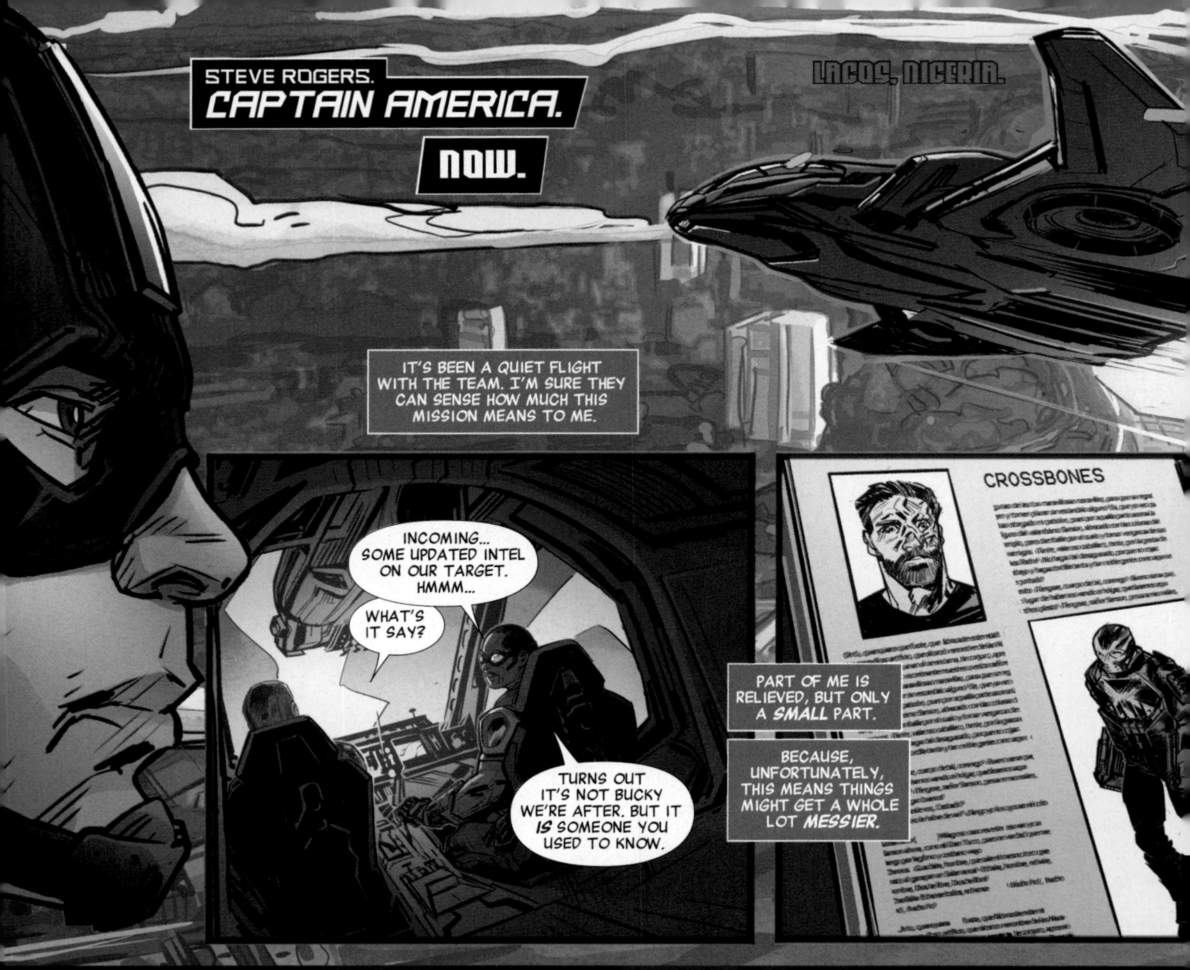
STEVE ROGERS.
CAPTAIN AMERICA.
NOW.
LAGOS, NIGERIA.
IT'S BEEN A QUIET FLIGHT WITH THE TEAM. I'M SURE THEY CAN SENSE HOW MUCH THIS MISSION MEANS TO ME.
INCOMING... SOME UPDATED INTEL ON OUR TARGET. HMMM...
WHAT'S IT SAY?
TURNS OUT IT'S NOT BUCKY WE'RE AFTER. BUT IT IS SOMEONE YOU USED TO KNOW.
CROSSBONES
PART OF ME IS RELIEVED, BUT ONLY A SMALL PART.
BECAUSE, UNFORTUNATELY, THIS MEANS THINGS MIGHT GET A WHOLE LOT MESSIER.

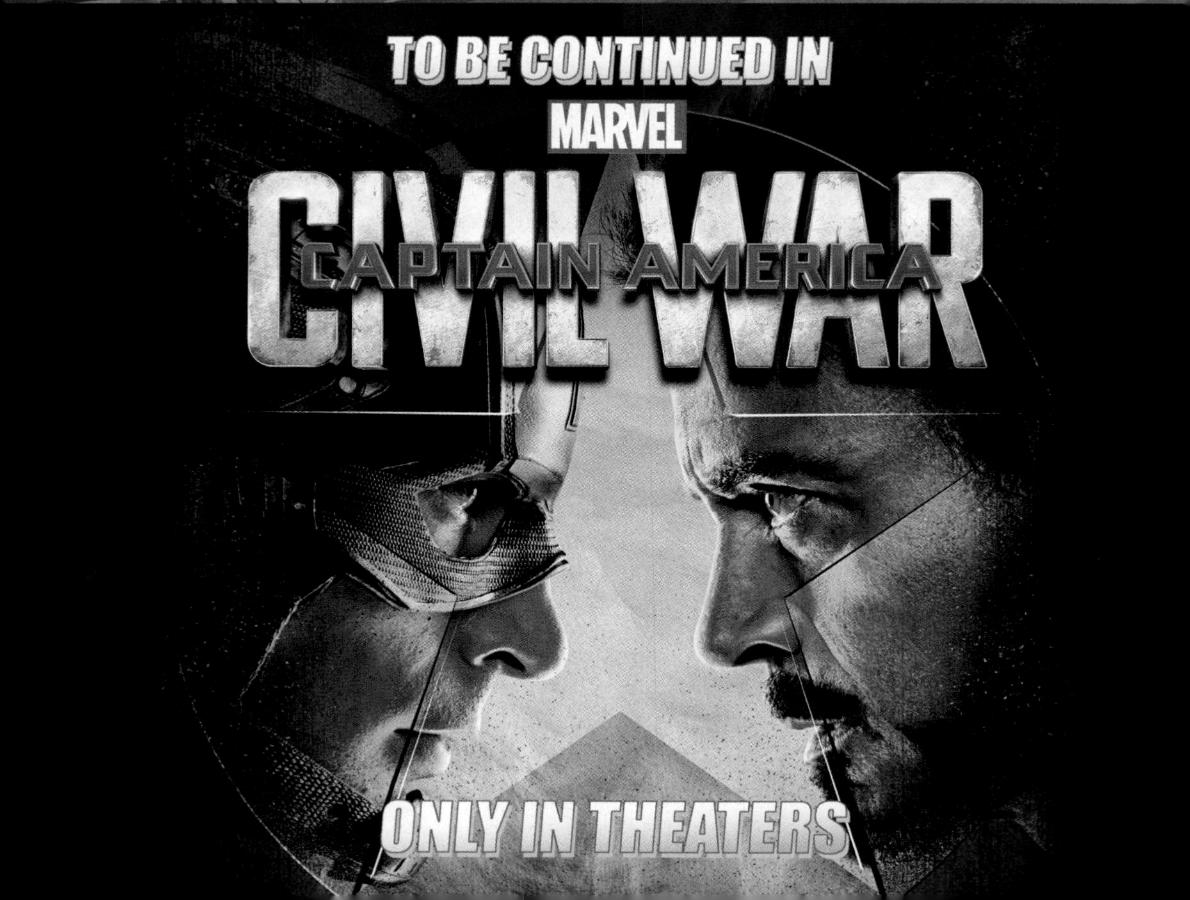
TO BE CONTINUED IN
MARVEL
CAPTAIN AMERICA
CIVIL WAR
ONLY IN THEATERS

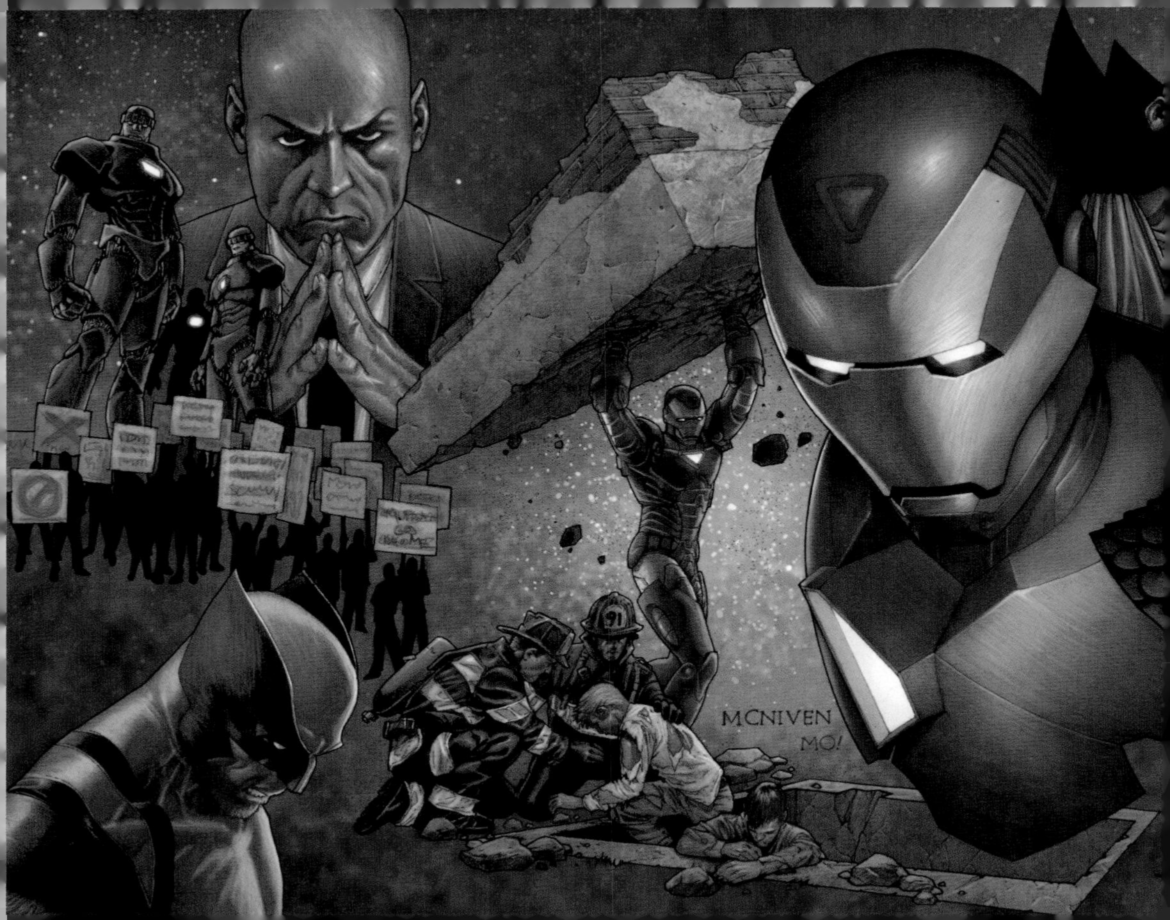
91
MCNIVEN
MO!

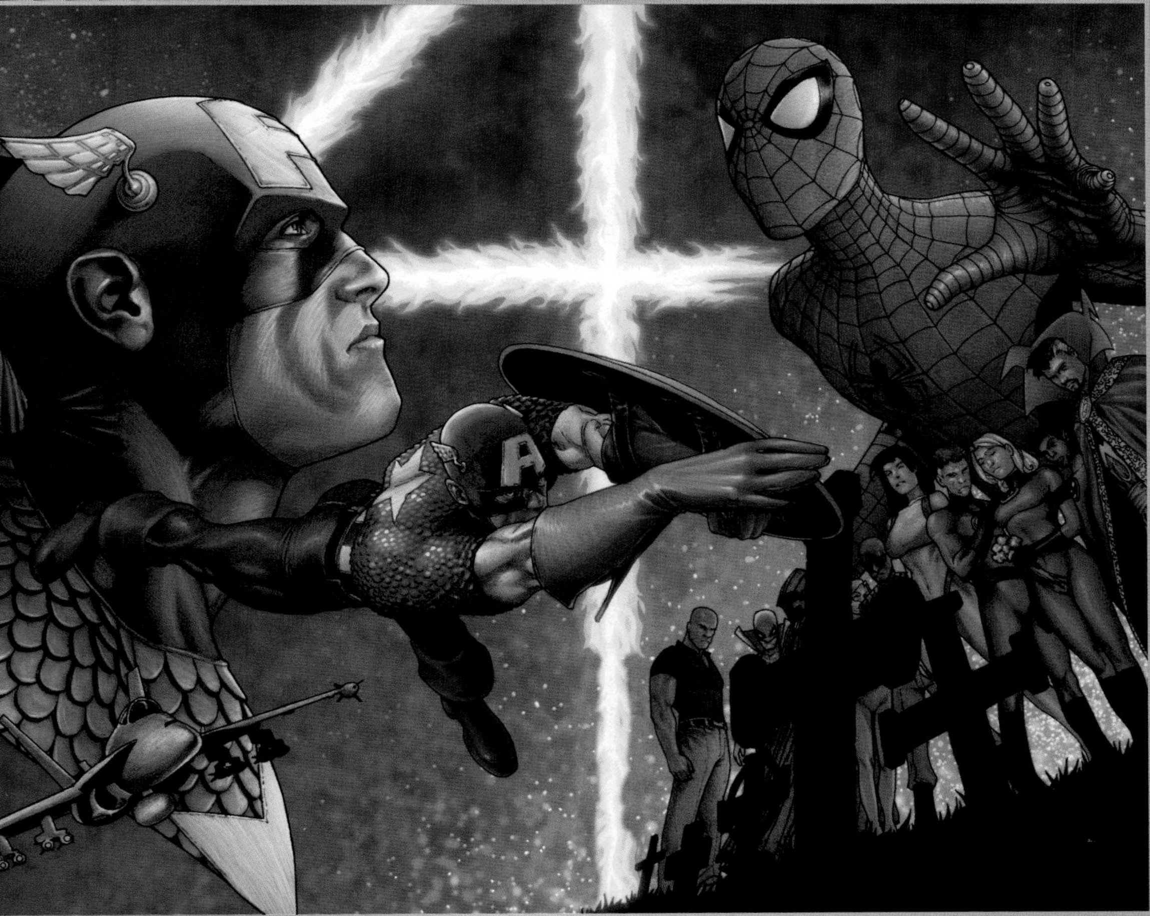

CIVIL WAR #1

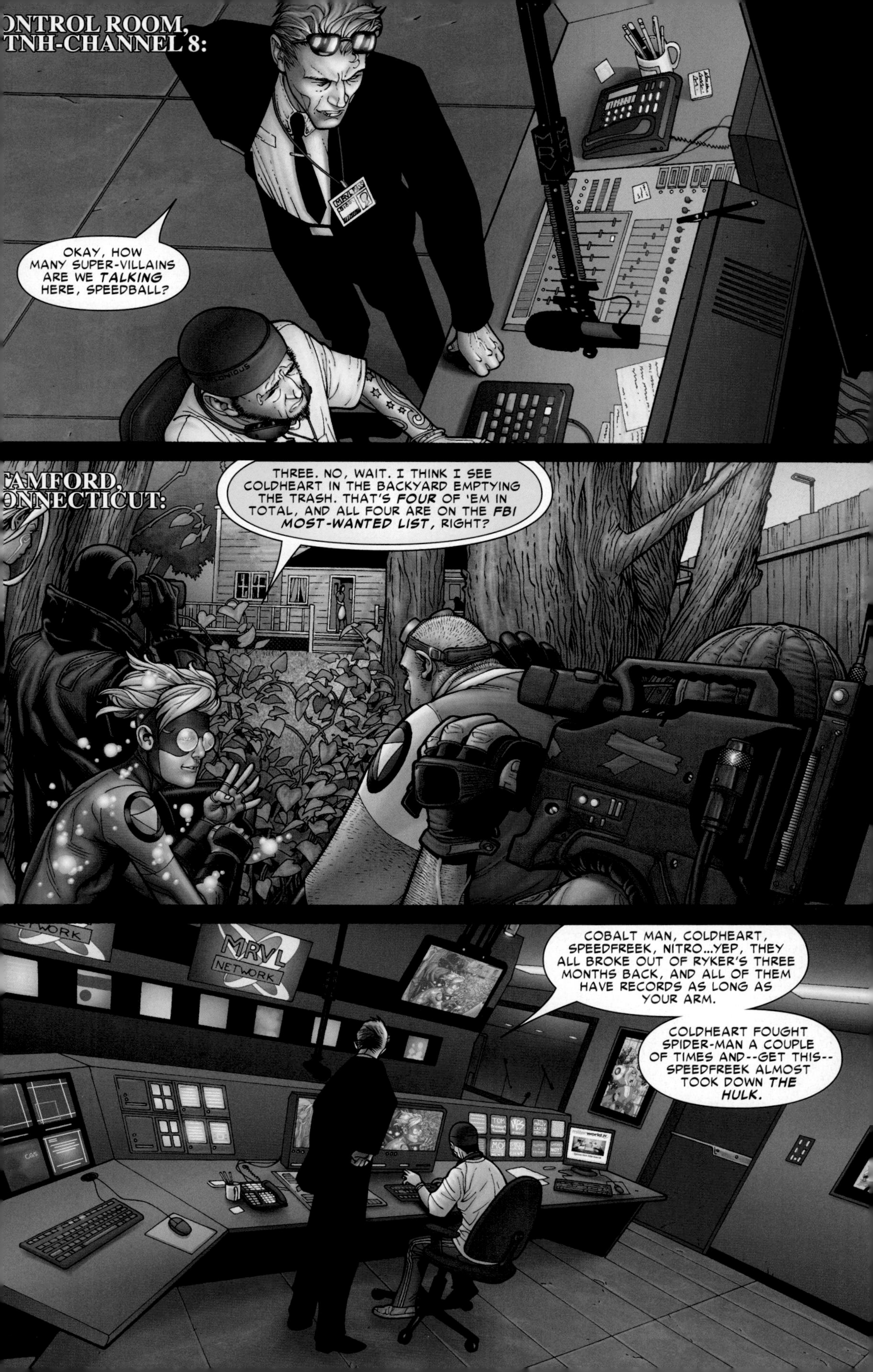

ONTROL ROOM,
TNH-CHANNEL 8:
OKAY, HOW MANY SUPER-VILLAINS ARE WE TALKING HERE, SPEEDBALL?
AMFORD,
ONNECTICUT:
THREE. NO, WAIT. I THINK I SEE COLDHEART IN THE BACKYARD EMPTYING THE TRASH. THAT'S FOUR OF 'EM IN TOTAL, AND ALL FOUR ARE ON THE FBI MOST-WANTED LIST, RIGHT?
MRVL NETWORK
COBALT MAN, COLDHEART, SPEEDFREEK, NITRO...YEP, THEY ALL BROKE OUT OF RYKER'S THREE MONTHS BACK, AND ALL OF THEM HAVE RECORDS AS LONG AS YOUR ARM.
COLDHEART FOUGHT SPIDER-MAN A COUPLE OF TIMES AND--GET THIS--SPEEDFREEK ALMOST TOOK DOWN THE HULK.

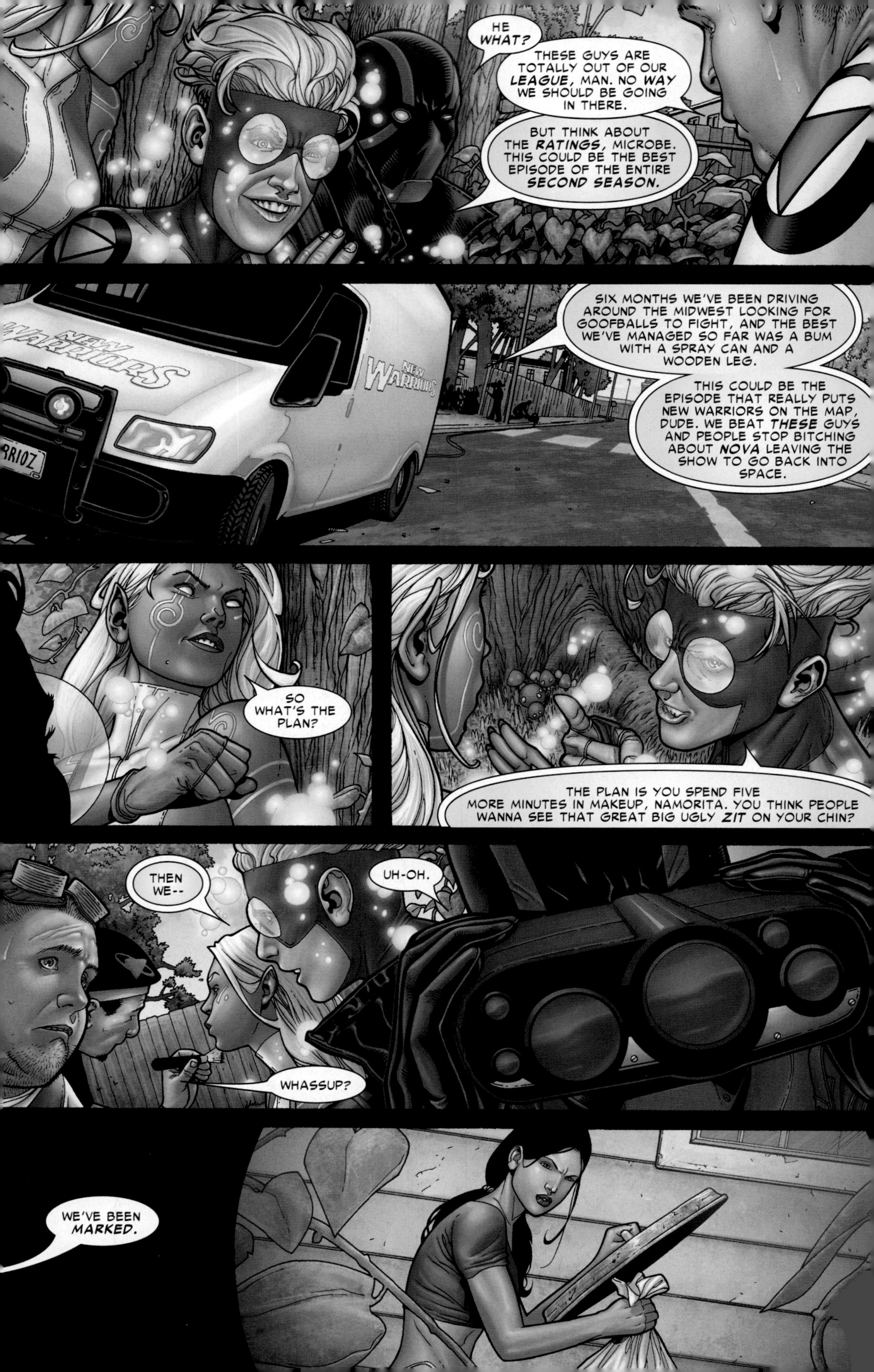
HE WHAT?
THESE GUYS ARE TOTALLY OUT OF OUR LEAGUE, MAN. NO WAY WE SHOULD BE GOING IN THERE.
BUT THINK ABOUT THE RATINGS, MICROBE. THIS COULD BE THE BEST EPISODE OF THE ENTIRE SECOND SEASON.
NEW WARRIORS
NEW WARRIORS
SIX MONTHS WE'VE BEEN DRIVING AROUND THE MIDWEST LOOKING FOR GOOFBALLS TO FIGHT, AND THE BEST WE'VE MANAGED SO FAR WAS A BUM WITH A SPRAY CAN AND A WOODEN LEG.
THIS COULD BE THE EPISODE THAT REALLY PUTS NEW WARRIORS ON THE MAP, DUDE. WE BEAT THESE GUYS AND PEOPLE STOP BITCHING ABOUT NOVA LEAVING THE SHOW TO GO BACK INTO SPACE.
SO WHAT'S THE PLAN?
THE PLAN IS YOU SPEND FIVE MORE MINUTES IN MAKEUP, NAMORITA. YOU THINK PEOPLE WANNA SEE THAT GREAT BIG UGLY ZIT ON YOUR CHIN?
THEN WE--
UH-OH.
WHASSUP?
WE'VE BEEN MARKED.

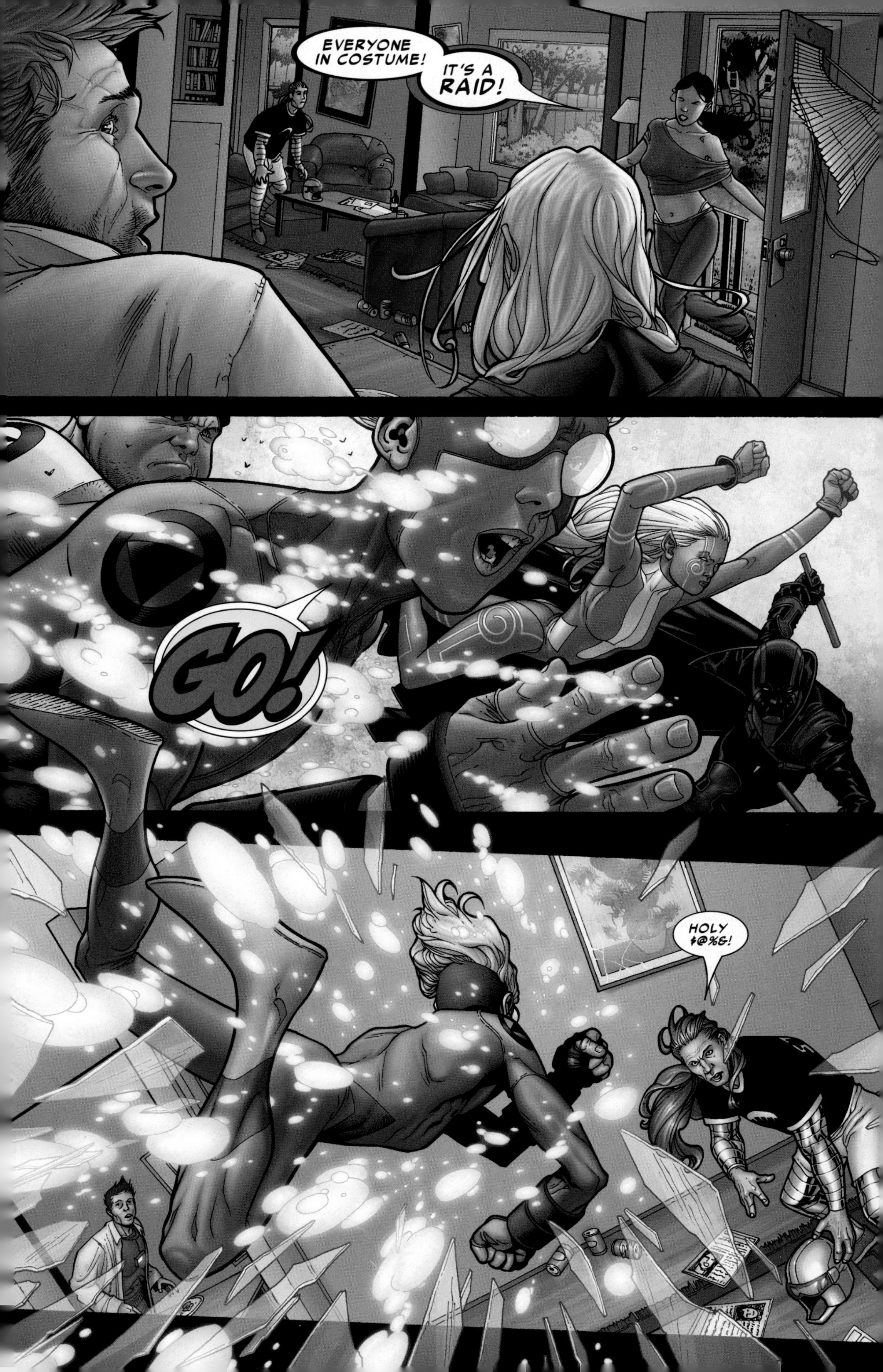
EVERYONE IN COSTUME!
IT'S A RAID!
GO!
HOLY $@%&!

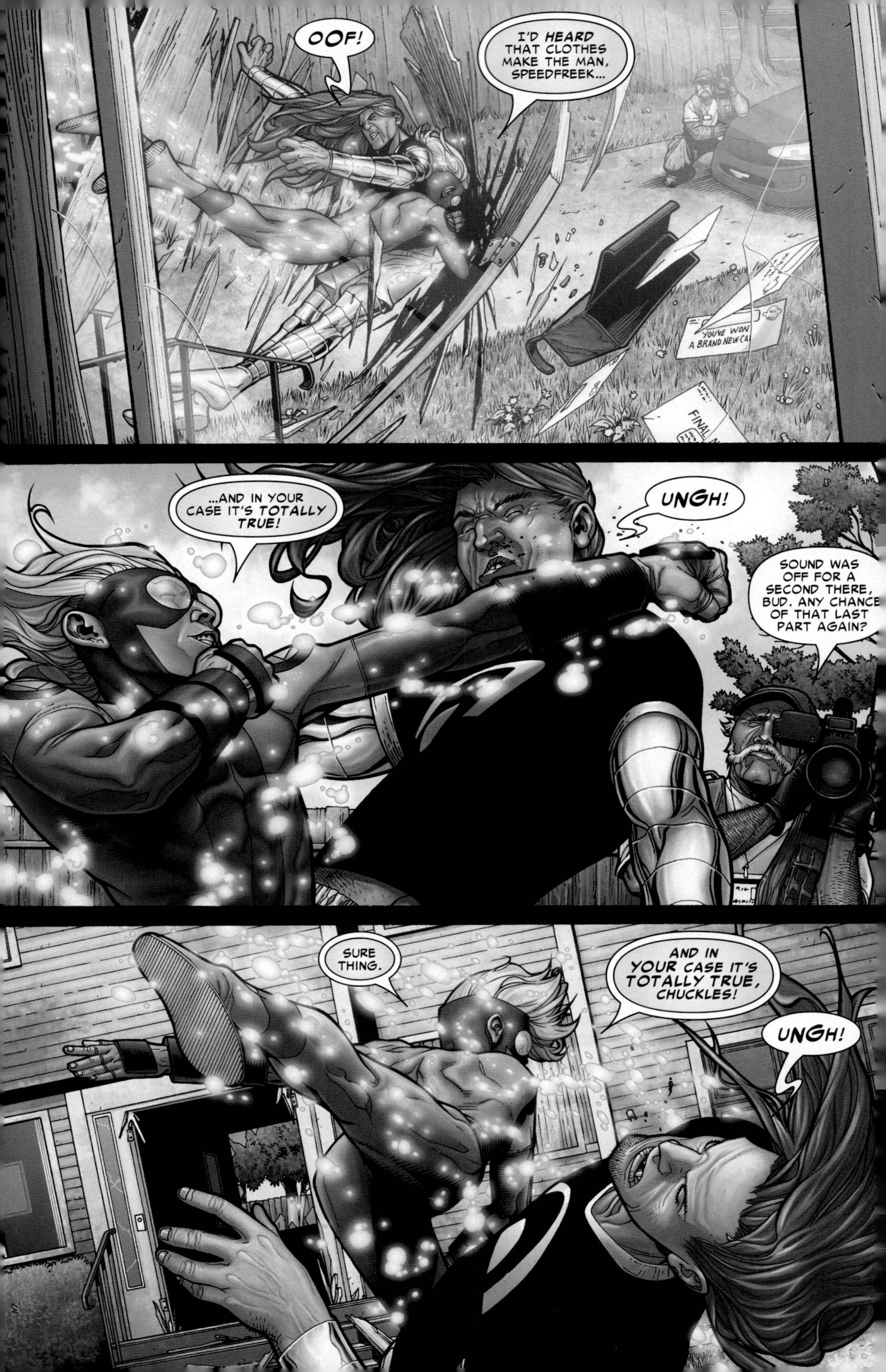
OOF!
I'D HEARD THAT CLOTHES MAKE THE MAN, SPEEDFREEK...
YOU'VE WON A BRAND NEW CA
FINAL
...AND IN YOUR CASE IT'S TOTALLY TRUE!
UNGH!
SOUND WAS OFF FOR A SECOND THERE, BUD. ANY CHANCE OF THAT LAST PART AGAIN?
SURE THING.
AND IN YOUR CASE IT'S TOTALLY TRUE, CHUCKLES!
UNGH!

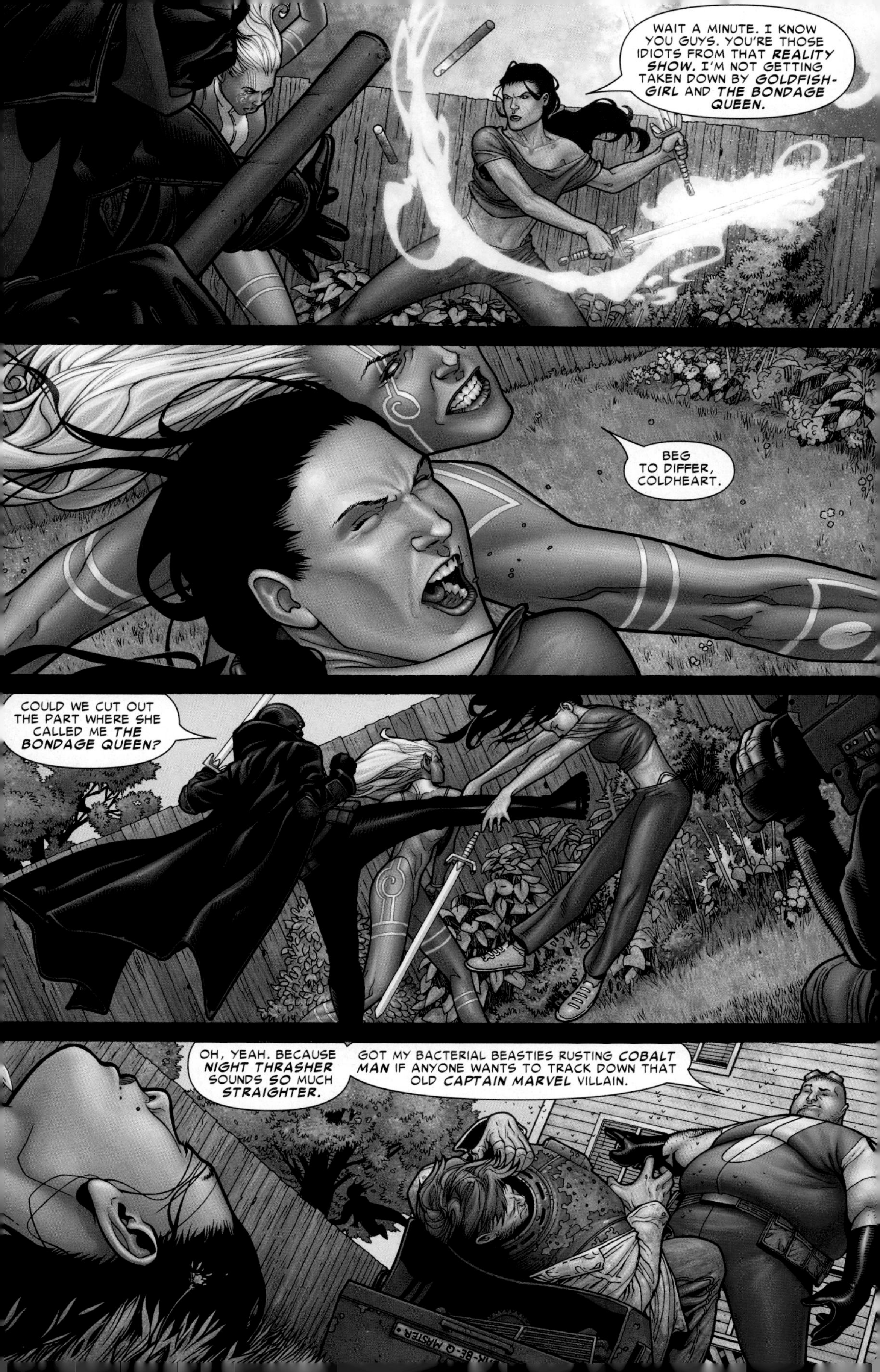
WAIT A MINUTE. I KNOW YOU GUYS. YOU'RE THOSE IDIOTS FROM THAT REALITY SHOW. I'M NOT GETTING TAKEN DOWN BY GOLDFISH-GIRL AND THE BONDAGE QUEEN.
BEG TO DIFFER, COLDHEART.
COULD WE CUT OUT THE PART WHERE SHE CALLED ME THE BONDAGE QUEEN?
OH, YEAH. BECAUSE NIGHT THRASHER SOUNDS SO MUCH STRAIGHTER.
GOT MY BACTERIAL BEASTIES RUSTING COBALT MAN IF ANYONE WANTS TO TRACK DOWN THAT OLD CAPTAIN MARVEL VILLAIN.

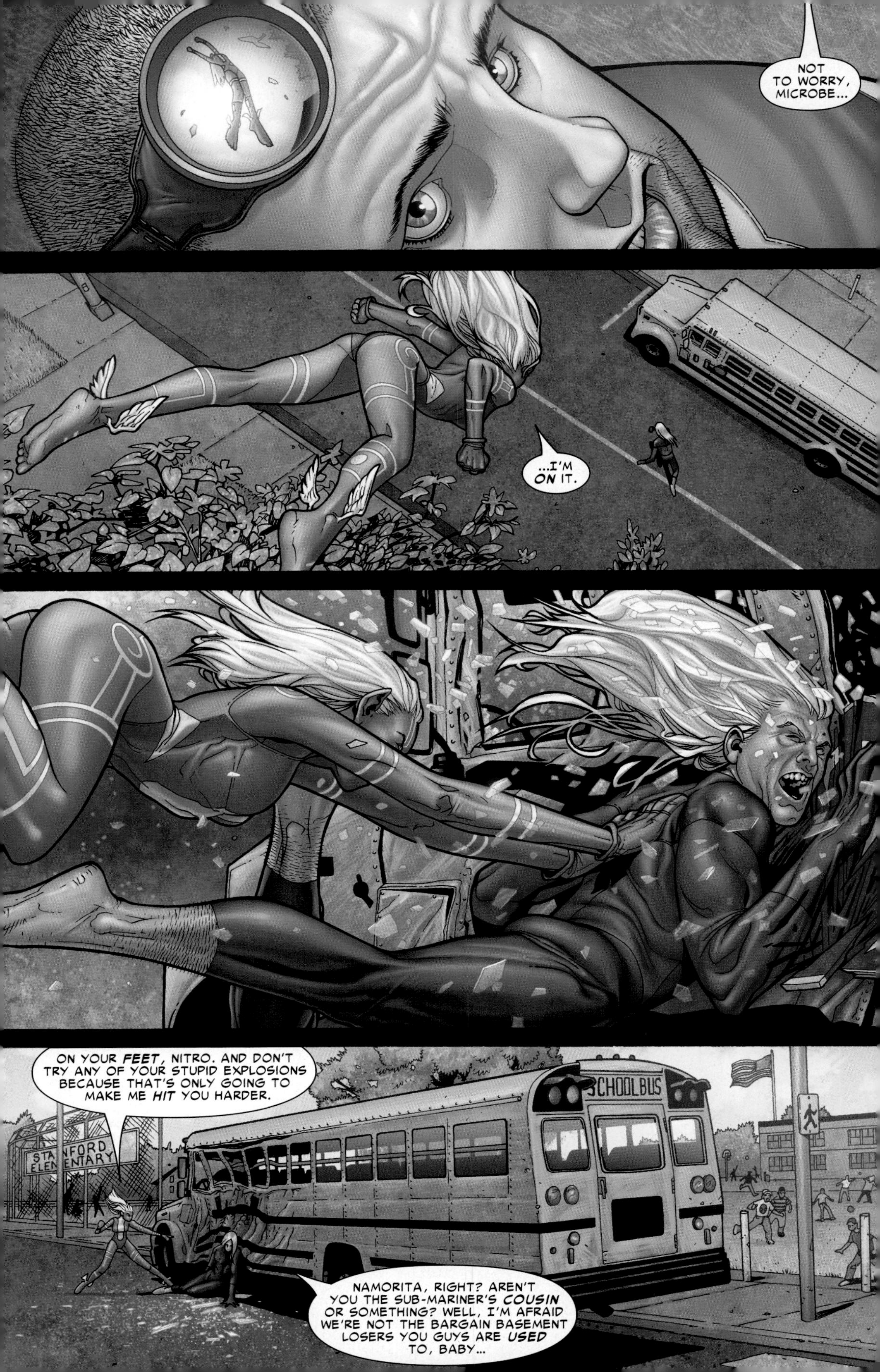
NOT TO WORRY, MICROBE...
...I'M ON IT.
ON YOUR FEET, NITRO. AND DON'T TRY ANY OF YOUR STUPID EXPLOSIONS BECAUSE THAT'S ONLY GOING TO MAKE ME HIT YOU HARDER.
SCHOOL BUS
STANFORD ELEMENTARY
NAMORITA, RIGHT? AREN'T YOU THE SUB-MARINER'S COUSIN OR SOMETHING? WELL, I'M AFRAID WE'RE NOT THE BARGAIN BASEMENT LOSERS YOU GUYS ARE USED TO, BABY...

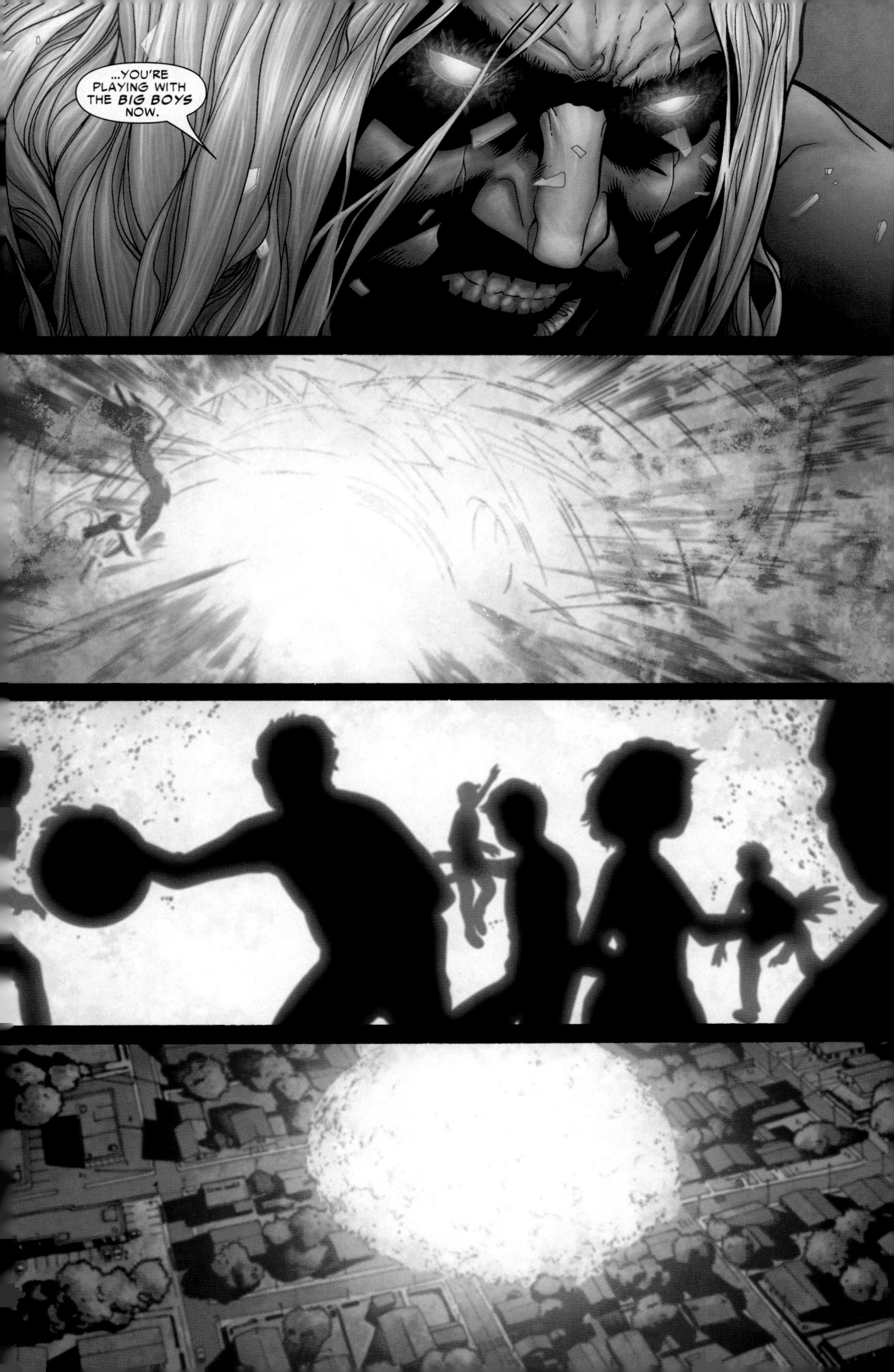
...YOU'RE PLAYING WITH THE *BIG BOYS* NOW.

MARK MILLAR
WRITER

STEVE McNIVEN
PENCILER

DEXTER VINES
INKER

MORRY HOLLOWELL
COLORIST

CHRIS ELIOPOULOS
LETTERER

P R E

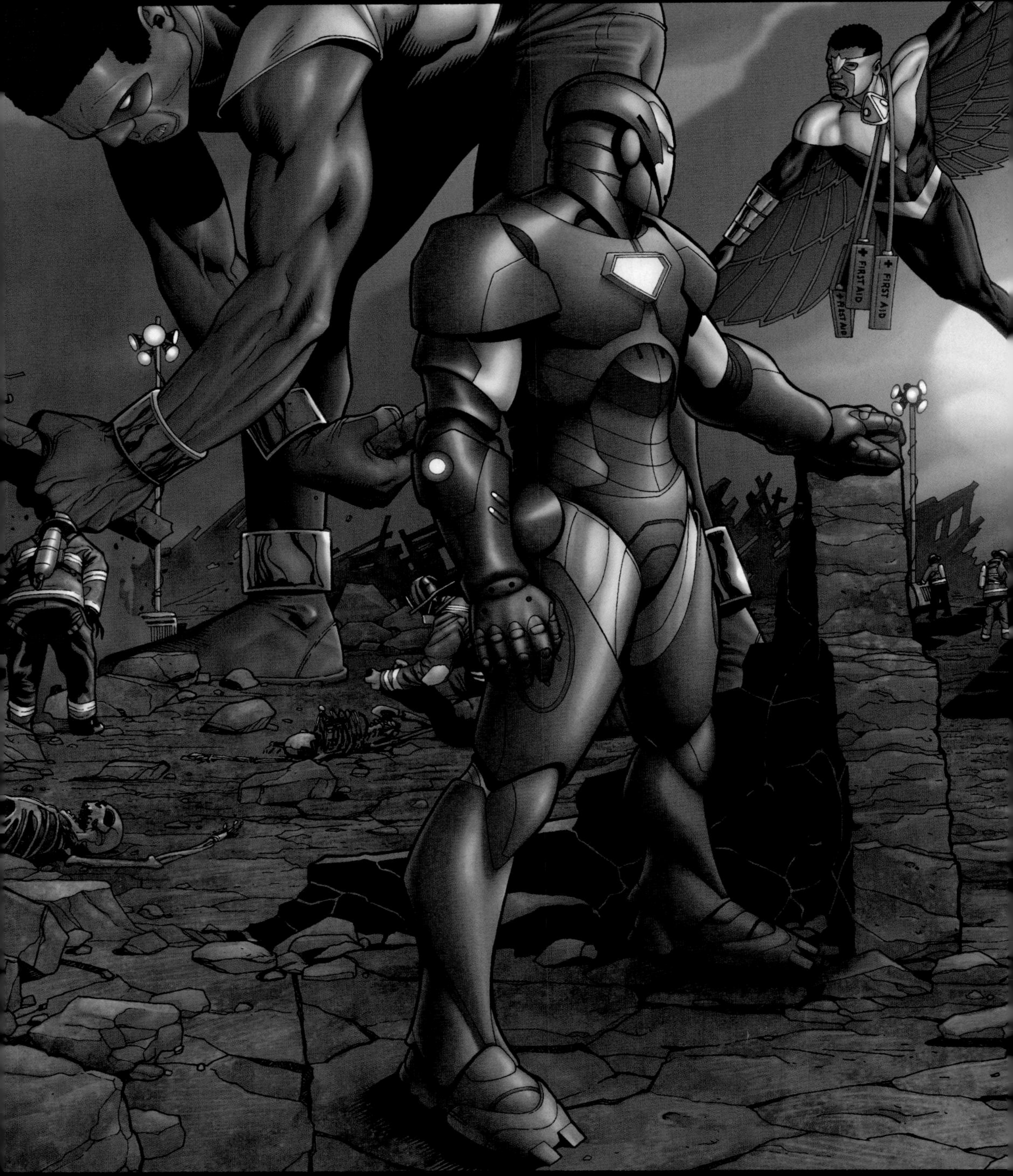

FIRST AID
FIRST AID
FIRST AID

CIVIL

MOLLY LAZER AND AUBREY SITTERSON — ASSISTANT EDITORS
ANDY SCHMIDT — ASSOCIATE EDITOR
TOM BREVOORT — EDITOR
JOE QUESADA — EDITOR IN CHIEF
DAN BUCKLEY — PUBLISHER

E N T :

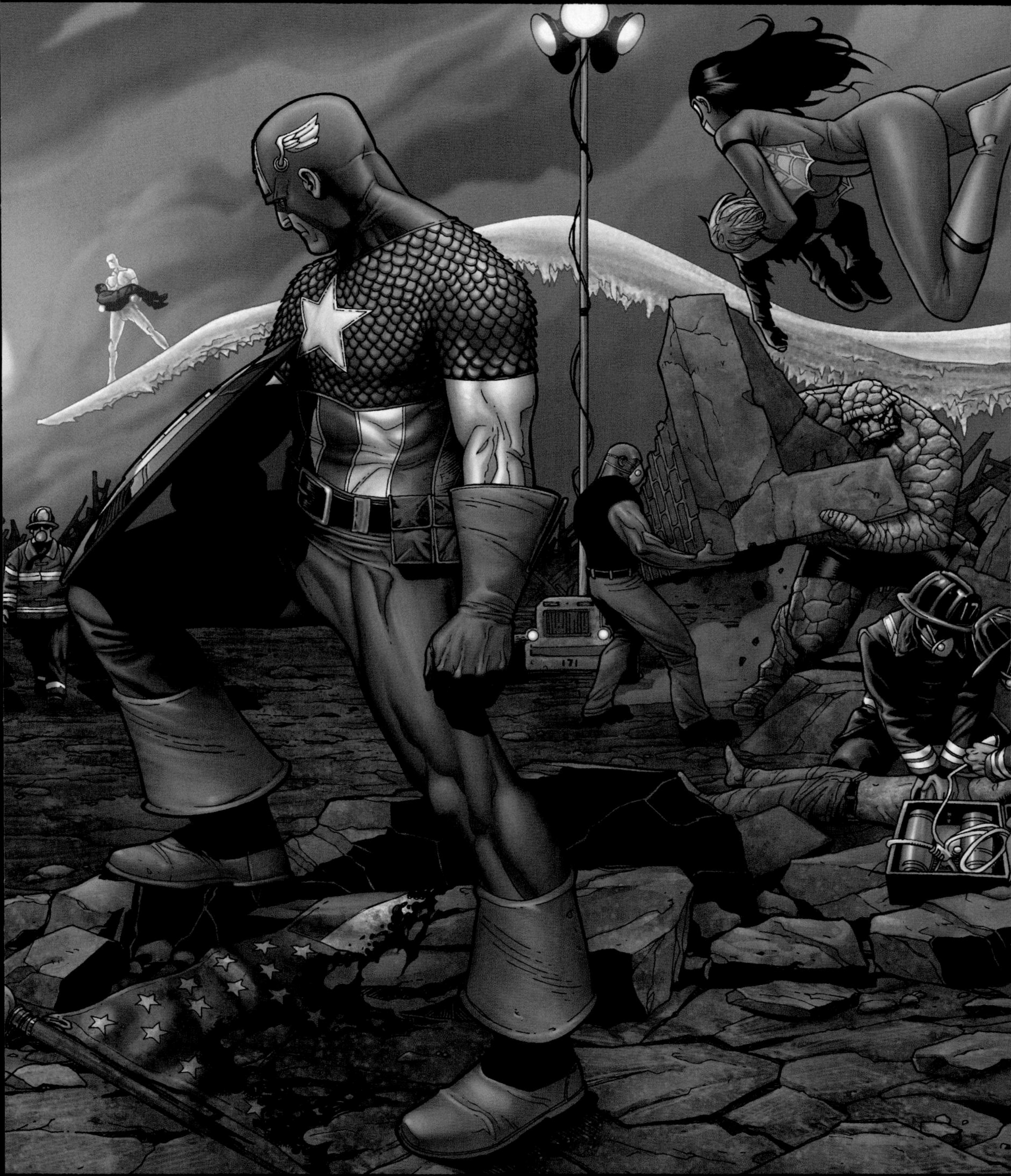

WAR

PART ONE OF SEVEN

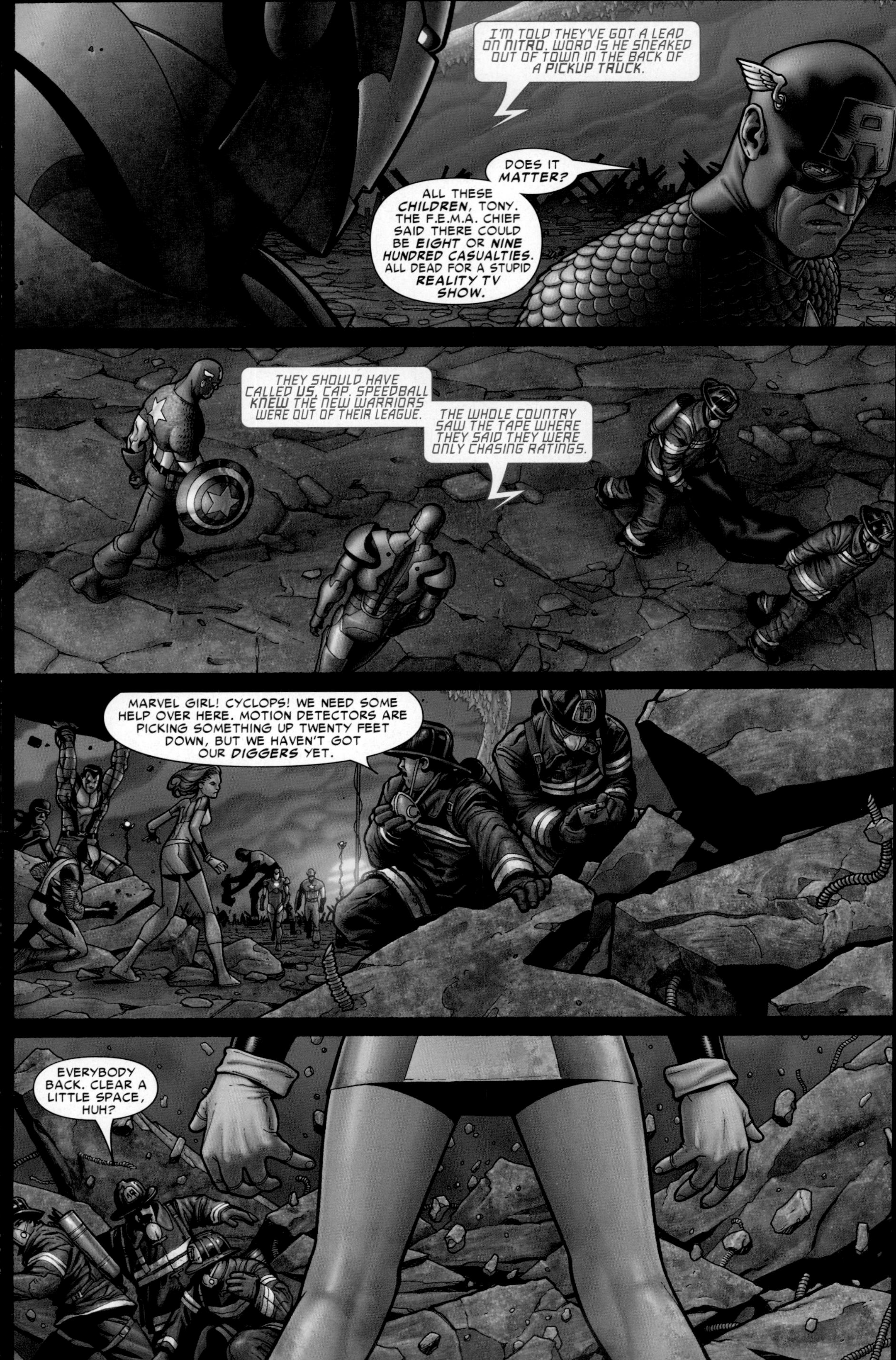
I'M TOLD THEY'VE GOT A LEAD ON NITRO. WORD IS HE SNEAKED OUT OF TOWN IN THE BACK OF A PICKUP TRUCK.
DOES IT MATTER?
ALL THESE CHILDREN, TONY. THE F.E.M.A. CHIEF SAID THERE COULD BE EIGHT OR NINE HUNDRED CASUALTIES. ALL DEAD FOR A STUPID REALITY TV SHOW.
THEY SHOULD HAVE CALLED US, CAP. SPEEDBALL KNEW THE NEW WARRIORS WERE OUT OF THEIR LEAGUE.
THE WHOLE COUNTRY SAW THE TAPE WHERE THEY SAID THEY WERE ONLY CHASING RATINGS.
MARVEL GIRL! CYCLOPS! WE NEED SOME HELP OVER HERE. MOTION DETECTORS ARE PICKING SOMETHING UP TWENTY FEET DOWN, BUT WE HAVEN'T GOT OUR DIGGERS YET.
EVERYBODY BACK. CLEAR A LITTLE SPACE, HUH?

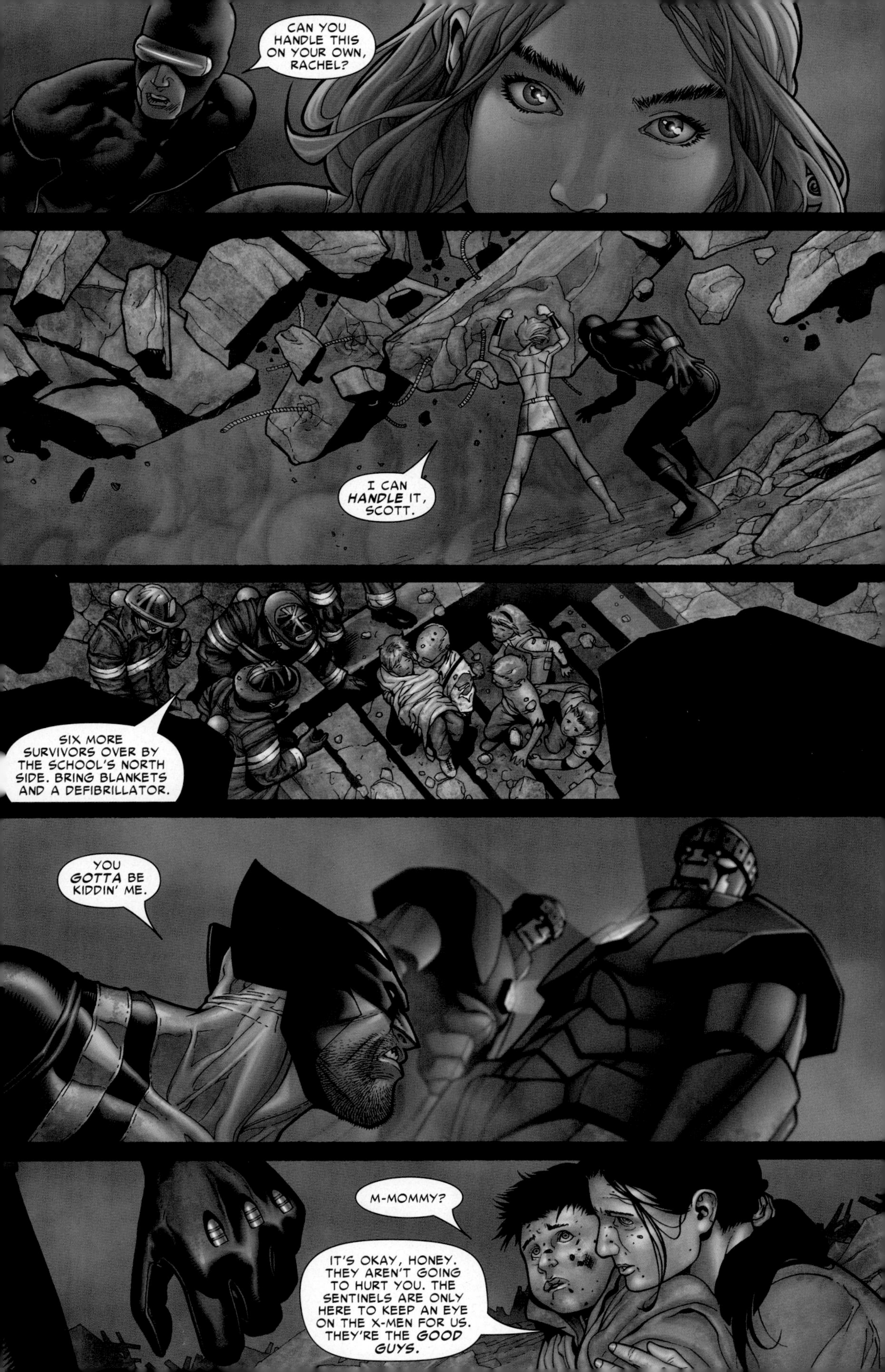
CAN YOU HANDLE THIS ON YOUR OWN, RACHEL?
I CAN *HANDLE* IT, SCOTT.
SIX MORE SURVIVORS OVER BY THE SCHOOL'S NORTH SIDE. BRING BLANKETS AND A DEFIBRILLATOR.
YOU *GOTTA* BE KIDDIN' ME.
M-MOMMY?
IT'S OKAY, HONEY. THEY AREN'T GOING TO HURT YOU. THE SENTINELS ARE ONLY HERE TO KEEP AN EYE ON THE X-MEN FOR US. THEY'RE THE *GOOD GUYS*.

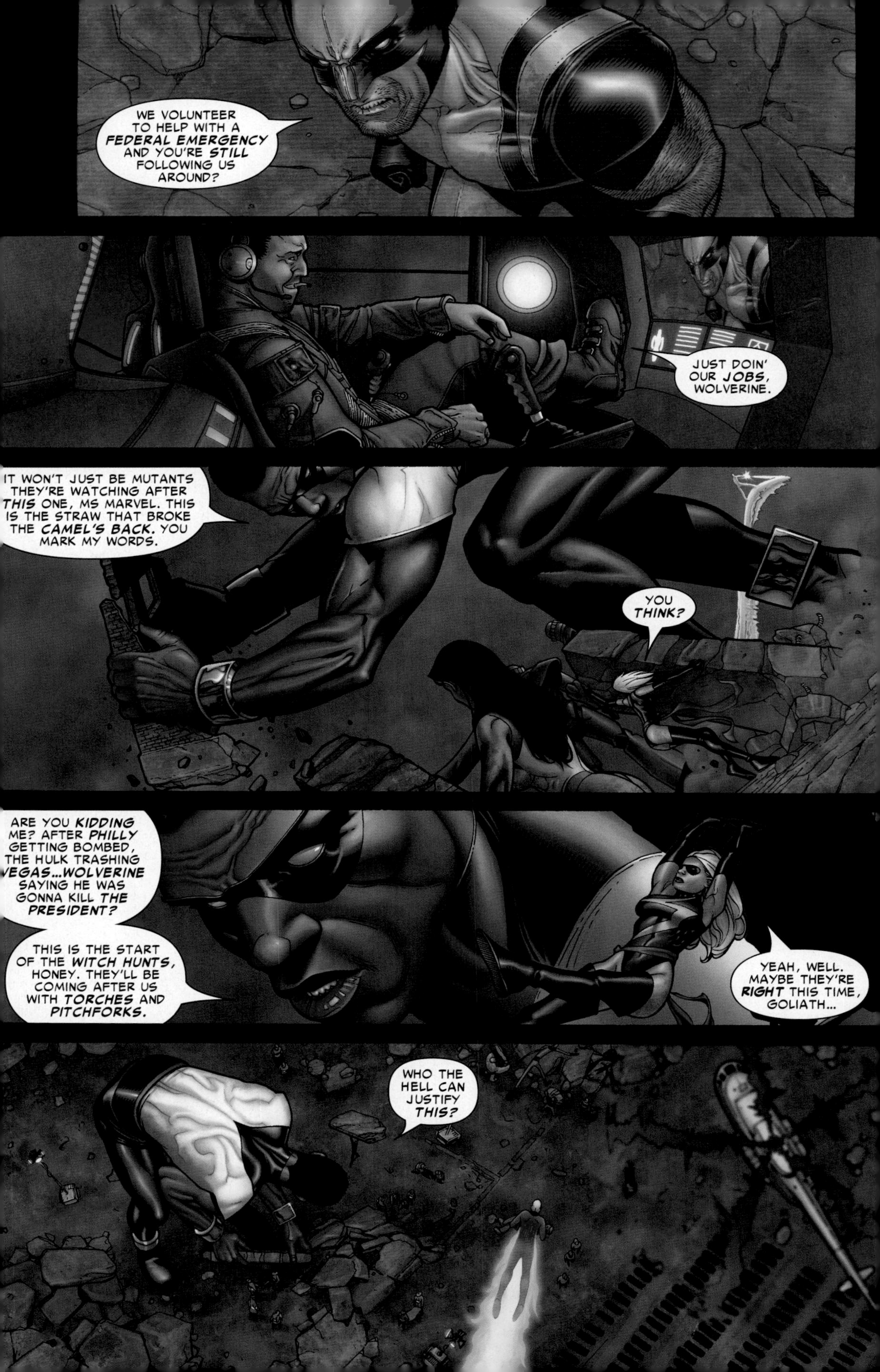
WE VOLUNTEER TO HELP WITH A FEDERAL EMERGENCY AND YOU'RE STILL FOLLOWING US AROUND?
JUST DOIN' OUR JOBS, WOLVERINE.
IT WON'T JUST BE MUTANTS THEY'RE WATCHING AFTER THIS ONE, MS MARVEL. THIS IS THE STRAW THAT BROKE THE CAMEL'S BACK. YOU MARK MY WORDS.
YOU THINK?
ARE YOU KIDDING ME? AFTER PHILLY GETTING BOMBED, THE HULK TRASHING VEGAS...WOLVERINE SAYING HE WAS GONNA KILL THE PRESIDENT?
THIS IS THE START OF THE WITCH HUNTS, HONEY. THEY'LL BE COMING AFTER US WITH TORCHES AND PITCHFORKS.
YEAH, WELL. MAYBE THEY'RE RIGHT THIS TIME, GOLIATH...
WHO THE HELL CAN JUSTIFY THIS?

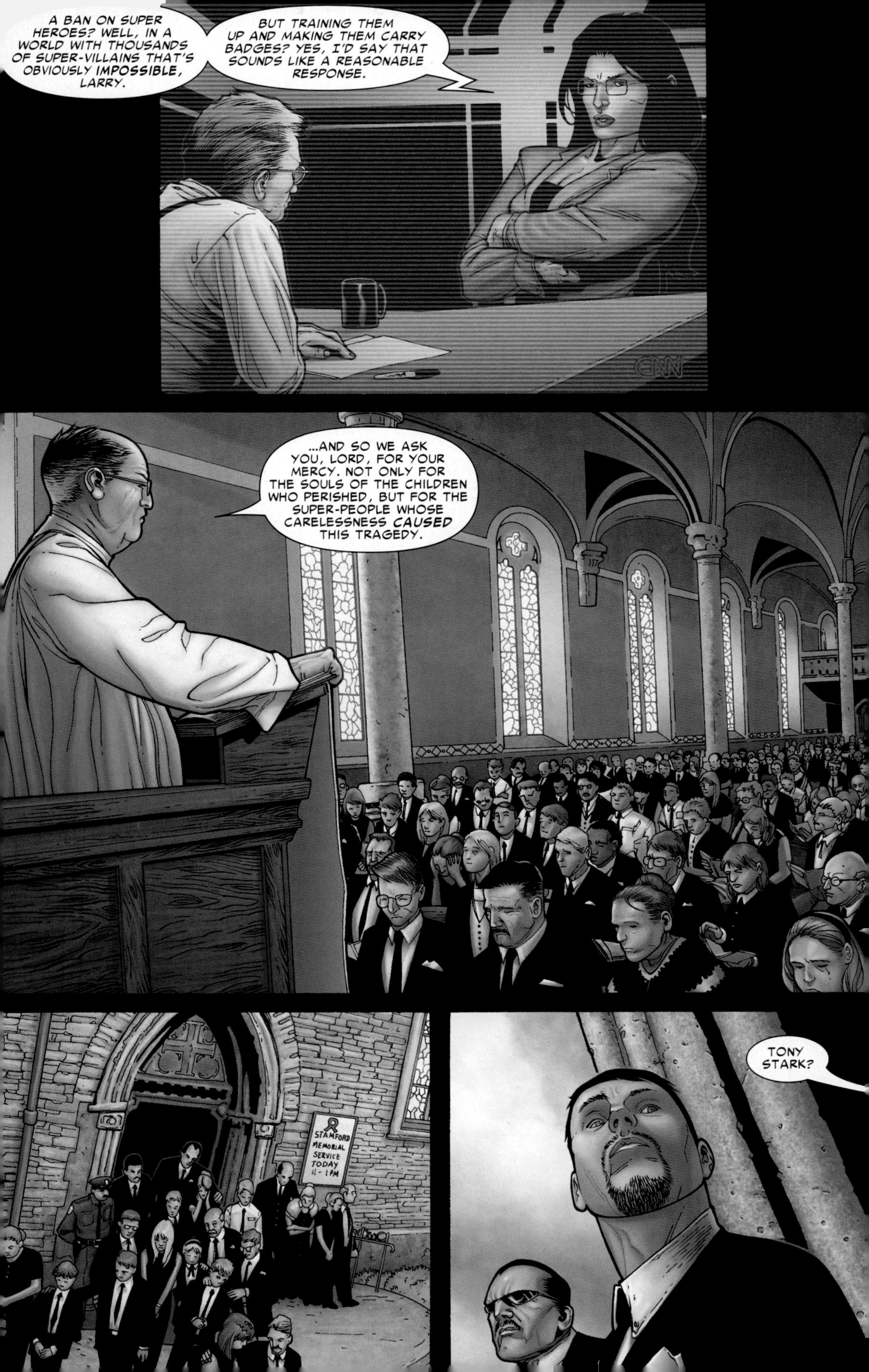

A BAN ON SUPER HEROES? WELL, IN A WORLD WITH THOUSANDS OF SUPER-VILLAINS THAT'S OBVIOUSLY IMPOSSIBLE, LARRY.
BUT TRAINING THEM UP AND MAKING THEM CARRY BADGES? YES, I'D SAY THAT SOUNDS LIKE A REASONABLE RESPONSE.
CNN
...AND SO WE ASK YOU, LORD, FOR YOUR MERCY. NOT ONLY FOR THE SOULS OF THE CHILDREN WHO PERISHED, BUT FOR THE SUPER-PEOPLE WHOSE CARELESSNESS CAUSED THIS TRAGEDY.
STAMFORD MEMORIAL SERVICE TODAY 11 - 1PM
TONY STARK?

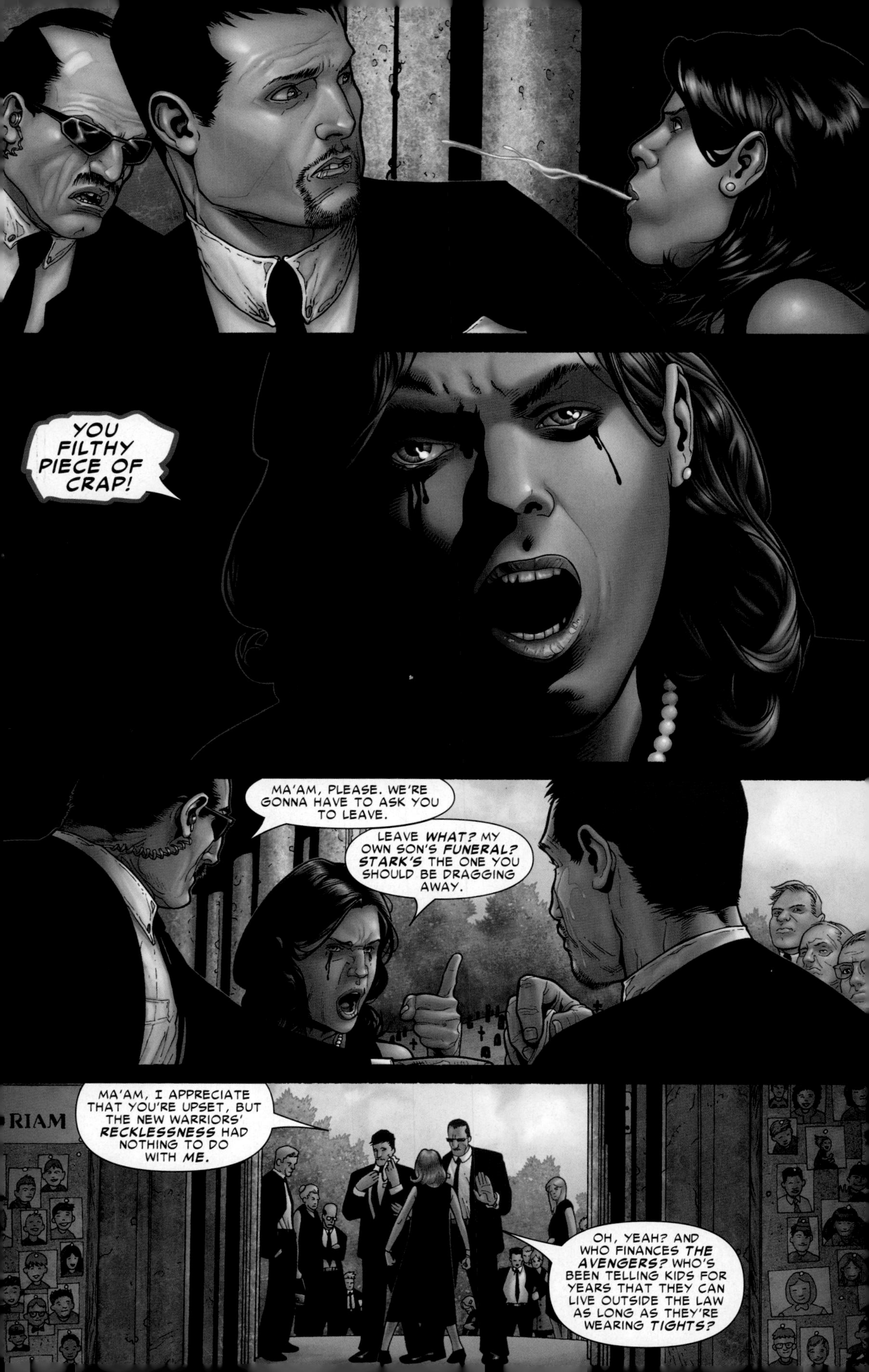

YOU FILTHY PIECE OF CRAP!
MA'AM, PLEASE. WE'RE GONNA HAVE TO ASK YOU TO LEAVE.
LEAVE WHAT? MY OWN SON'S FUNERAL? STARK'S THE ONE YOU SHOULD BE DRAGGING AWAY.
RIAM
MA'AM, I APPRECIATE THAT YOU'RE UPSET, BUT THE NEW WARRIORS' RECKLESSNESS HAD NOTHING TO DO WITH ME.
OH, YEAH? AND WHO FINANCES THE AVENGERS? WHO'S BEEN TELLING KIDS FOR YEARS THAT THEY CAN LIVE OUTSIDE THE LAW AS LONG AS THEY'RE WEARING TIGHTS?

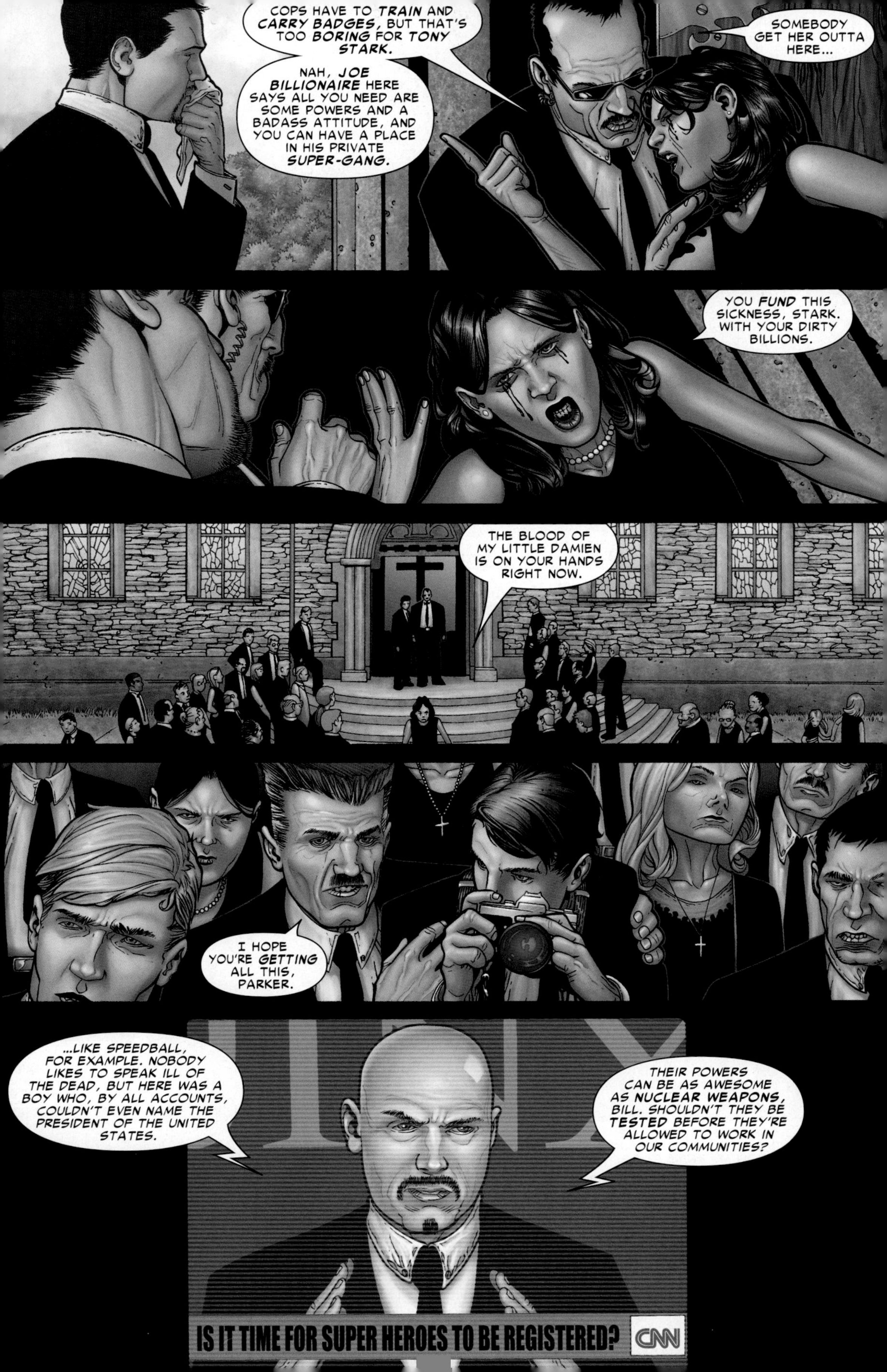
COPS HAVE TO TRAIN AND CARRY BADGES, BUT THAT'S TOO BORING FOR TONY STARK.
NAH, JOE BILLIONAIRE HERE SAYS ALL YOU NEED ARE SOME POWERS AND A BADASS ATTITUDE, AND YOU CAN HAVE A PLACE IN HIS PRIVATE SUPER-GANG.
SOMEBODY GET HER OUTTA HERE...
YOU FUND THIS SICKNESS, STARK. WITH YOUR DIRTY BILLIONS.
THE BLOOD OF MY LITTLE DAMIEN IS ON YOUR HANDS RIGHT NOW.
I HOPE YOU'RE GETTING ALL THIS, PARKER.
...LIKE SPEEDBALL, FOR EXAMPLE. NOBODY LIKES TO SPEAK ILL OF THE DEAD, BUT HERE WAS A BOY WHO, BY ALL ACCOUNTS, COULDN'T EVEN NAME THE PRESIDENT OF THE UNITED STATES.
THEIR POWERS CAN BE AS AWESOME AS NUCLEAR WEAPONS, BILL. SHOULDN'T THEY BE TESTED BEFORE THEY'RE ALLOWED TO WORK IN OUR COMMUNITIES?
IS IT TIME FOR SUPER HEROES TO BE REGISTERED?
CNN

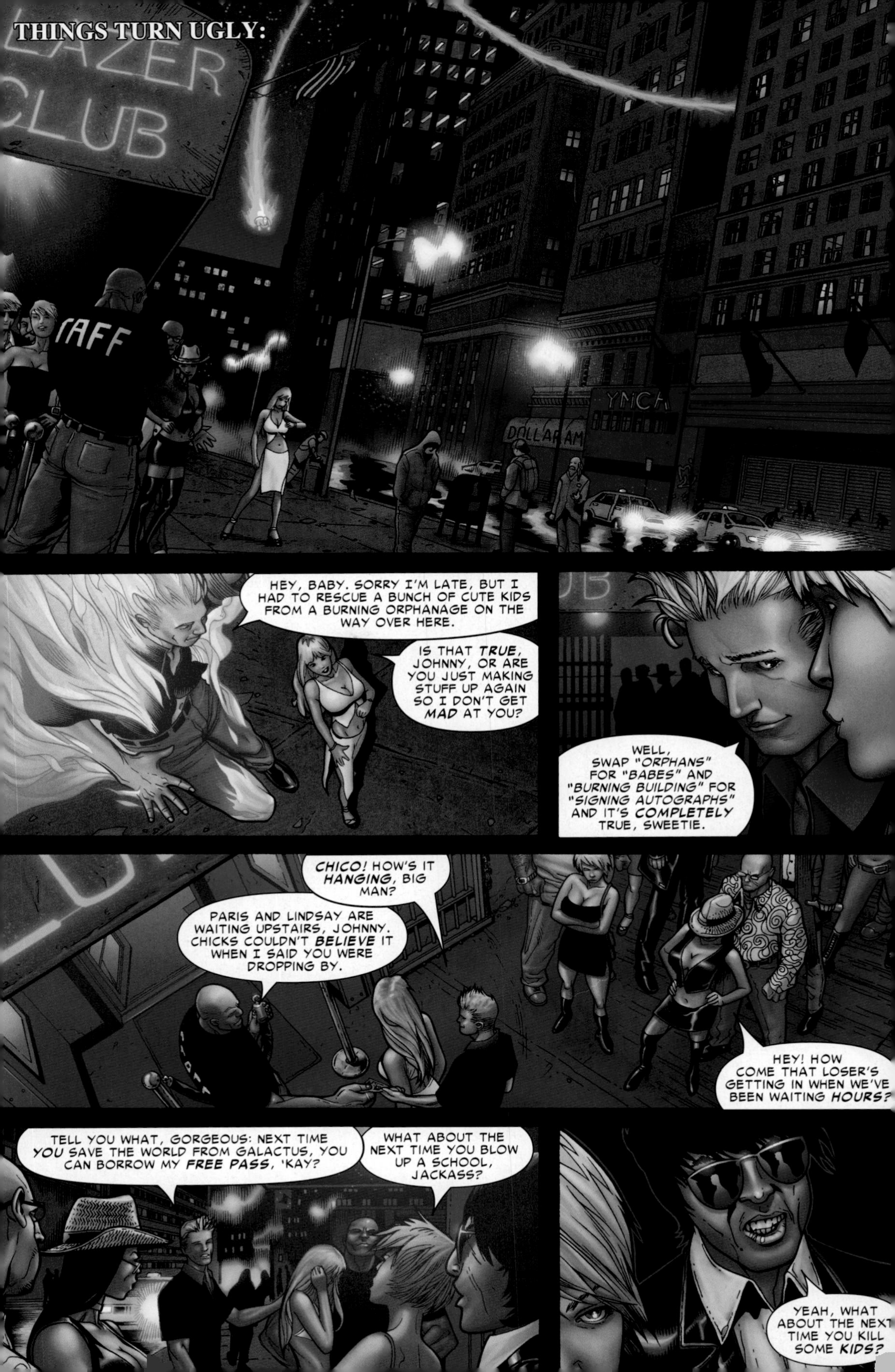
THINGS TURN UGLY:
LAZER CLUB
STAFF
YMCA
DOLLARAMA
HEY, BABY. SORRY I'M LATE, BUT I HAD TO RESCUE A BUNCH OF CUTE KIDS FROM A BURNING ORPHANAGE ON THE WAY OVER HERE.
IS THAT TRUE, JOHNNY, OR ARE YOU JUST MAKING STUFF UP AGAIN SO I DON'T GET MAD AT YOU?
WELL, SWAP "ORPHANS" FOR "BABES" AND "BURNING BUILDING" FOR "SIGNING AUTOGRAPHS" AND IT'S COMPLETELY TRUE, SWEETIE.
CHICO! HOW'S IT HANGING, BIG MAN?
PARIS AND LINDSAY ARE WAITING UPSTAIRS, JOHNNY. CHICKS COULDN'T BELIEVE IT WHEN I SAID YOU WERE DROPPING BY.
HEY! HOW COME THAT LOSER'S GETTING IN WHEN WE'VE BEEN WAITING HOURS?
TELL YOU WHAT, GORGEOUS: NEXT TIME YOU SAVE THE WORLD FROM GALACTUS, YOU CAN BORROW MY FREE PASS, 'KAY?
WHAT ABOUT THE NEXT TIME YOU BLOW UP A SCHOOL, JACKASS?
YEAH, WHAT ABOUT THE NEXT TIME YOU KILL SOME KIDS?

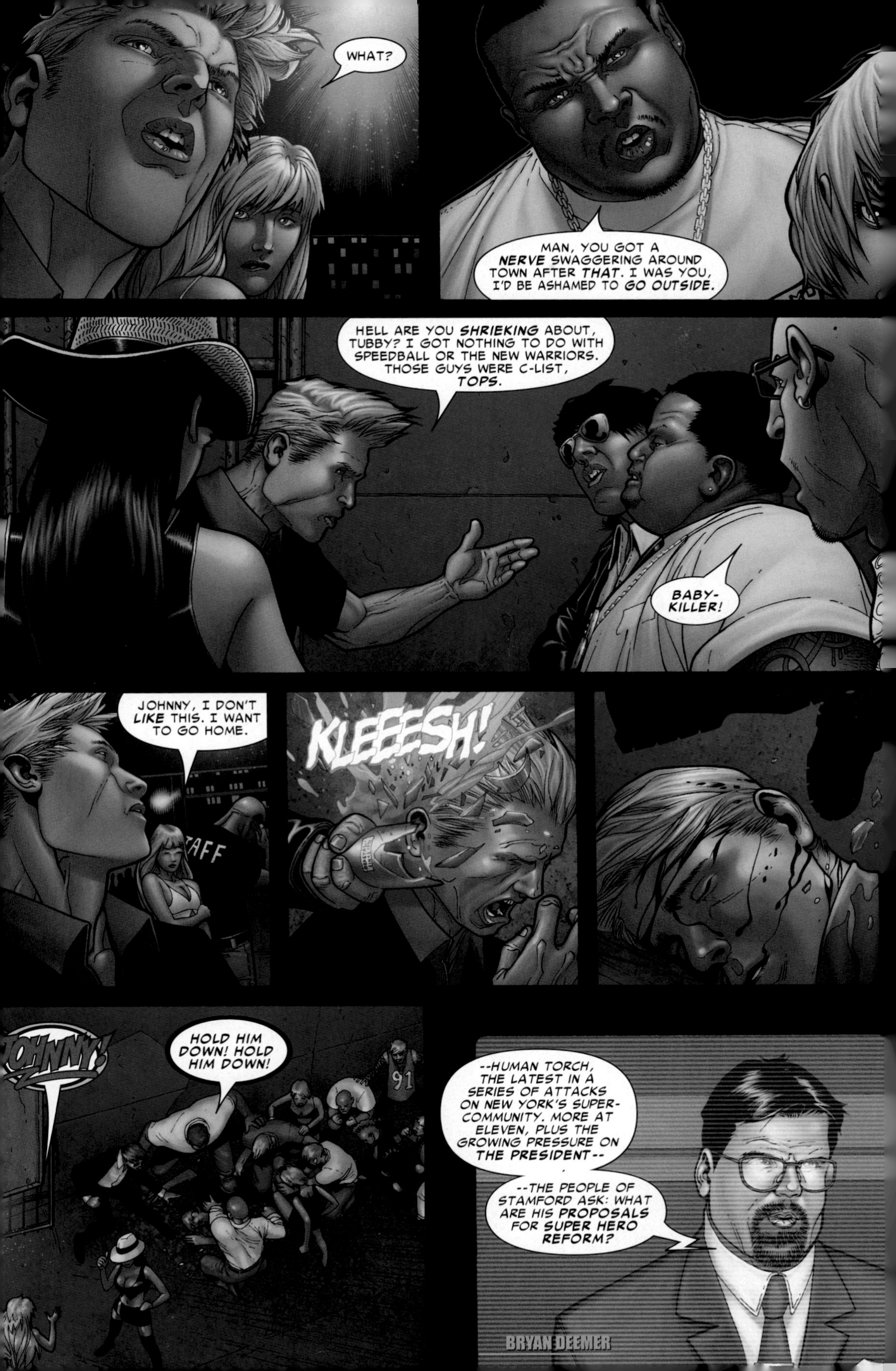
WHAT?
MAN, YOU GOT A NERVE SWAGGERING AROUND TOWN AFTER THAT. I WAS YOU, I'D BE ASHAMED TO GO OUTSIDE.
HELL ARE YOU SHRIEKING ABOUT, TUBBY? I GOT NOTHING TO DO WITH SPEEDBALL OR THE NEW WARRIORS. THOSE GUYS WERE C-LIST, TOPS.
BABY-KILLER!
JOHNNY, I DON'T LIKE THIS. I WANT TO GO HOME.
KLEEESH!
JOHNNY!
HOLD HIM DOWN! HOLD HIM DOWN!
--HUMAN TORCH, THE LATEST IN A SERIES OF ATTACKS ON NEW YORK'S SUPER-COMMUNITY. MORE AT ELEVEN, PLUS THE GROWING PRESSURE ON THE PRESIDENT--
--THE PEOPLE OF STAMFORD ASK: WHAT ARE HIS PROPOSALS FOR SUPER HERO REFORM?
BRYAN DEEMER

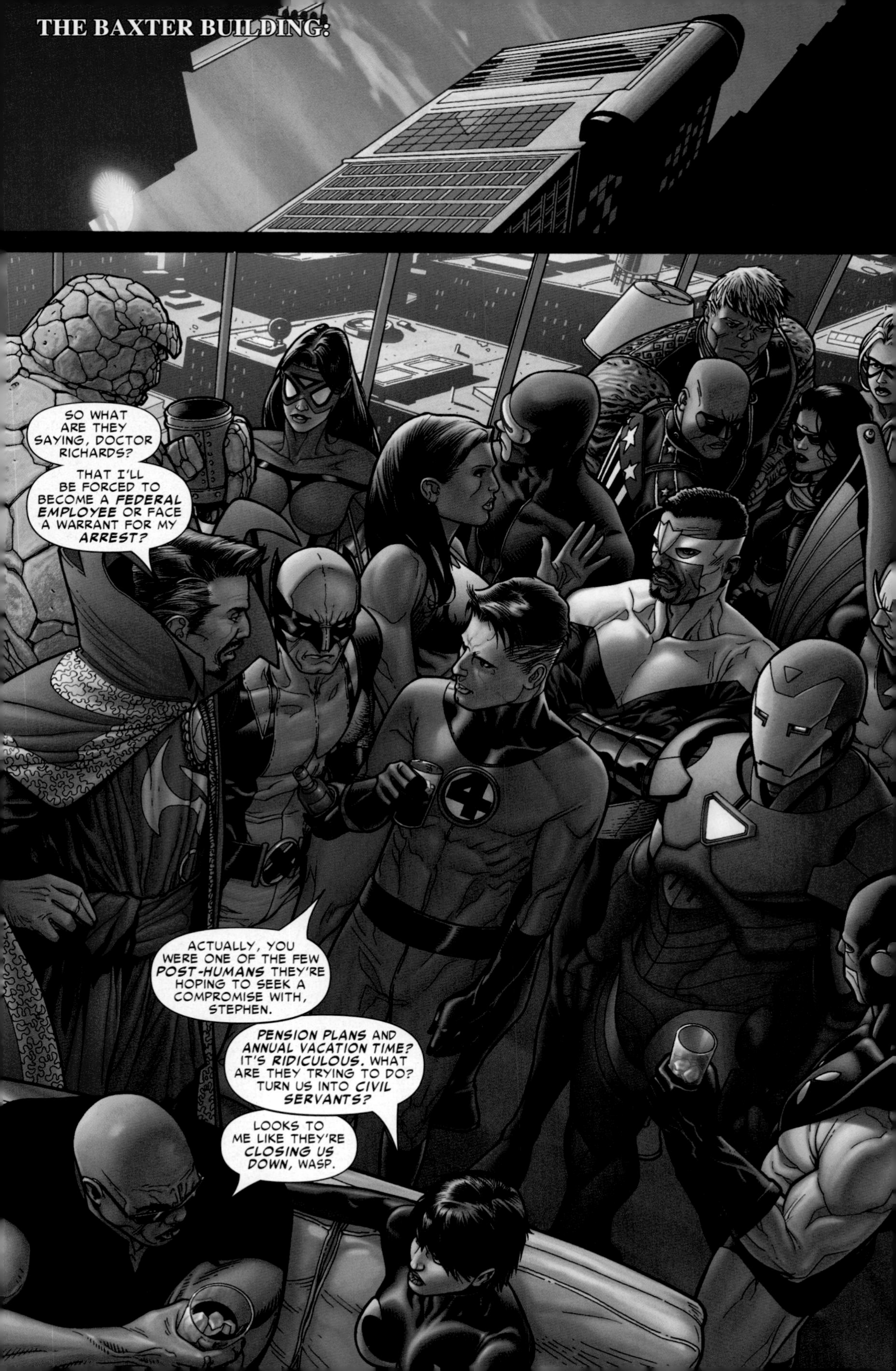
THE BAXTER BUILDING:
SO WHAT ARE THEY SAYING, DOCTOR RICHARDS?
THAT I'LL BE FORCED TO BECOME A FEDERAL EMPLOYEE OR FACE A WARRANT FOR MY ARREST?
ACTUALLY, YOU WERE ONE OF THE FEW POST-HUMANS THEY'RE HOPING TO SEEK A COMPROMISE WITH, STEPHEN.
PENSION PLANS AND ANNUAL VACATION TIME? IT'S RIDICULOUS. WHAT ARE THEY TRYING TO DO? TURN US INTO CIVIL SERVANTS?
LOOKS TO ME LIKE THEY'RE CLOSING US DOWN, WASP.

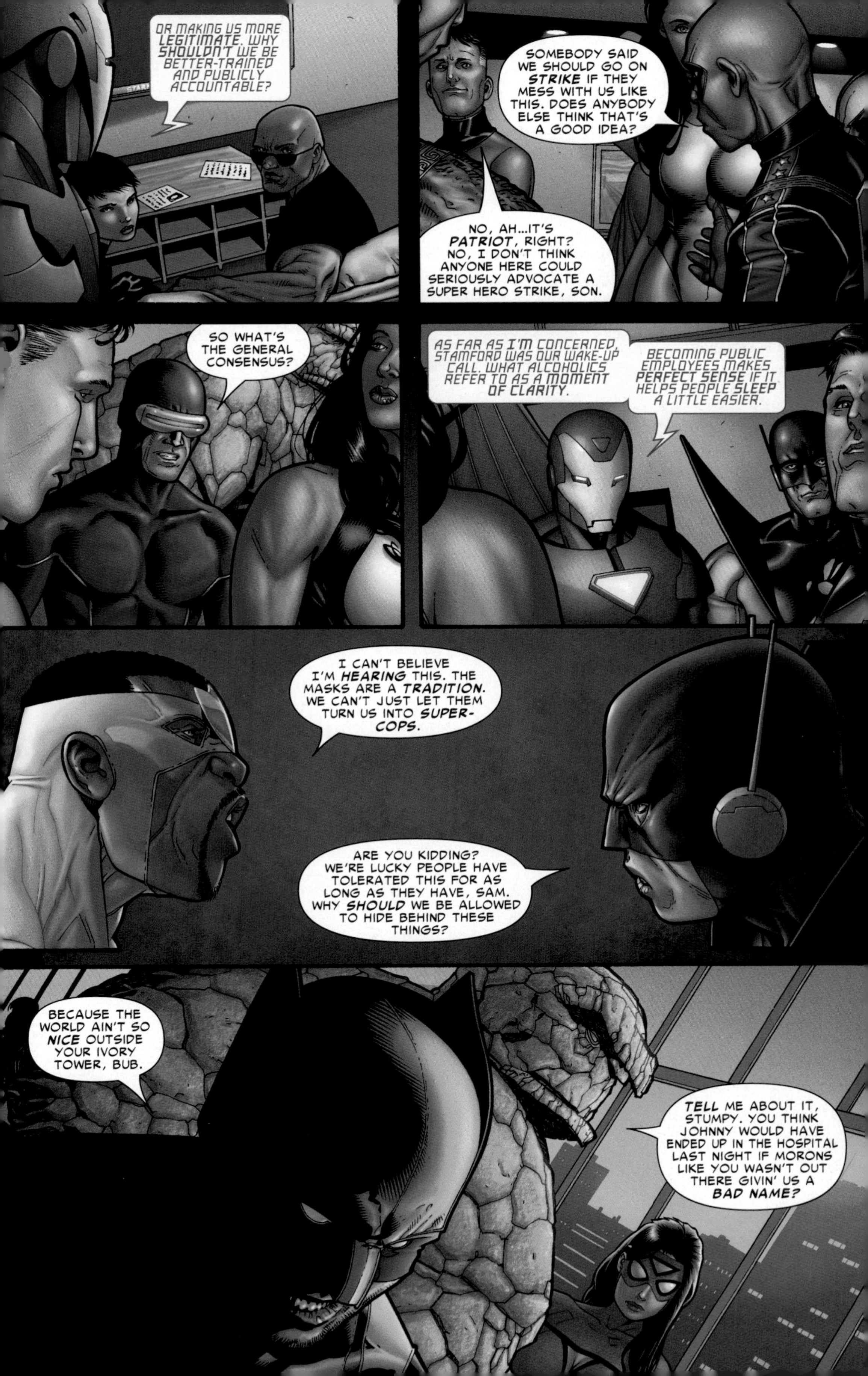
OR MAKING US MORE LEGITIMATE. WHY SHOULDN'T WE BE BETTER-TRAINED AND PUBLICLY ACCOUNTABLE?
SOMEBODY SAID WE SHOULD GO ON STRIKE IF THEY MESS WITH US LIKE THIS. DOES ANYBODY ELSE THINK THAT'S A GOOD IDEA?
NO, AH...IT'S PATRIOT, RIGHT? NO, I DON'T THINK ANYONE HERE COULD SERIOUSLY ADVOCATE A SUPER HERO STRIKE, SON.
SO WHAT'S THE GENERAL CONSENSUS?
AS FAR AS I'M CONCERNED, STAMFORD WAS OUR WAKE-UP CALL. WHAT ALCOHOLICS REFER TO AS A MOMENT OF CLARITY.
BECOMING PUBLIC EMPLOYEES MAKES PERFECT SENSE IF IT HELPS PEOPLE SLEEP A LITTLE EASIER.
I CAN'T BELIEVE I'M HEARING THIS. THE MASKS ARE A TRADITION. WE CAN'T JUST LET THEM TURN US INTO SUPER-COPS.
ARE YOU KIDDING? WE'RE LUCKY PEOPLE HAVE TOLERATED THIS FOR AS LONG AS THEY HAVE, SAM. WHY SHOULD WE BE ALLOWED TO HIDE BEHIND THESE THINGS?
BECAUSE THE WORLD AIN'T SO NICE OUTSIDE YOUR IVORY TOWER, BUB.
TELL ME ABOUT IT, STUMPY. YOU THINK JOHNNY WOULD HAVE ENDED UP IN THE HOSPITAL LAST NIGHT IF MORONS LIKE YOU WASN'T OUT THERE GIVIN' US A BAD NAME?

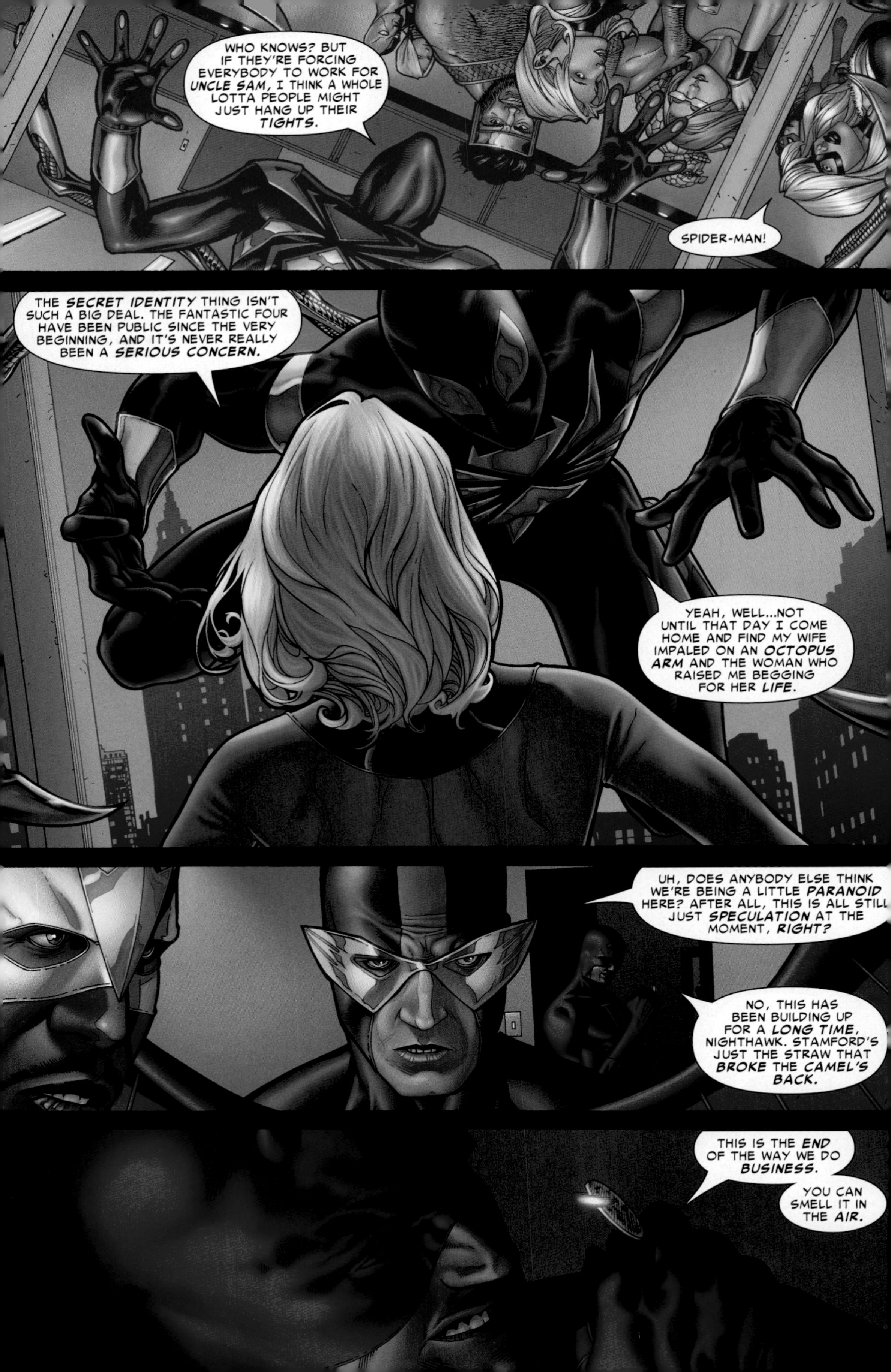
WHO KNOWS? BUT IF THEY'RE FORCING EVERYBODY TO WORK FOR UNCLE SAM, I THINK A WHOLE LOTTA PEOPLE MIGHT JUST HANG UP THEIR TIGHTS.
SPIDER-MAN!
THE SECRET IDENTITY THING ISN'T SUCH A BIG DEAL. THE FANTASTIC FOUR HAVE BEEN PUBLIC SINCE THE VERY BEGINNING, AND IT'S NEVER REALLY BEEN A SERIOUS CONCERN.
YEAH, WELL...NOT UNTIL THAT DAY I COME HOME AND FIND MY WIFE IMPALED ON AN OCTOPUS ARM AND THE WOMAN WHO RAISED ME BEGGING FOR HER LIFE.
UH, DOES ANYBODY ELSE THINK WE'RE BEING A LITTLE PARANOID HERE? AFTER ALL, THIS IS ALL STILL JUST SPECULATION AT THE MOMENT, RIGHT?
NO, THIS HAS BEEN BUILDING UP FOR A LONG TIME, NIGHTHAWK. STAMFORD'S JUST THE STRAW THAT BROKE THE CAMEL'S BACK.
THIS IS THE END OF THE WAY WE DO BUSINESS.
YOU CAN SMELL IT IN THE AIR.

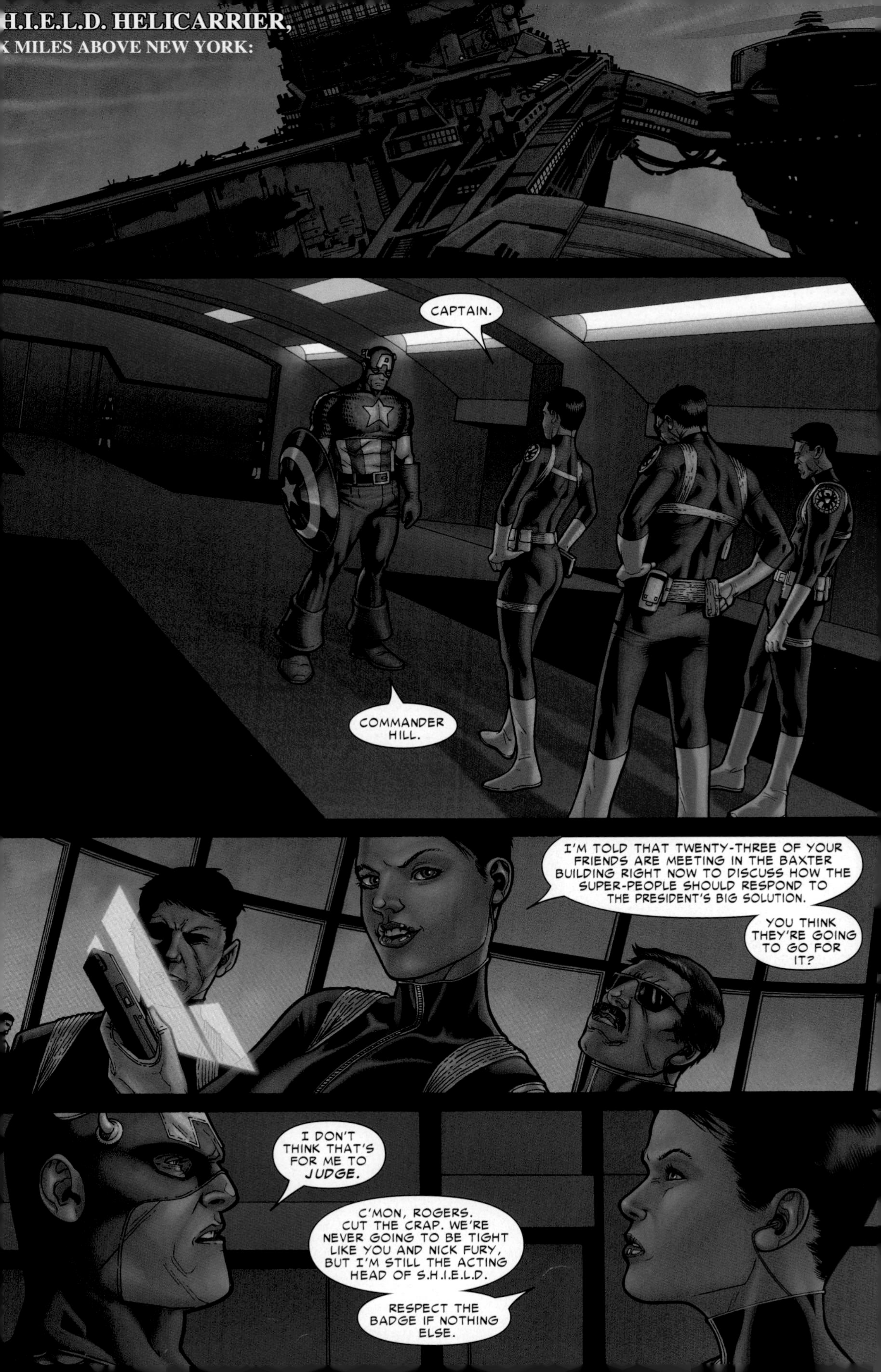

H.I.E.L.D. HELICARRIER,
X MILES ABOVE NEW YORK:
CAPTAIN.
COMMANDER HILL.
I'M TOLD THAT TWENTY-THREE OF YOUR FRIENDS ARE MEETING IN THE BAXTER BUILDING RIGHT NOW TO DISCUSS HOW THE SUPER-PEOPLE SHOULD RESPOND TO THE PRESIDENT'S BIG SOLUTION.
YOU THINK THEY'RE GOING TO GO FOR IT?
I DON'T THINK THAT'S FOR ME TO JUDGE.
C'MON, ROGERS. CUT THE CRAP. WE'RE NEVER GOING TO BE TIGHT LIKE YOU AND NICK FURY, BUT I'M STILL THE ACTING HEAD OF S.H.I.E.L.D.
RESPECT THE BADGE IF NOTHING ELSE.

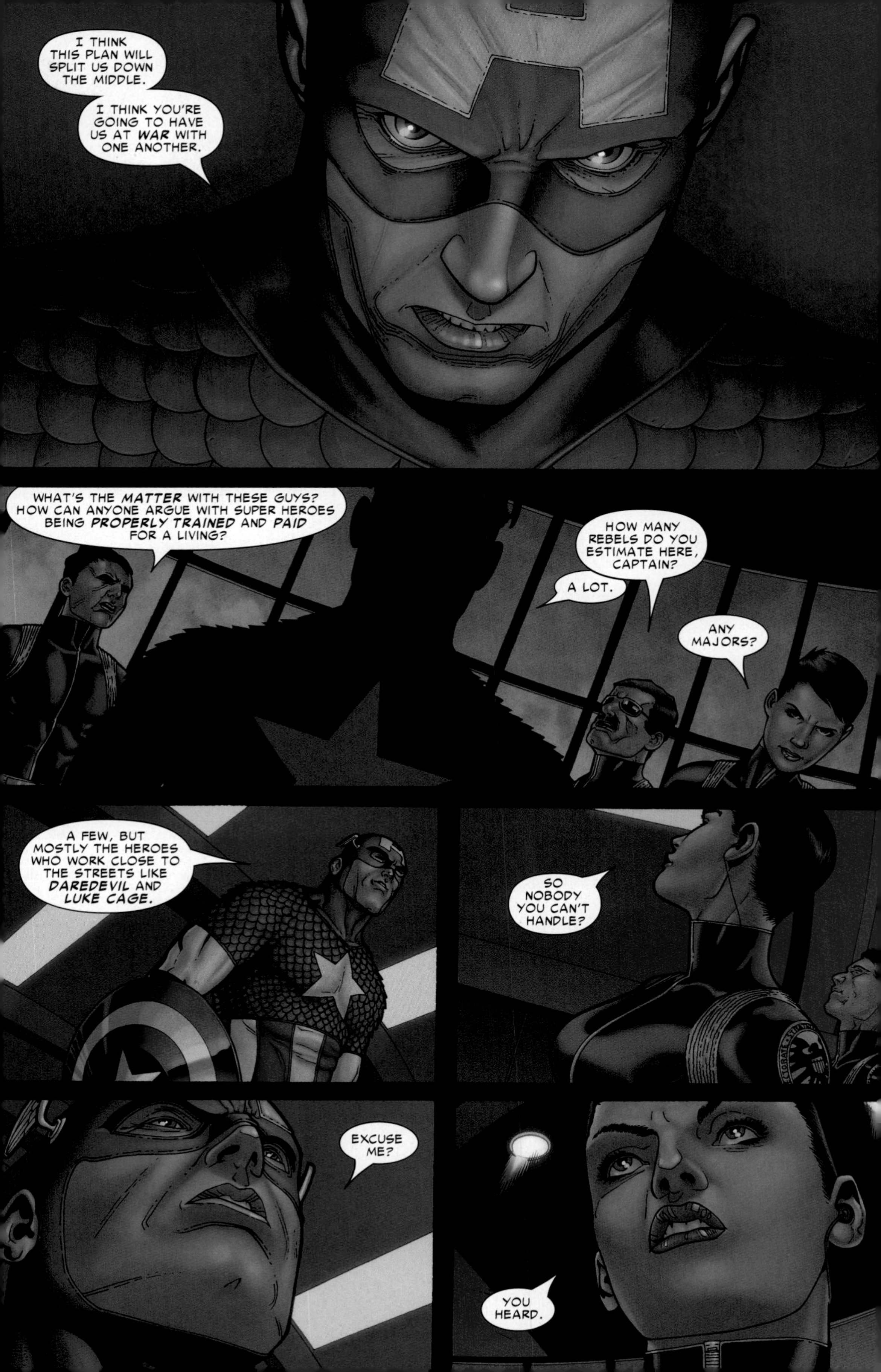

I THINK THIS PLAN WILL SPLIT US DOWN THE MIDDLE.
I THINK YOU'RE GOING TO HAVE US AT WAR WITH ONE ANOTHER.
WHAT'S THE MATTER WITH THESE GUYS? HOW CAN ANYONE ARGUE WITH SUPER HEROES BEING PROPERLY TRAINED AND PAID FOR A LIVING?
HOW MANY REBELS DO YOU ESTIMATE HERE, CAPTAIN?
A LOT.
ANY MAJORS?
A FEW, BUT MOSTLY THE HEROES WHO WORK CLOSE TO THE STREETS LIKE DAREDEVIL AND LUKE CAGE.
SO NOBODY YOU CAN'T HANDLE?
EXCUSE ME?
YOU HEARD.

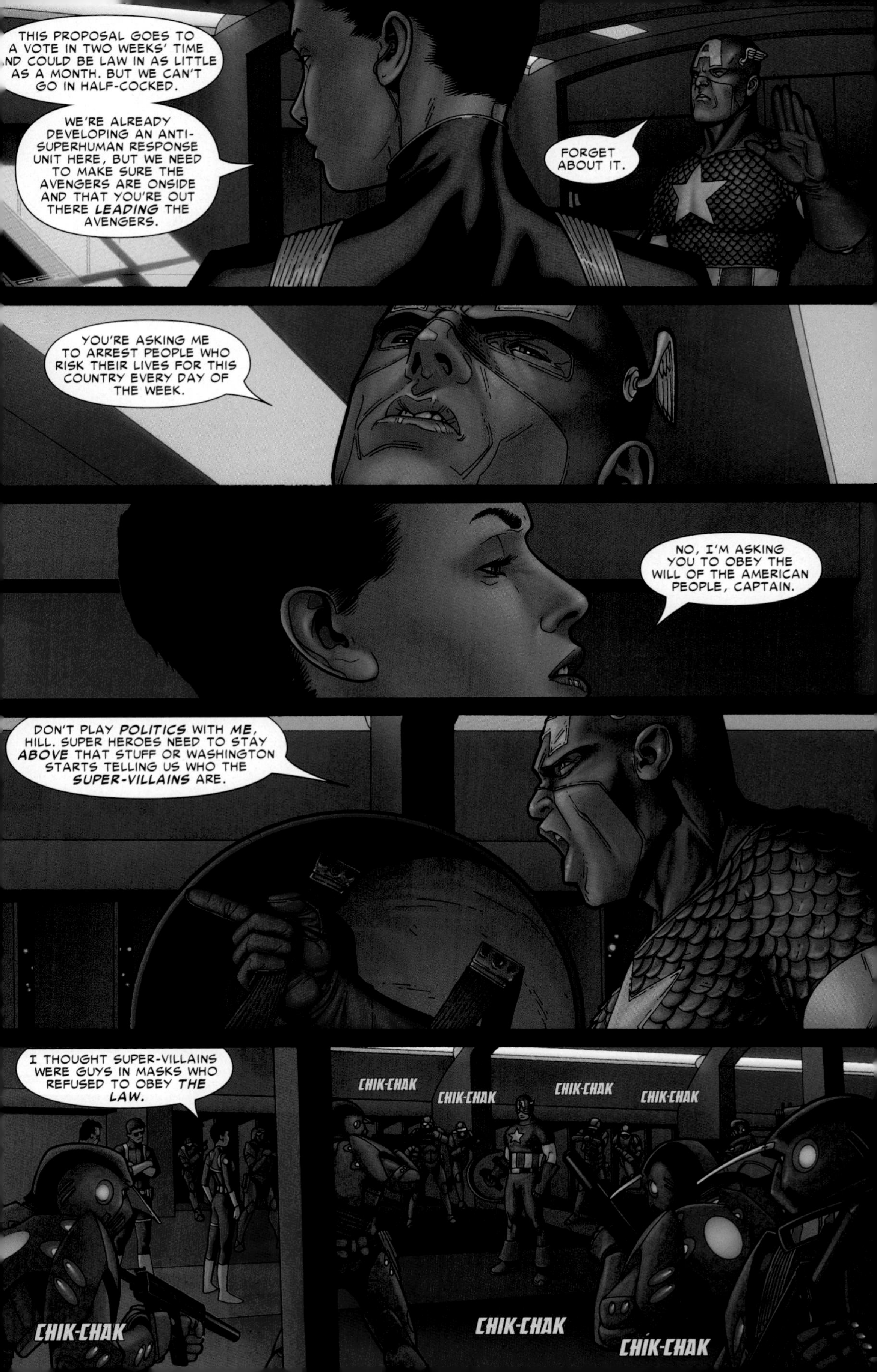
THIS PROPOSAL GOES TO A VOTE IN TWO WEEKS' TIME ND COULD BE LAW IN AS LITTLE AS A MONTH. BUT WE CAN'T GO IN HALF-COCKED.
WE'RE ALREADY DEVELOPING AN ANTI-SUPERHUMAN RESPONSE UNIT HERE, BUT WE NEED TO MAKE SURE THE AVENGERS ARE ONSIDE AND THAT YOU'RE OUT THERE *LEADING* THE AVENGERS.
FORGET ABOUT IT.
YOU'RE ASKING ME TO ARREST PEOPLE WHO RISK THEIR LIVES FOR THIS COUNTRY EVERY DAY OF THE WEEK.
NO, I'M ASKING YOU TO OBEY THE WILL OF THE AMERICAN PEOPLE, CAPTAIN.
DON'T PLAY *POLITICS* WITH *ME*, HILL. SUPER HEROES NEED TO STAY *ABOVE* THAT STUFF OR WASHINGTON STARTS TELLING US WHO THE *SUPER-VILLAINS* ARE.
I THOUGHT SUPER-VILLAINS WERE GUYS IN MASKS WHO REFUSED TO OBEY *THE LAW*.
CHIK-CHAK
CHIK-CHAK
CHIK-CHAK
CHIK-CHAK
CHIK-CHAK
CHIK-CHAK
CHIK-CHAK

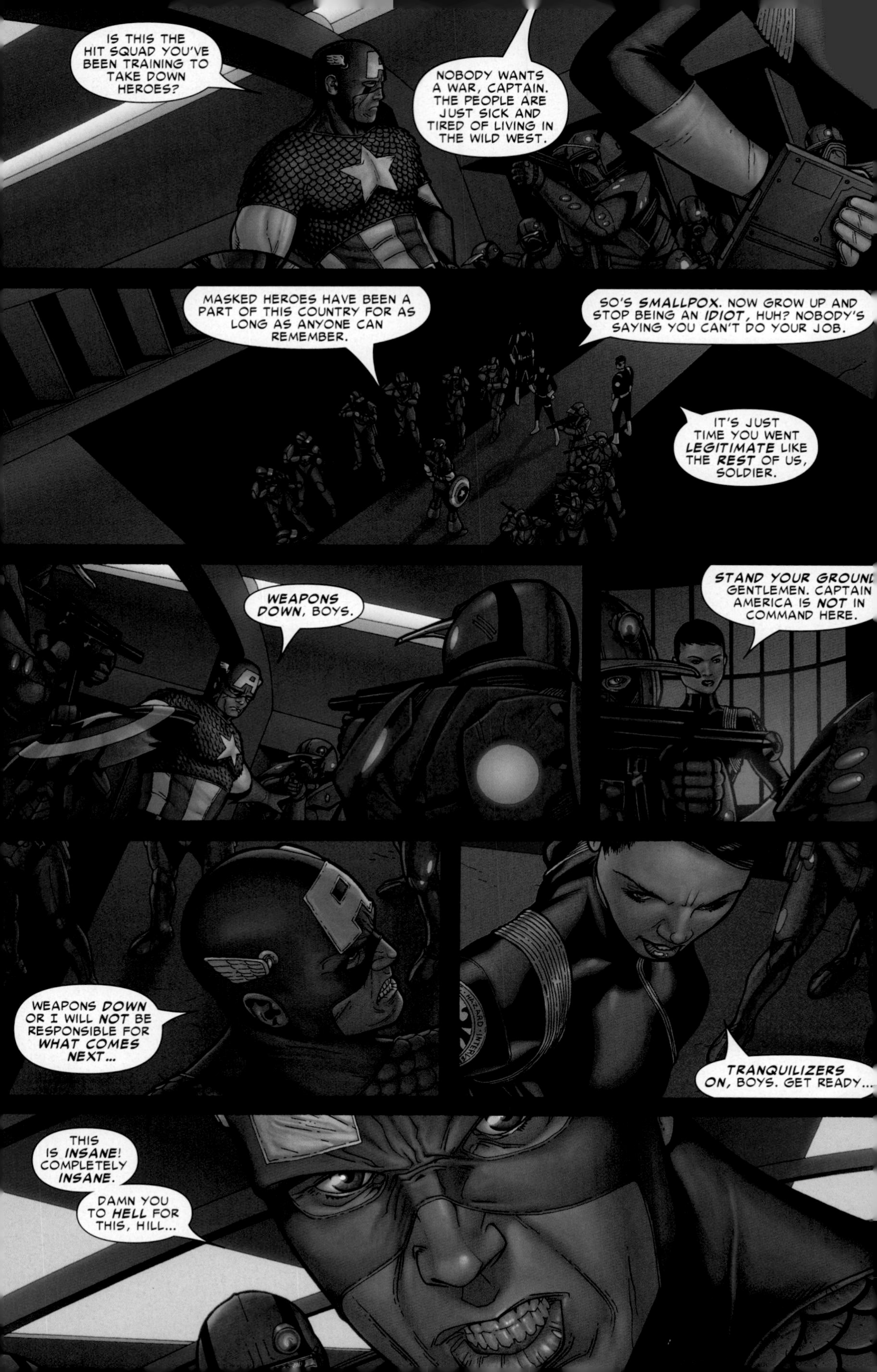
IS THIS THE HIT SQUAD YOU'VE BEEN TRAINING TO TAKE DOWN HEROES?
NOBODY WANTS A WAR, CAPTAIN. THE PEOPLE ARE JUST SICK AND TIRED OF LIVING IN THE WILD WEST.
MASKED HEROES HAVE BEEN A PART OF THIS COUNTRY FOR AS LONG AS ANYONE CAN REMEMBER.
SO'S SMALLPOX. NOW GROW UP AND STOP BEING AN IDIOT, HUH? NOBODY'S SAYING YOU CAN'T DO YOUR JOB.
IT'S JUST TIME YOU WENT LEGITIMATE LIKE THE REST OF US, SOLDIER.
WEAPONS DOWN, BOYS.
STAND YOUR GROUND GENTLEMEN. CAPTAIN AMERICA IS NOT IN COMMAND HERE.
WEAPONS DOWN OR I WILL NOT BE RESPONSIBLE FOR WHAT COMES NEXT...
TRANQUILIZERS ON, BOYS. GET READY...
THIS IS INSANE! COMPLETELY INSANE.
DAMN YOU TO HELL FOR THIS, HILL...

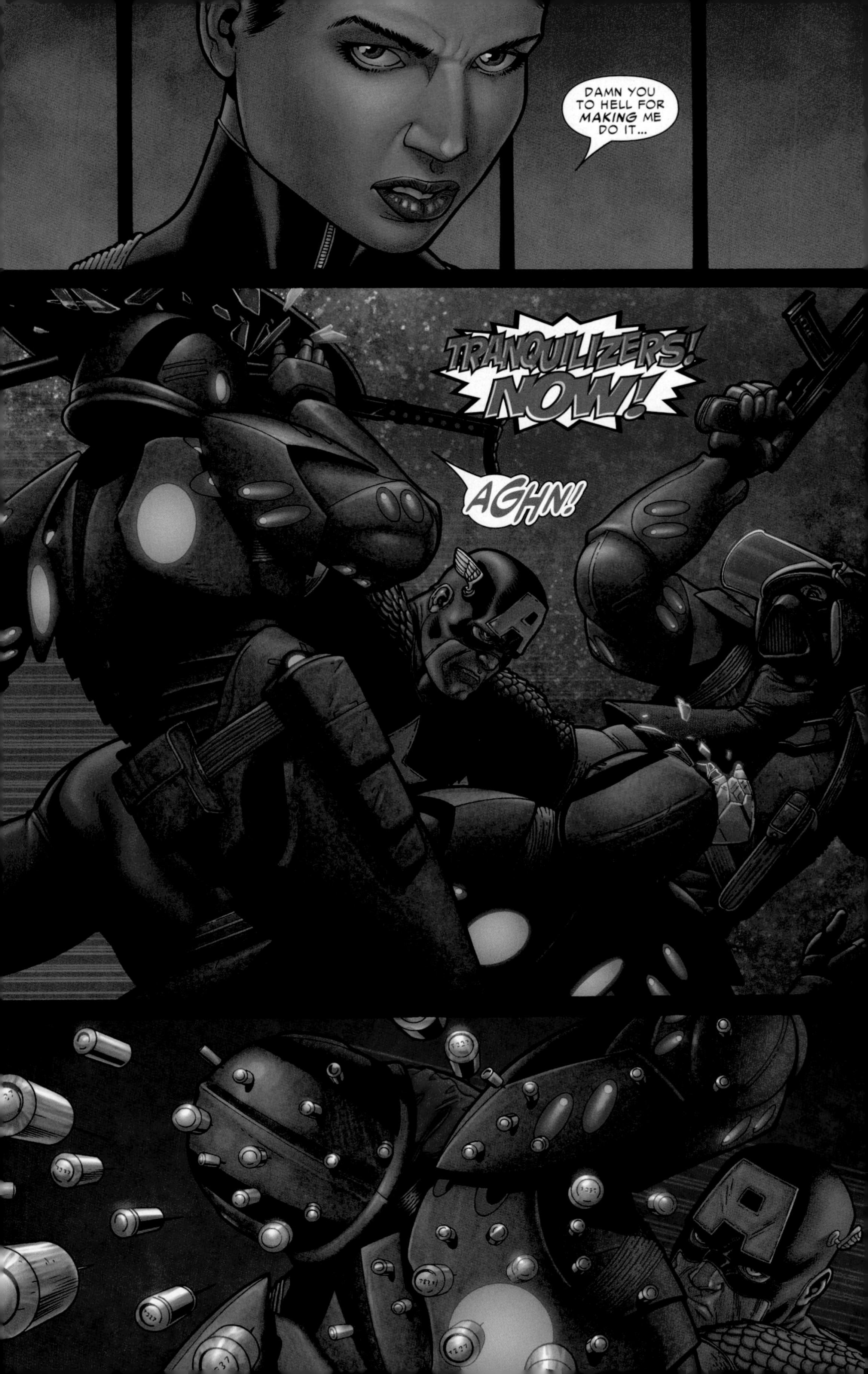
DAMN YOU TO HELL FOR MAKING ME DO IT...
TRANQUILIZERS! NOW!
AGHN!

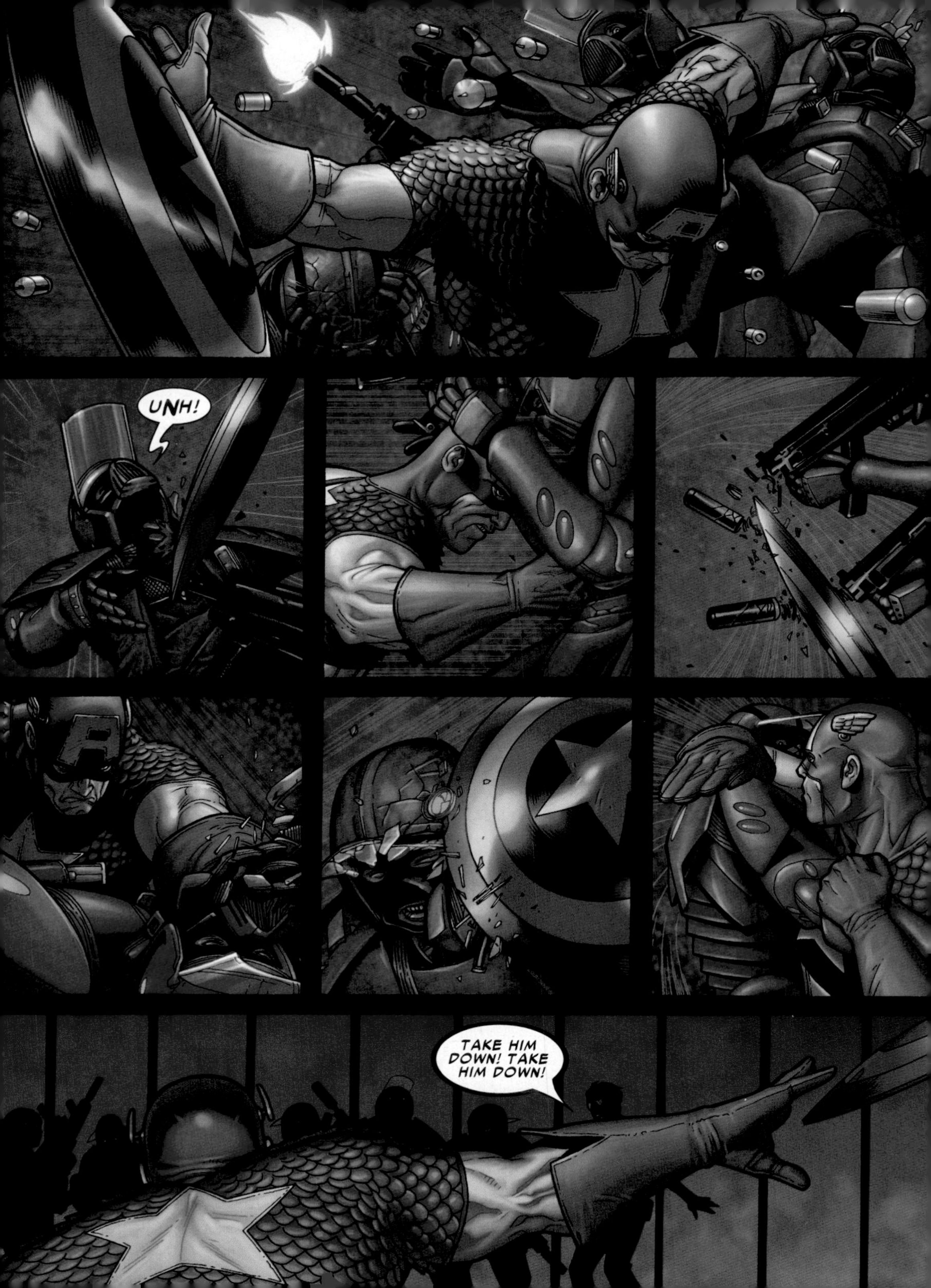
UNH!
TAKE HIM DOWN! TAKE HIM DOWN!

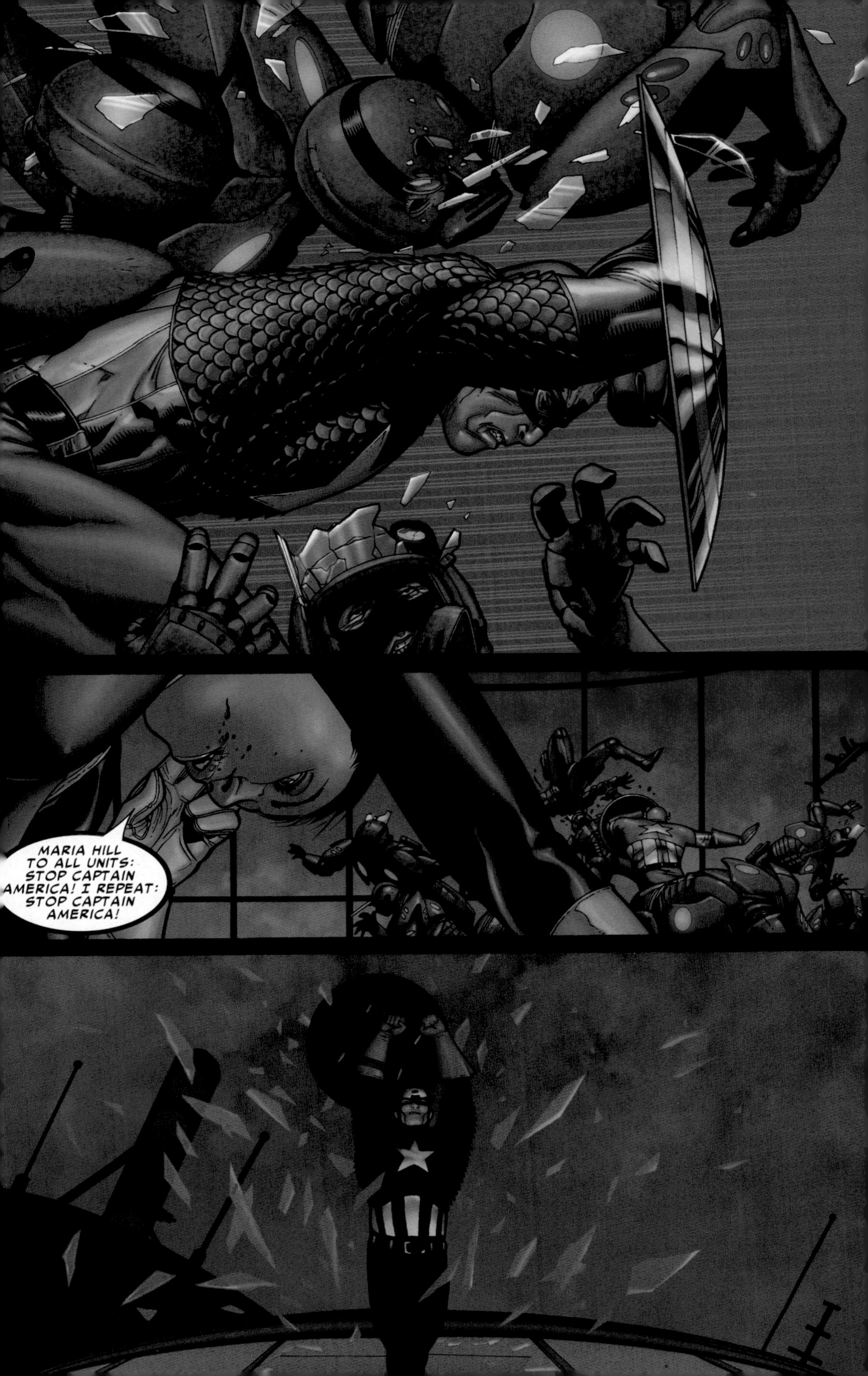
MARIA HILL TO ALL UNITS: STOP CAPTAIN AMERICA! I REPEAT: STOP CAPTAIN AMERICA!

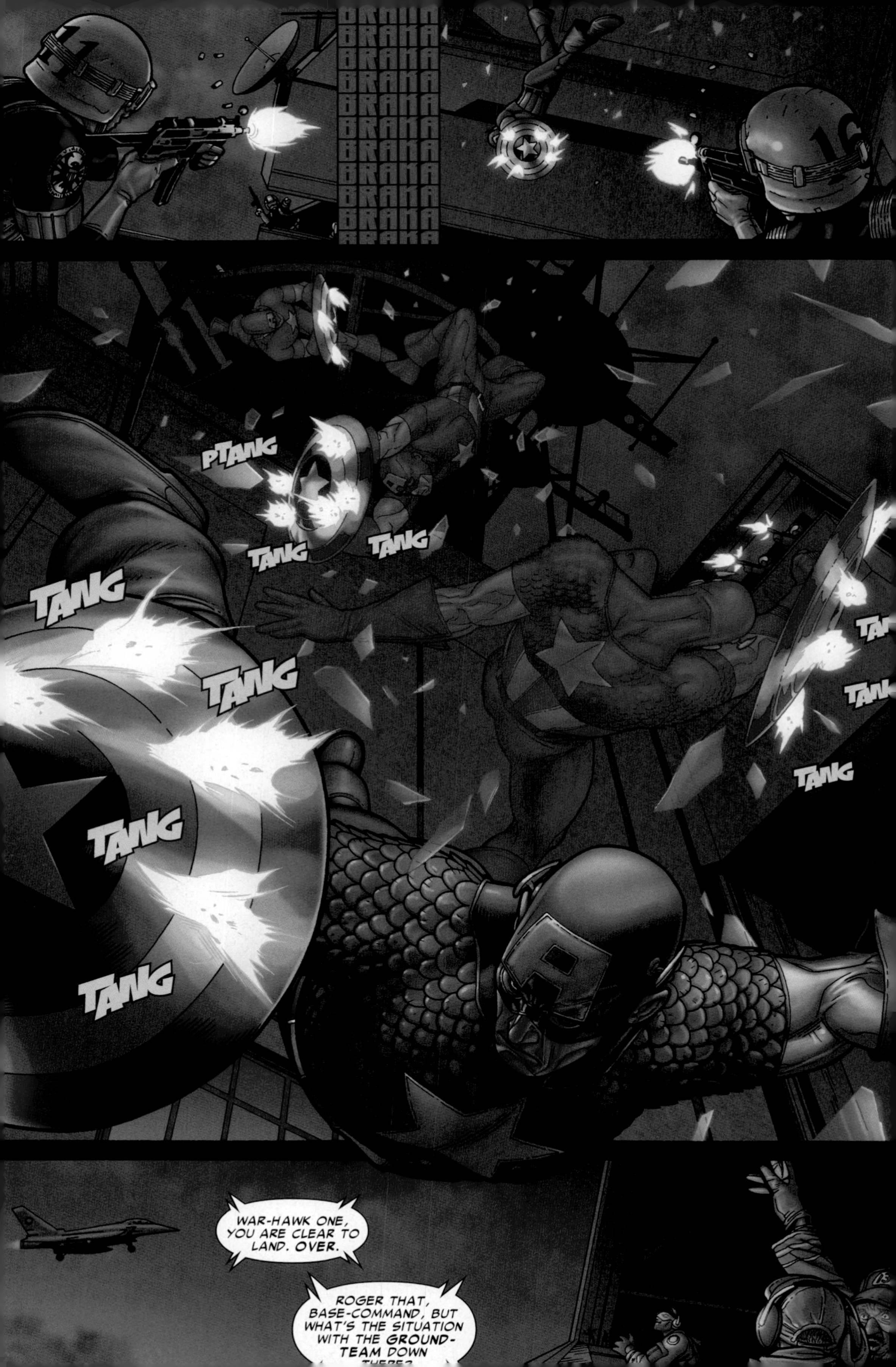
BRAKA
BRAKA
BRAKA
BRAKA
BRAKA
BRAKA
BRAKA
BRAKA
PTANG
TANG
TANG
TANG
TANG
TANG
TANG
TANG
WAR-HAWK ONE, YOU ARE CLEAR TO LAND. OVER.
ROGER THAT, BASE-COMMAND, BUT WHAT'S THE SITUATION WITH THE GROUND-TEAM DOWN

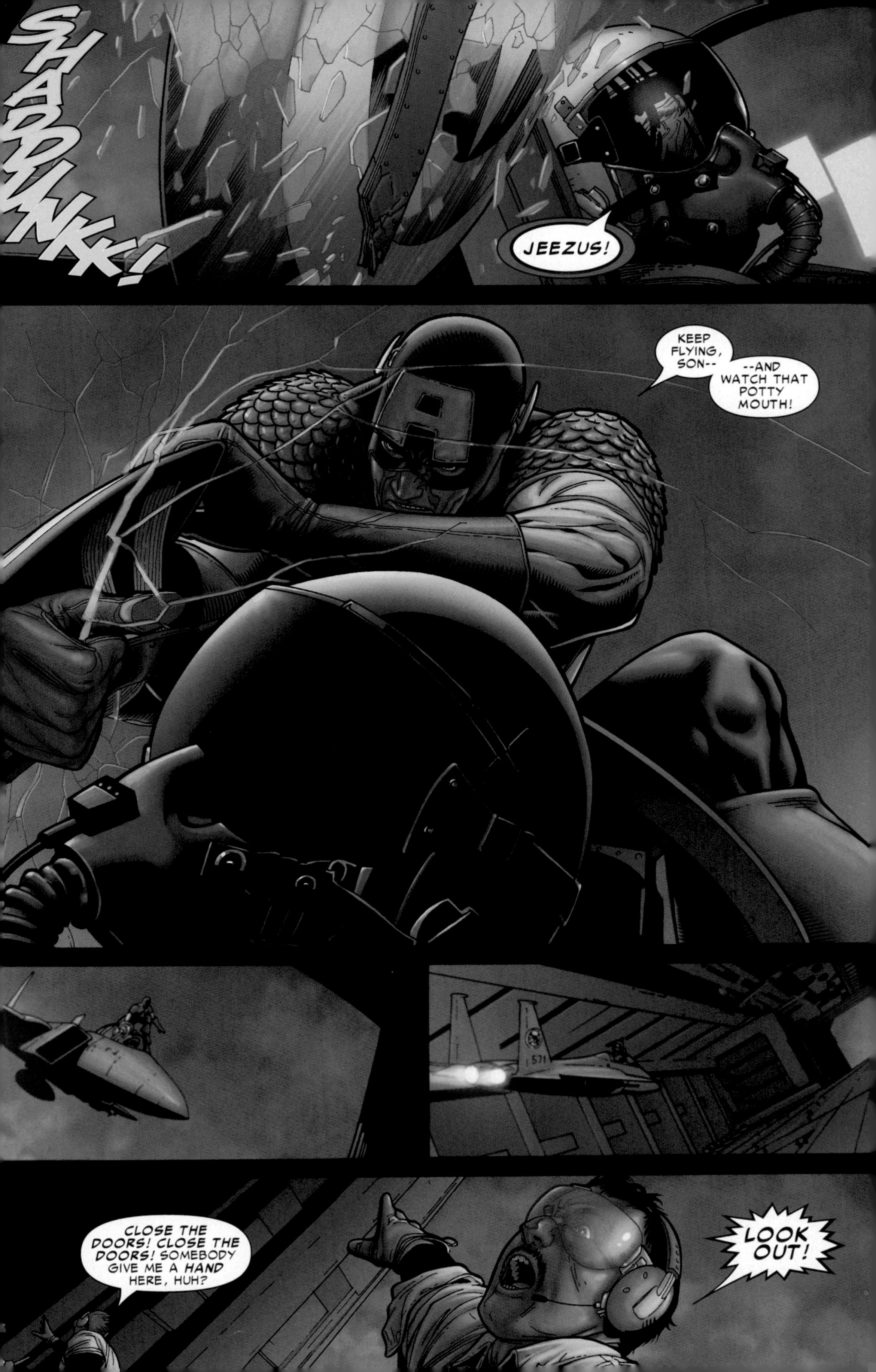
SHADUNKK!
JEEZUS!
KEEP FLYING, SON--
--AND WATCH THAT POTTY MOUTH!
CLOSE THE DOORS! CLOSE THE DOORS! SOMEBODY GIVE ME A HAND HERE, HUH?
LOOK OUT!

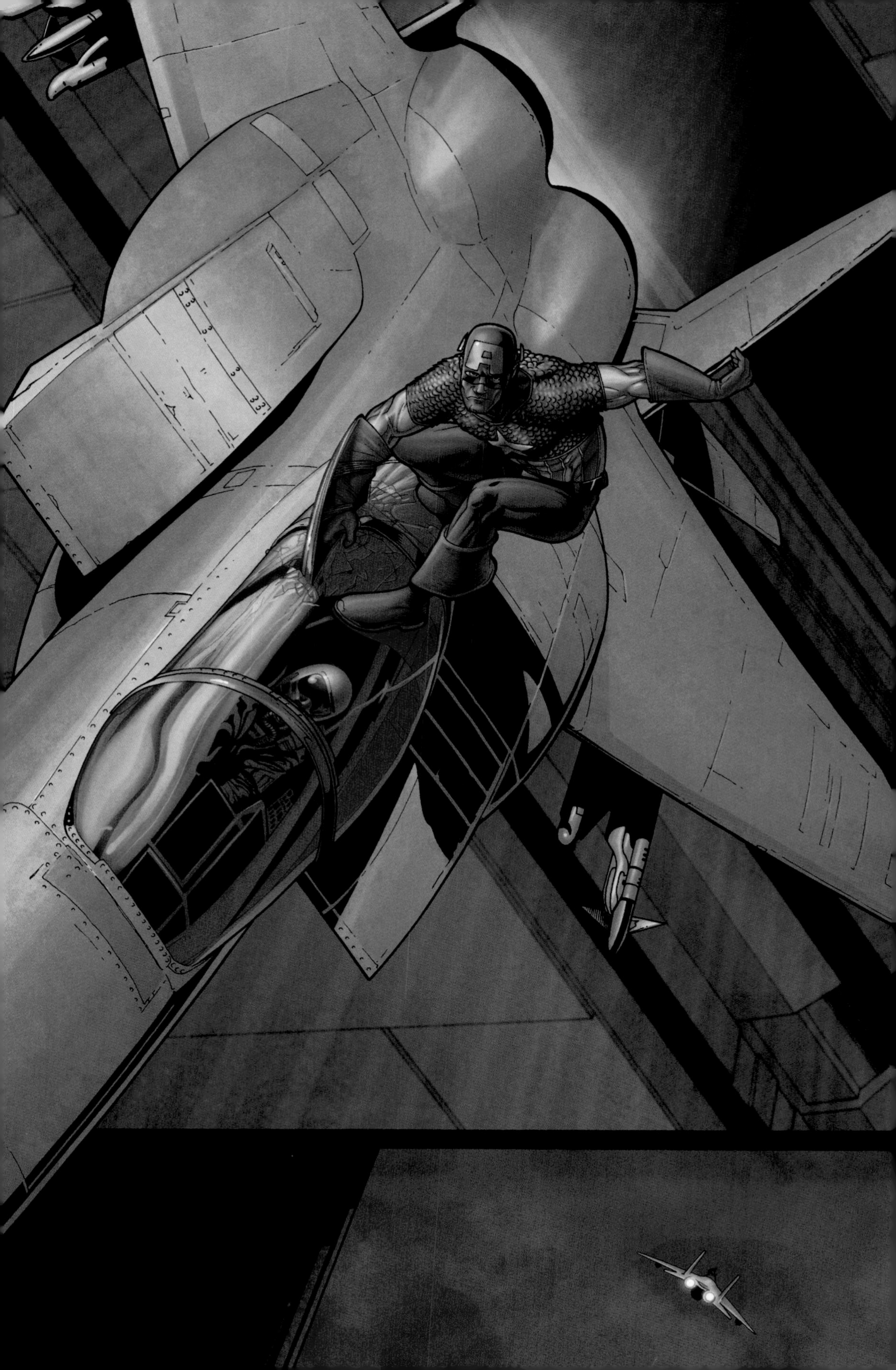

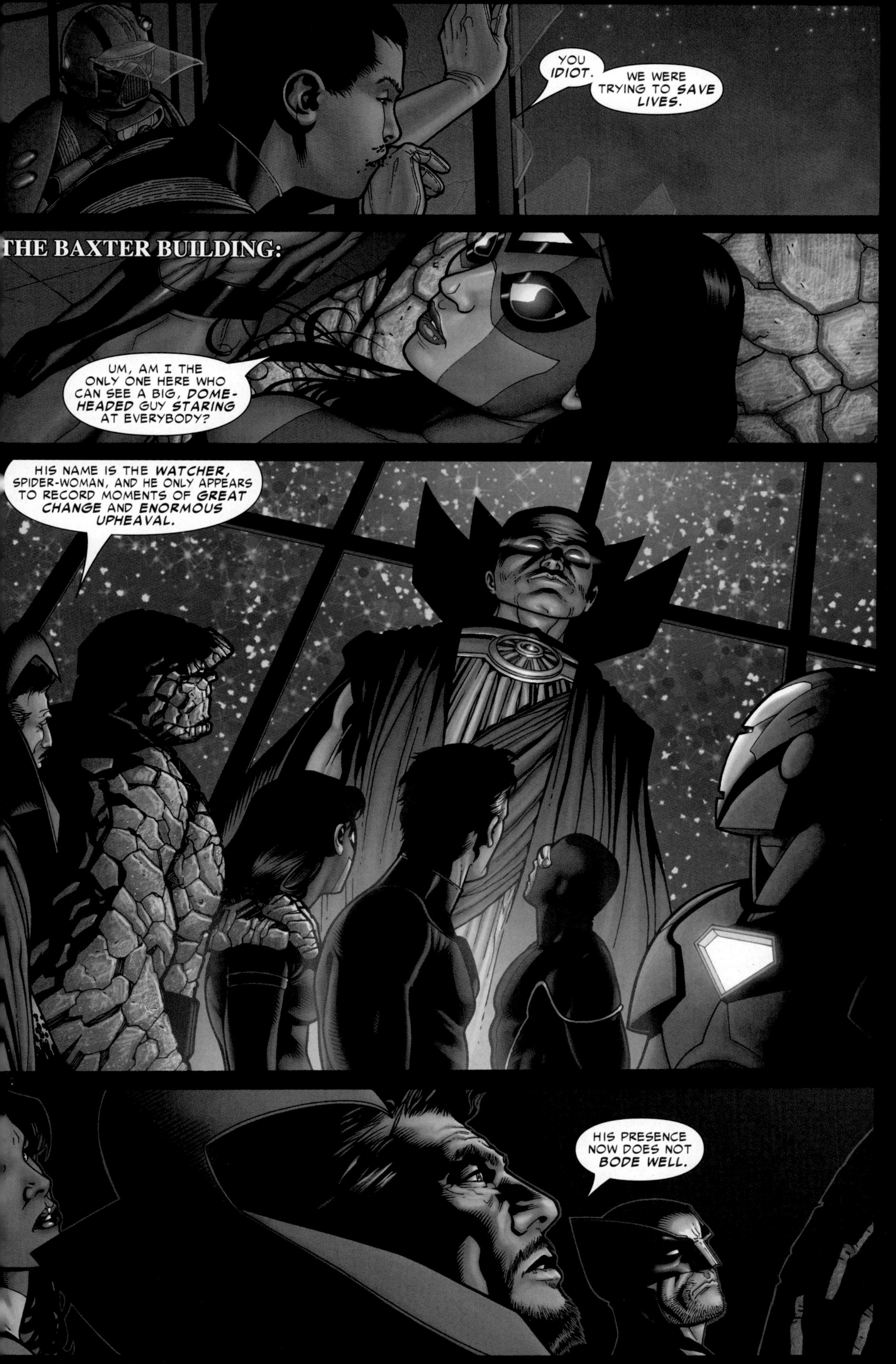

YOU IDIOT.
WE WERE TRYING TO SAVE LIVES.
THE BAXTER BUILDING:
UM, AM I THE ONLY ONE HERE WHO CAN SEE A BIG, DOME-HEADED GUY STARING AT EVERYBODY?
HIS NAME IS THE WATCHER, SPIDER-WOMAN, AND HE ONLY APPEARS TO RECORD MOMENTS OF GREAT CHANGE AND ENORMOUS UPHEAVAL.
HIS PRESENCE NOW DOES NOT BODE WELL.

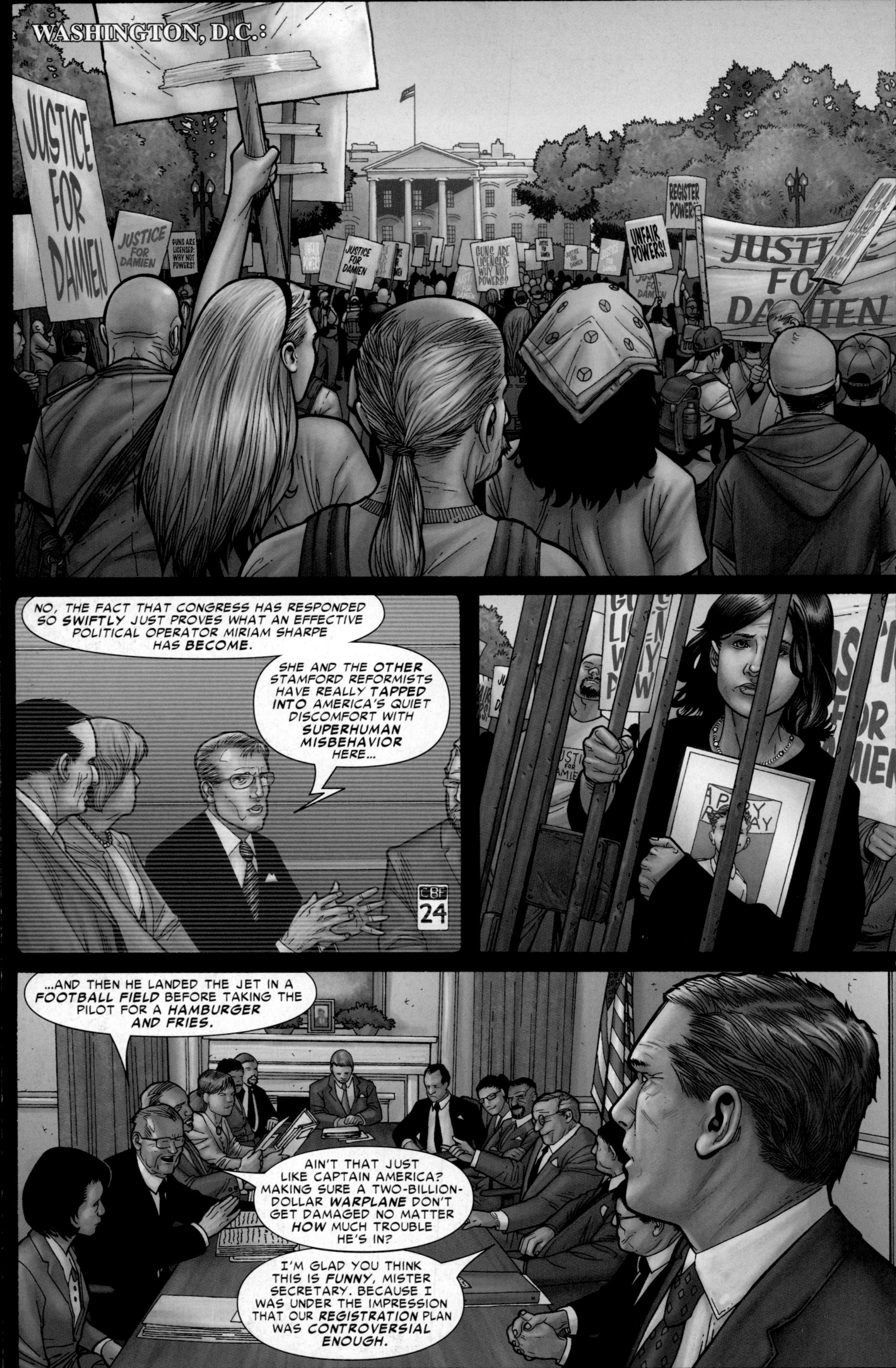
WASHINGTON, D.C.:
JUSTICE FOR DAMIEN
JUSTICE FOR DAMIEN
GUNS ARE LICENSED: WHY NOT POWERS?
UNFAIR POWERS!
JUSTICE FOR DAMIEN
GUNS ARE LICENSED: WHY NOT POWERS?
UNFAIR POWERS!
REGISTER POWERS!
JUSTICE FOR DAMIEN
NO, THE FACT THAT CONGRESS HAS RESPONDED SO SWIFTLY JUST PROVES WHAT AN EFFECTIVE POLITICAL OPERATOR MIRIAM SHARPE HAS BECOME.
SHE AND THE OTHER STAMFORD REFORMISTS HAVE REALLY TAPPED INTO AMERICA'S QUIET DISCOMFORT WITH SUPERHUMAN MISBEHAVIOR HERE...
CBF 24
...AND THEN HE LANDED THE JET IN A FOOTBALL FIELD BEFORE TAKING THE PILOT FOR A HAMBURGER AND FRIES.
AIN'T THAT JUST LIKE CAPTAIN AMERICA? MAKING SURE A TWO-BILLION-DOLLAR WARPLANE DON'T GET DAMAGED NO MATTER HOW MUCH TROUBLE HE'S IN?
I'M GLAD YOU THINK THIS IS FUNNY, MISTER SECRETARY. BECAUSE I WAS UNDER THE IMPRESSION THAT OUR REGISTRATION PLAN WAS CONTROVERSIAL ENOUGH.

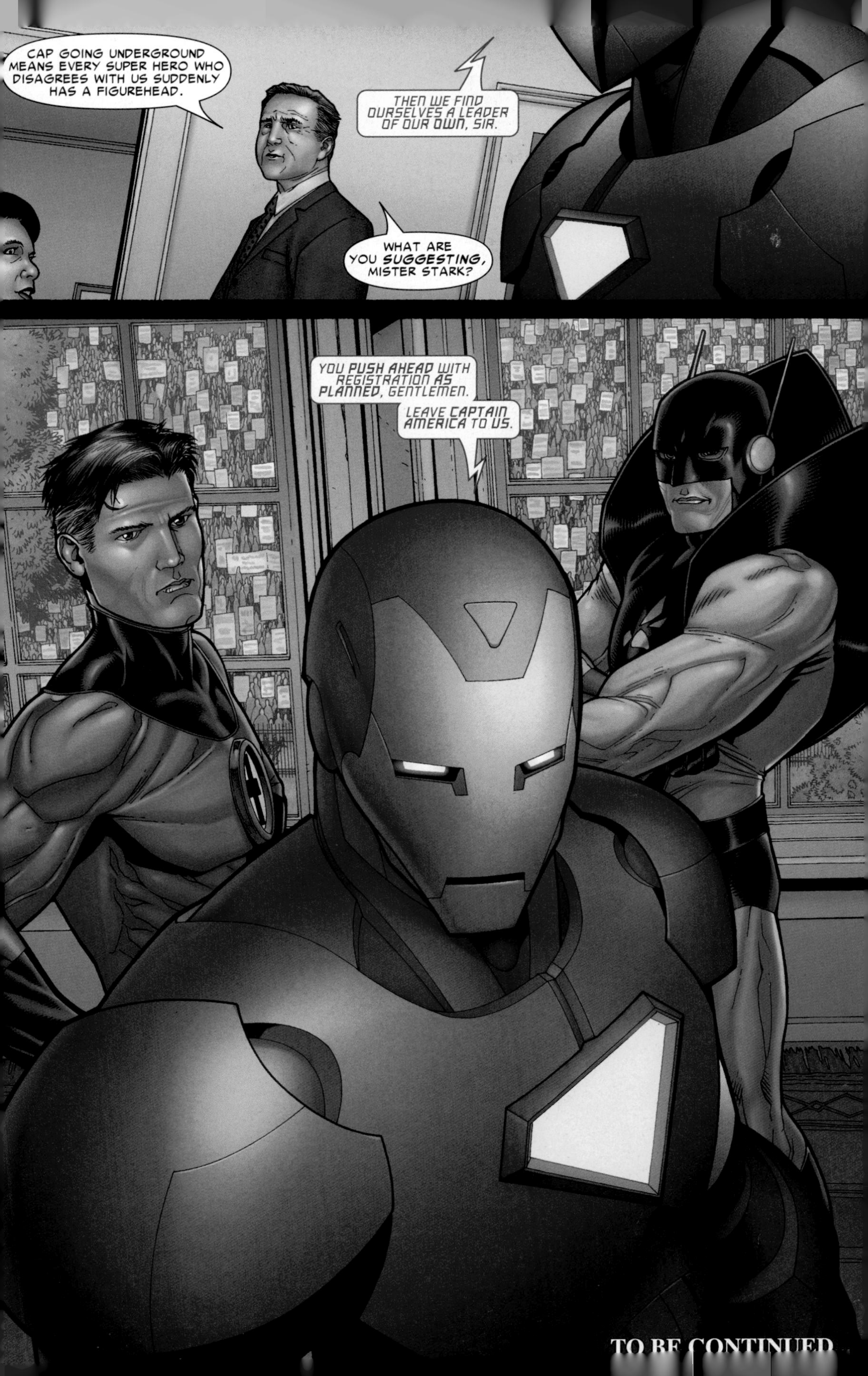
CAP GOING UNDERGROUND MEANS EVERY SUPER HERO WHO DISAGREES WITH US SUDDENLY HAS A FIGUREHEAD.
THEN WE FIND OURSELVES A LEADER OF OUR OWN, SIR.
WHAT ARE YOU SUGGESTING, MISTER STARK?
YOU PUSH AHEAD WITH REGISTRATION AS PLANNED, GENTLEMEN.
LEAVE CAPTAIN AMERICA TO US.
TO BE CONTINUED